GOLD-PLATED POLITICS

GOLD-PLATED POLITICS

THE 1992 CONGRESSIONAL RACES

DWIGHT MORRIS
AND
MURIELLE E. GAMACHE

Congressional Quarterly Inc.
Washington, D.C.

Copyright © 1994 Congressional Quarterly Inc.
1414 22nd Street, N.W., Washington, D.C. 20037

Printed in the United States of America

Cover design: Ben Santora

Library of Congress Cataloging-in-Publication Data

Morris, Dwight, 1952-
    Gold-plated politics : the 1992 congressional races / Dwight
Morris and Murielle E. Gamache.
        p.   cm.
    Includes index.
    ISBN 0-87187-998-0
    1. Campaign funds--United States   2. United States.   Congress--
Elections, 1992.   I. Gamache, Murielle E., 1964-   .   II. Title.
JK1991.M77   1994
324.7'8'097309049--dc20   93-50218
                                                                   CIP

For challenging us intellectually, for encouraging us to look beneath what might at first appear obvious, for picking us up the thousands of times we fell, we lovingly dedicate this book to Herbert Morris and Pauline Alice Masse Gamache.

Contents

List of Tables and Boxes

Tables

Boxes

Preface

For years, journalists have struggled to explain the exploding cost of political campaigns but have been stymied by a lack of real information. Each year, thousands of pages of campaign expenditure data are filed with the Federal Election Commission (FEC), which microfiches the documents and places paper copies in filing cabinets for the curious public to peruse. However, unlike the information it routinely collects on political contributions, the FEC has never computerized the expenditure data, making any comprehensive analysis extremely difficult.

Lacking information and needing an explanation for the high cost of modern campaigns, journalists turned to the "experts," and a mythology was born. According to conventional wisdom, politicians used their campaign treasuries to pay for yard signs, buttons, bumper stickers, and various get-out-the-vote efforts. Most importantly, candidates were thought to be locked in a constant chase for campaign contributions in order to pay for increasingly expensive advertising, primarily on television. Until 1990, few bothered to question whether or not advertising was truly the villain of the campaign finance drama.

In the spring of 1990, the *Los Angeles Times* decided to test the campaign spending myths empirically, and the Washington bureau's special investigations unit was given the task of building a database that ultimately contained 437,753 separate expenditures reported to the FEC by congressional candidates who contested the November general elections. Analysis of that database punched gaping holes in the spending mythology, revealing that House candidates invested an average of only 22 percent of their campaign treasuries in advertising. The comparable figure for Senate candidates was a surprisingly low 33 percent.

What the investigations unit discovered gave rise to a series of articles by reporter Sara Fritz and Dwight Morris, editor for special investigations, that detailed questionable and improper expenditures by a host of congressional candidates. The information gleaned from this 1990 database also served as the basis for the first edition of *Gold-Plated Politics: Running for Congress in the 1990s* and its expanded reference edition, the *Handbook of Campaign Spending: Money in the 1990 Congressional Races,* both coauthored by Fritz and Morris.

Candidates in 1992 had to contend with redistricting, a supposed surge of anti-incumbent sentiment sweeping through the electorate, and the seemingly endless debate over campaign finance reform. Many observers believed there was a distinct possibility that campaigns would dramatically alter their spending habits, rendering moot many of the issues raised in the first edition of *Gold-Plated Politics.* We decided to test that hypothesis.

Although the *Times* decided to limit its inquiry to California candidates in 1992, we felt the nationwide project was too important to drop. Moving the project into our basements and onto our home computers, we spent nearly two years coding and verifying the 1992 data.

We discovered that little had changed. While members of Congress continued to debate the subject of campaign finance reform, the questionable and improper spending practices uncovered in 1990 continued unabated in 1992. While spending on broadcast advertising increased significantly, so did spending on everything else. The result was only a modest shift in the allocation of funds. The forces that drove campaign spending in 1990 had been largely unaffected by either the electorate's mood or redistricting.

This second look at campaign spending is based on an analysis of 524,024 expenditures reported to the FEC by 933 candidates who sought congressional office in 1992. To ensure that our analysis was as complete and as accurate as possible, we contacted every campaign that spent at least $25,000 to clarify all ambiguous expenditures. In all but a few cases, candidates and their advisers were willing to cooperate.

Our analysis of House campaigns includes all expenditures during the two-year election cycle beginning January 1, 1991, and ending December 31, 1992. For Senate races, this book examines all campaign outlays during the six-year cycle beginning January 1, 1987, and ending December 31, 1992. No attempt was made to analyze the campaign expenditures of senators who were not up for reelection in 1992. In those instances where special elections were held during the cycle to fill House vacancies, the book includes data from the special election as well as the subsequent primary and general elections. In the case of Sen. Harris Wofford (D-Pa.), who was elected in 1991 to fill the vacancy created by the death of Sen. John Heinz, we have included only his special election spending. Wofford will be up for reelection in 1994.

Readers interested in the individual race-by-race analyses that are summarized here should refer to the *Handbook of Campaign Spending: Money in the 1992 Congressional Races*. In that edition, tables show how each campaign allotted its money in all the major spending categories, including overhead, fund raising, advertising, and constituent entertainment.

It is important to note that very few of the spending practices outlined in this book are illegal. Rather, they are part of a continuously developing campaign system that has few strict rules. That, we believe, is the main problem.

Dwight Morris
Murielle E. Gamache
July 1994

Acknowledgments

This book could not have been written had it not been for the support of a small army of friends and colleagues who volunteered thousands of hours of their time. While most people were out having fun after work and on weekends, James Peterson, Charlotte Huff, and Michael Cheek gave generously of themselves to help us code and check data. Gary Feld spent nights and weekends chained to his computer, formatting and cranking out the tables that fed our analysis.

When we desperately needed help in entering data into our home computers, Jenifer Morris was there to make certain the work was done. Although unable to lend physical support, Monique Gamache Venne, Janine Gamache Triller, Daniel Charles Gamache, Jordan Morris, Herbert Morris, Minette Morris, and Gloria Morris provided much needed moral support.

For nearly one year, we committed virtually every free moment to this project, and we would like to thank Helen K. Duval for insisting that Murielle go out on an occasional Saturday night. Elizabeth Franzese, Kathleen Richards, and Melissa Michelsen were Helen's co-conspirators in keeping Murielle sane, and we are grateful to them as well. Thanks to Michael Casey Griffen for giving Murielle his enthusiastic backing and sympathetic ear. Deborah Hofmann and Gregory Henschel provided both moral support and periodic comic relief for Dwight.

We would also like to thank Deborah Hofmann of the *New York*

Times for her work with Dwight in assembling campaign spending information during the heat of the 1982 campaign. While that study was more anecdotal than systematic, the ideas Dwight and Deborah generated during that hectic period laid the foundation for the massive spending project we began in 1990.

For their patience and understanding during the past year, we would like to give a special thanks to Jeanne Ferris and Kerry Kern, our editors in the Book Department at Congressional Quarterly. Although we sometimes cringed when the telephone rang, we knew their gentle prodding was matched by a tremendous belief in the value of the project.

We both owe a great deal to former political science professors who encouraged us to argue rather than sit quietly in class. Thanks to Dr. William K. Hall, whose love of politics was infectious and, without knowing it at the time, made Dwight realize that attending law school would be a mistake. Thanks to Dr. J. Barron Boyd for teaching Murielle many of the analytical skills necessary to do this book, even though she protested strenuously at the time.

Our work would have been far more difficult had it not been for Phil Ruiz, who set up our home computer systems and made certain they ran to perfection. Few people would have stayed in Dwight's basement until 9:00 on a Saturday night to troubleshoot a problem that was totally unrelated to his job.

We would also like to thank several of those who made the 1990 edition of this book possible. Thanks to Sara Fritz, who was responsible for developing the concept of this book and who coauthored the first edition. For their assistance in writing that first edition, we would also like to thank Richard S. Dunham, Eric Woodman, and Lisa Hoffman. A special thanks to Stephanie Grace for helping us create the original database.

A Guide to the Tables

The analysis that follows is based on an extensive examination of all 524,024 separate expenditures reported to the Federal Election Commission (FEC) by 933 candidates who sought congressional office in 1992.

Copies of each campaign's financial reports were obtained from the FEC and entered into a database under 1 of 143 categories. To ensure that the categorization was accurate, we contacted officials of each campaign that spent $25,000 or more and asked for clarification of all vaguely reported expenditures. We also inquired about the work performed by every consultant employed by the campaign.

While most campaigns were cooperative, some were not. In cases where neither the candidate nor the campaign employees provided sufficient information, we contacted the consultants directly. In all, we conducted more than 800 interviews with candidates, campaign staff, and consultants.

In calculating expenditure totals, transfers between authorized committees, payments of debts from prior election cycles, contribution refunds, and loan repayments have been excluded in order to avoid double counting expenditures. All debts to vendors reported at the end of the 1992 cycle have been included.

The expenditures were subsequently assigned to one of eight major spending categories. Five categories were broken further into specific areas of spending. The following is a description of the categories and the types of items included in each.

OVERHEAD

Office furniture/supplies: Furniture and basic office supplies, telephone answering services, messenger and overnight delivery services, monthly cable television payments, newspaper and magazine subscriptions, clipping services, payments for file storage, small postage and photocopying charges, office moving expenses, and improvements or upkeep of the office (including office cleaning, garbage pickup, repairs, plumbers, and locksmiths).

Rent/utilities: Rent and utility payments for campaign offices. Purchases and leases of vehicles used as mobile offices, as well as their maintenance costs, are also included.

Salaries: Salary payments and employee benefits, including health insurance. In addition to payments specifically described as salary, this category includes regular payments to those people who performed routine office tasks, which were frequently misrepresented in campaign finance reports as "consulting." Whenever a housing allowance was part of a campaign employee's compensation package, it was considered to be salary.

Taxes: All federal and state taxes paid by the campaign, including payroll taxes and income taxes paid on the campaign's investments.

Bank/investment fees: Interest payments on outstanding loans, annual credit card fees, check charges, investment fees, and investment losses.

Lawyers/accountants: Fees paid for their services as well as any other expenses incurred by the campaign's lawyers and accountants. Five Senate and thirty-one House campaigns paid fines related to violations of federal or state election laws, and those fines have been included as part of legal fees.

Telephone: Purchases of telephone equipment (including cellular telephones and beepers), monthly payments for local and long-distance service, installation fees, repairs, and reimbursements to staff for telephone expenses.

Campaign automobile: All payments for the purchase or lease of a campaign vehicle (except mobile offices), maintenance, insurance, registration, licensing, and gasoline.

Computers/office equipment: All payments related to the purchase, lease, and repair of office equipment, such as computer equipment and software, typewriters, photocopiers, FAX machines, telephone answering machines, televisions, radios, and VCRs.

Travel: All general travel expenses, such as air fare and hotels, rental cars, taxies, daily parking, and entries such as "food for travel." Expenses for the national party conventions, including the costs of receptions and other entertainment, are also included.

Food/meetings: Meeting expenses (for example, steering committees, finance committees, state delegations) and other food costs not specifically related to fund raising, constituent entertainment, or travel.

Fund Raising

Events: All costs related to fund-raising events, including invitations, postage, planning meetings, travel costs, room rental, food and catering costs, liquor, flowers, bartenders, follow-up thank-you cards, in-kind fund-raising expenses, general reimbursements to individuals for fund raising, tickets to sporting or theater events that served a fund-raising purpose, and fees paid to consultants who planned the events.

Direct mail: All costs related to fund-raising solicitations via the mail, including the purchase of mailing lists, computer charges, postage, printing, caging services, and consultant fees and expenses. Mailings that served a dual purpose, both to raise funds and inform voters, were included in this category.

Telemarketing: All expenses related to a telephone operation designed to raise money, including consultant fees, list purchases, and computer costs. Campaigns use the terms *telemarketing* and *phonebanking* loosely. Some items listed as telemarketing in campaign reports to the FEC were found to be inaccurately identified and were assigned to their proper category.

POLLING

All polling costs, including payments to consultants as well as in-kind contributions of polling results to the campaign.

ADVERTISING

Electronic media: All payments to consultants, separate purchases of broadcast time, and production costs associated with the development of radio and television advertising.

Other media: Campaign videos; payments for billboards; advertising in newspapers, journals, magazines, and publications targeted to religious groups, senior citizens, and other special constituencies; as well as program ads purchased from local charitable and booster organizations.

OTHER CAMPAIGN ACTIVITY

Persuasion mail/brochures: All costs associated with strictly promotional mailings and other campaign literature, including artwork, printing of brochures or other literature, postage, the purchase of mailing lists, as well as consultant fees and consultant expenses.

Actual campaigning: Filing fees and costs of petition drives, announcement parties, state party conventions, campaign rallies and parades, campaign training schools, opposition research, posters, signs, buttons, bumper stickers, speech writers and coaches, get-out-the-vote efforts, election day poll watchers, and all campaign promotional material (T-shirts, jackets, hats, embossed pencils, pens, nail files, pot holders, etc.). Fees and expenses billed by campaign management firms and general consultants for services unrelated to advertising, fund raising, and persuasion mail are also included.

Staff/volunteers: All food expenses for staff and volunteers, including phonebank and get-out-the-vote volunteers. These expenses included bottled water, soda machines, monthly coffee service, and food purchases that are specifically for the campaign office. Also included were expenditures for recruitment of volunteers, gifts for staff and volunteers, and staff retreats.

CONSTITUENT GIFTS/ENTERTAINMENT

Meals purchased for constituents, the costs of events that were designed purely for constituent entertainment (for example, a local dominos tournament), constituent gifts of all kinds, flowers, holiday greeting cards, awards and plaques, inaugural parties, and costs associated with the annual congressional art contest.

DONATIONS

To candidates (both in-state and out-of-state): Direct contributions to other candidates as well as the purchase price of fund-raiser tickets.

To civic organizations: Contributions to charitable organizations, such as the American Cancer Society, as well as local booster groups, such as the Chamber of Commerce and local high school athletic associations. Includes the cost of tickets to events sponsored by such groups.

To ideological groups: Contributions to ideological organizations, such as the NAACP, the National Organization for Women, and the Sierra Club.

To political parties: Contributions to national, state, and local party organizations, including tickets to party-sponsored fund-raising events.

UNITEMIZED EXPENSES

Candidates are not required to report expenditures of less than $200, and many do not list them on their FEC reports. This category also includes expenditures described in FEC reports merely as "petty cash," unitemized credit card purchases, and all reimbursements that were vaguely worded, such as "reimbursement," "political expenses," or "campaign expenses."

CHAPTER 1

1992

The Year of Change?

There is a ferocious tide against incumbents running across the country, and I could not swim strongly enough to offset it.
Rep. Guy Vander Jagt (R-Mich.),
following his August 4, 1992 primary loss

C hange. In some respects no word better symbolized the 1992 campaigns, as Rep. Guy Vander Jagt (R-Mich.) would undoubtedly attest. Democratic presidential nominee Bill Clinton vowed to reinvent government. Independent presidential aspirant H. Ross Perot promised to get "under the hood" of a gridlocked federal bureaucracy. An August 24 cover story in *U.S. News & World Report* proposed to tell readers "Why George Bush Can't Change."

Incumbency, it seemed, had become a dirty word. In September 1991 the House of Representatives was rocked by revelations that members had routinely written checks against their accounts at the House bank without having sufficient funds to cover them. On October 1, 1991 freshman Rep. Jim Nussle (R-Iowa) took the House floor to decry the leadership's decision not to make public the names of those who had overdrawn their accounts. Wearing a brown paper bag over his head, Nussle theatrically declared that it was "time to take the mask off this institution. It is time to expose the check-writing scandal that I like to call Rubbergate. It is time to bring some honor back to this institution." When, after six months of political wrangling, the names were finally made public, voters learned that Rep. Ronald V. Dellums (D-Calif.) had overdrawn his account 851 times over a thirty-nine-month period and ranked fifth on the overdraft list. At the other end of the spectrum, Rep. Jolene Unsoeld (D-Wash.) had overdrawn her account only once, and then by just thirty-eight cents.

1

Although no public funds were involved, the media jumped on the story, turning the overdrafts into "bounced checks." That nomenclature was quickly adopted by Vander Jagt and other Republicans who saw an opportunity to gain political advantage from their colleagues' misadventures. "There will be many, many members who will be taken out, lose their reelection because of their record of bounced checks," Vander Jagt told reporters. "I am absolutely overjoyed," he quickly added. Ultimately, challengers on both sides of the political aisle made these checks one of the central issues of the campaign, although the number of times a member had overdrawn his or her account frequently proved to be a poor predictor of the issue's impact.

The House bank scandal was one of several, both large and small. Federal prosecutors launched an investigation into allegations that Democratic Reps. Dan Rostenkowski (Ill.) and Joe Kolter (Pa.) had embezzled thousands of dollars through the House post office. A parallel investigation led to the conviction of six former employees of the House post office on drug and embezzlement charges. In addition, it was revealed that seven House members had abused their post office privileges by setting up special post office boxes to receive campaign donations.

In October 1991 it was revealed that many incumbents had failed to pay bills totaling more than $370,000 at the House restaurant, a report that proved grossly inaccurate. In October 1990 a *PrimeTime Live* hidden camera had caught members of Congress playing golf and frolicking on a beach in Barbados, all paid for by corporate lobbyists. House members were pilloried for the fact that they paid only $100 each year for the use of the House gymnasium. There were revelations that members of both chambers could have pictures framed for free, obtain free prescription drugs through the Office of Attending Physician, have their hair cut for under $5, park free at National and Dulles airports in suburban Washington, D.C., and have parking tickets fixed.

Scandals and "perkomania," as one challenger dubbed it, were not the only black marks on Congress's image. In 1991 Anita F. Hill, a professor of law at the University of Oklahoma, had come forth with allegations that she had been sexually harassed by Supreme Court nominee Clarence Thomas, her former supervisor at the Equal Employment Opportunity Commission. The Senate Judiciary Committee's nationally televised hearings into those allegations served for many as evidence that the institution was insensitive to women's concerns and produced several high-profile challengers to House and Senate campaigns.

Few women centered their campaigns entirely around Hill's treatment, but virtually all of the ninety-four women who challenged incumbents or contested open House or Senate seats in the general election ran "outsider" campaigns. State senator Patty Murray (D-Wash.) ran for the Senate as "the mom in tennis shoes." Community activist Claire Sargent (D-Ariz.) said it was time to "start electing senators with breasts; we've had boobs long enough." When Rep. Charles E. Bennett (D-Fla.) opted to retire, leaving Jacksonville City Council member Tillie Fowler (R-Fla.) without an incumbent to attack, she simply leveled her charges at the entire House. One of Fowler's ads scrolled across the screen the names of all congressional staffers who made more than $100,000.

As the negative news reports continued to mount, so too did voter anger. Frustrated voters forced term limit initiatives onto the ballot in fourteen states, including California, Florida, Michigan, Ohio, and House Speaker Thomas S. Foley's home state of Washington. Buffeted by a rising tide of anti-incumbent sentiment, fifty-two House members and seven senators chose to leave politics rather than seek reelection. Thirteen House members retired in order to make Senate or gubernatorial bids.

Among those voluntarily relinquishing their House seats was Rep. Bill Dickinson (R-Ala.), ranking member of the Armed Services Committee, who noted that Congress just was not "fun any more." Saying that he was "simply not ready to engage in character assassination and mud wrestling to win a campaign," six-term Rep. Bill Lowery (R-Calif.) stepped aside rather than wage a primary battle with fellow Republican Rep. Randy "Duke" Cunningham in California's District 51. Disillusioned with what he called "the money chase," forty-one-year-old Rep. Dennis E. Eckart (D-Ohio) walked away after six terms. Pointing to his growing frustration with "the scandals, the anti-incumbency, the term-limitation movement," Rep. William S. Broomfield (R-Mich.) decided to move on after thirty-six years in the House.

In announcing he would not seek a third term, Sen. Warren B. Rudman (R-N.H.) said he was "terribly frustrated" by Congress's failure to reduce the federal budget deficit and added that he felt

Congress was incapable of "doing what has to be done while we still have time to do it." Hampered by negative publicity over his ties to the savings and loan industry and identified with a proposal to create a Senate bank modeled after the infamous House bank, Sen. Tim Wirth (D-Colo.) opted to retire after a single term. Among Wirth's reasons were the "continuous money chase," "the hysterical superficiality in the electronic media's focus on sensational themes," and "the stalemate to which economic mismanagement and partisan pettiness have reduced the work of our government."

Redistricting added to the woes of many House incumbents who opted to fight it out. In Georgia, which gained one seat following the census, the Democratic-dominated redistricting committee obliterated Republican Rep. Newt Gingrich's former district, parceling out his constituents to several other districts. Facing a totally new constituency, Gingrich survived the Republican primary in the redrawn District 6 by just 980 votes. In Illinois, which faced the loss of two House seats, a Republican-dominated plan set up Democratic primary battles between Reps. Glenn Poshard and Terry L. Bruce, William O. Lipinski and Marty Russo, and Dan Rostenkowski and Frank Annunzio. Annunzio opted to retire rather than fight; Bruce and Russo lost bitter contests. In California, which gained seven new seats, Democratic Rep. Anthony C. Beilenson found himself faced with a choice between waging an expensive primary battle with fellow Democratic Rep. Henry A. Waxman or waging an expensive general election campaign in a more heavily Republican district. He chose to avoid intraparty fratricide.

While the power of incumbency had historically discouraged spirited challenges in House campaigns, the surge of anti-incumbent sentiment brought forth scores of challengers in 1992. In 1990, 52 of the 405 House incumbents who sought reelection had won without facing either a primary or general election opponent. Only 8 of the 349 incumbents seeking reelection were so fortunate in 1992. Few challengers passed up the opportunity to portray themselves as agents of change.

More importantly, challengers seeking House seats in 1992 were able to spend $40,123 more on average than their 1990 counterparts to deliver that outsider message, an increase of 30 percent. Challengers involved in hotly contested races—those in which the winner received no more than 60 percent of the vote—spent $64,291 more than their 1990 counterparts, a 29 percent increase.

In some cases, the additional funding was a result of an ability to tap personal wealth. Businessman Michael Huffington poured about $3.5 million into the Republican primary in California's District 22, virtually all of it his own money. The continuous media blitz his money bought carried Huffington to a narrow upset victory over veteran Rep. Robert J. Lagomarsino, who spent $747,536. In the general election campaign, Huffington again dipped into his own bank account, putting together a $1.9 million effort to defeat Santa Barbara County Supervisor Gloria Ochoa, who spent $706,338. Huffington's total expenditures topped $5.4 million, making this the most expensive House campaign in history—more then doubling the previous record.

Although less dramatic, spending by Senate challengers increased from an average of $1,686,616 in 1990 to $1,922,001 in 1992, a modest 14 percent rise. Former San Francisco mayor Dianne Feinstein (D-Calif.) led all challengers, spending $8,041,099 to defeat Republican Sen. John Seymour. At the low end of the spending spectrum, independent candidate Jon Khachaturian (La.) spent only $94,920 on a token challenge to Democratic Sen. John B. Breaux, who spent $1.8 million.

Burdened by a litany of institutional negatives and faced by better funded challengers, many incumbents were forced to work considerably harder in 1992 than they had in 1990. In the 1990 election cycle, 127 of the 405 House members who managed to secure their party's nomination were involved in hotly contested primary or general election campaigns, including 15 incumbents who lost. The only House incumbent to lose a 1990 primary was Rep. Donald E. "Buz" Lukens (R-Ohio), who had been convicted on a misdemeanor charge stemming from his sexual encounter with a sixteen-year-old girl. Two years later, 150 of the 349 incumbents who won their party's nomination were involved in hotly contested races in the primary, the general election, or both, including 24 who were ousted on November 3. Another 19 House members never made it past the primary.

Twenty-eight incumbent senators were given the opportunity by their party to seek another term in 1992; of that total only nine received 61 percent of the vote or more in both their primary and general elections. Thirteen incumbents were held to 55 percent or less, including four who lost in the general election. In contrast, seventeen of the thirty-two senators who sought reelection in 1990 won easily, including three who ran unopposed and one whose only challenger was a supporter of fringe political activist Lyndon H. LaRouche, Jr. No senator who sought renomination failed to get it. Three incumbent senators opted to leave politics and one chose to run for governor. Only one incumbent senator was defeated.

Amidst this chaos, one might have anticipated that incumbents would feel the need to alter their approach to campaigning. One might have expected a significant change from 1990, when more than half the money invested in congressional elections was spent on items that had virtually nothing to do with pure election activity. Looking at the overall numbers, those expectations were only partially met.

Senate incumbents seeking reelection in 1992 spent slightly more on average than their 1990 counterparts. During the 1990 election cycle, senators seeking reelection spent a total of $131,242,807, an average of $4,101,338. Incumbents who contested the 1992 general election reported spending $116,177,549, an average of $4,149,198 (see Tables 1-1 and 1-2). This insignificant 1 percent increase resulted less from anti-incumbent fears than from the fact that three senators ran unopposed in 1990. The 1992 campaign also featured hotly contested races in California, New York, and Pennsylvania, all of which have expensive media markets and none of which had seats up for grabs during the previous election cycle.

Although the bottom line did not move for the average Senate incumbent, a cursory look at spending in various categories might lead one to conclude that priorities had shifted between 1990 and 1992. In fact, any shift in priorities was marginal, at most. Broadcast advertising expenditures, which represented 33 percent of spending by Senate incumbents in the 1990 election cycle, accounted for 40 percent of total outlays in 1992 (see Table 1-3). Again, this was more a reflection of the media markets represented in the two election cycles than a conscious change in behavior. As a percentage of total spending, outlays for overhead increased slightly, from 24 percent in 1990 to 25 percent in 1992. The percentage of total spending devoted to fund raising dropped significantly, from 31 percent in 1990 to 21 percent in 1992, but much of that difference is accounted for by the absence of Sen. Jesse Helms (R-N.C.) in the 1992 sample. In 1990 Helms led all incumbents in spending on direct-mail fund raising with outlays of $10,957,563. During the 1992 election cycle, combined spending on direct-mail solicitations by all twenty-eight incumbents totaled only $11,183,186.

On the other hand, average spending by House incumbents increased 46 percent from 1990 to 1992. During the 1990 election cycle, spending by incumbents totaled $156,545,183, an average of $390,387. Incumbents who contested the 1992 general election spent a total of $199,310,139, an average of $571,089 (see Tables 1-4 and 1-5).

The average House incumbent's investment in broadcast advertising nearly doubled, from $76,109 in 1990 to $141,791 in 1992. Average outlays for persuasion mail jumped from $37,825 to $70,198. Expenditures for yard signs, buttons, bumper stickers, rallies, get-out-the-vote-efforts, general strategic advice, and other items included under the rubric of "actual campaigning" climbed from $28,097 in 1990 to $42,196 in 1992.

Among those forced to alter their campaign style, at least temporarily, was Rep. Elton Gallegly (R-Calif.). Gallegly invested $434,418 in 1990 to defeat Democrat Richard D. Freiman, who spent just $18,018. In his solidly Republican district, only 15 percent of Gallegly's 1990 expenditures were devoted to direct appeals for votes.

Two significant problems confronted Gallegly in 1992. First, redistricting robbed him of almost three-quarters of his former constituency and handed him a new electorate in which registered Democrats slightly outnumbered Republicans. Perhaps more importantly, in a district where 30 percent of the population was Hispanic, Gallegly faced Democrat Anita Perez Ferguson, a Hispanic educational consultant who had taken 44 percent of the vote against Lagomarsino in 1990. As a result, Gallegly poured $851,701 into his 1992 campaign, and 53 percent of that total was invested in advertising, persuasion mail, and grass-roots campaigning.

Running unopposed in 1986, 1988, and 1990, Rep. Harold Rogers (R-Ky.) spent a combined total of $484,046. In 1991 his low-key, off-year campaign cost only $49,075. However, when redistricting transformed Rogers's safe Republican district into one in which 55 percent of the registered voters were Democrats, his days of relaxed campaigning quickly drew to a close. During the first six months of 1992, Rogers spent nearly $209,000—despite the fact that he was unopposed in the May primary. He then invested $627,624 over the final six months of the election cycle, more than half of which was spent in October, to defeat former state senator John Doug Hays.

For Rep. David E. Skaggs (D-Colo.) the problems were different, but the result was the same. In keeping with his 1990 pledge to hold down campaign spending, Skaggs spent only $68,315 to run his off-year campaign in 1991. With additional expenditures of roughly $140,000 through the first seven months of 1992, Skaggs looked as though he might contain his spending for the entire cycle to well under $400,000.

That was before Republican Bryan Day, a Southern Baptist minister with strong backing from both the evangelical Christian Coalition and the National Republican Congressional Committee, began hammering Skaggs over his fifty-seven overdrafts at the House bank. Skaggs spent more than $470,000 over the final months of the campaign, committing approximately $350,000 to the effort in October alone.

For the first time in his twenty-year congressional career, Rep. Ralph Regula (R-Ohio) ran a television commercial. Helped by rising anti-incumbent sentiment, underfunded college professor Warner D. Mendenhall had held Regula to 59 percent in 1990, and the incumbent worked hard to make certain their rematch would not be that close.

To reach voters in two counties added to his district, Regula invested about $25,000 to air one 30-second spot on Cleveland television stations. The ad, which dealt with his views on foreign trade and job creation, showed him on his farm, at a local steel mill, and at a trade school he helped establish. "It was an experiment," noted Regula in explaining his more aggressive campaign style. "This was the most expensive campaign I've ever been involved in."

As dramatic as these examples are, they suggest a far greater change in spending habits than actually occurred, even among House incumbents. Forty-nine percent of the money spent in the 1992 congressional elections went for purchases that had virtually nothing to do with appeals for votes: overhead, fund raising, constituent gifts and entertainment, donations, and unitemized expenditures (see Table 1-6). Of the $199,310,139 invested by House incumbents, 46 percent was spent by those whose reelection was never in doubt.

For example, Rep. John D. Dingell (D-Mich.) spent $1,085,395 to collect 65 percent of the vote against Republican Frank Beaumont, who spent just $5,402. Rep. Dennis Hastert (R-Ill.) spent $613,623 in winning 67 percent of the vote against Democrat Jonathan Abram

Reich, who spent less than $5,000. Rep. Jack Fields (R-Texas) spent $744,065 and grabbed 77 percent of the vote against Democrat Charles E. Robinson, who invested less than $5,000. None of the three incumbents had primary opposition.

Dingell's 1992 campaign was truly a study in excess. First elected in 1955, Dingell had never received less than 63 percent of the vote. He had already turned back one underfunded challenge by Beaumont in 1990, and redistricting had done little to improve Beaumont's chances for their rematch in 1992. Nevertheless, Dingell's 1992 spending spree represented an 82 percent increase over the $596,591 he spent during the 1990 campaign.

Virtually every aspect of Dingell's effort reflected this massive increase. Overhead rose 97 percent, from $124,441 in 1990 to $244,744 in 1992.. His 1992 fund-raising costs of $161,127 represented an increase of 73 percent over the $92,890 he spent to fill his 1990 treasury. Expenditures on broadcast advertising more than doubled from $100,981 to $211,779. The only exception to the trend was Dingell's outlays for constituent entertainment and gifts, which declined from $57,921 to a still hefty $54,707.

Similarly, prior to 1992 Rep. Bill Thomas (R-Calif.) had seen his winning percentage drop as low as 60 percent only once in six reelection bids. Yet, in a district carried comfortably by George Bush, Thomas spent $610,997 to defeat Democrat Deborah A. Vollmer, who spent roughly 4 percent of that total. "You never know what the results are going to be until election day," remarked Catherine M. Abernathy, Thomas's administrative assistant.

In the Senate, electoral pressures clearly had nothing to do with Breaux's decision to invest $1,840,676 to beat back the challenge of the underfunded Khachaturian. Sen. Richard C. Shelby (D-Ala.) did not need to spend $2,638,104 to fend off the $146,556 challenge of Republican Richard Sellers. Rick Reed's (R-Hawaii) $482,953 campaign did not require Democratic Sen. Daniel K. Inouye's $3,503,564 response.

What then was driving these huge outlays? It most assuredly was not television advertising, which conventional wisdom has long blamed for the skyrocketing cost of campaigns. While the average amount invested by House incumbents in television and radio advertising nearly doubled between 1990 and 1992, those expenditures still represented only 25 percent of their total outlays. While some members felt the need to increase their broadcast budgets, others were able to cut them dramatically.

In 1990 Rep. Nancy L. Johnson (R-Conn.) had pumped $231,629 into television and radio commercials, despite the fact that her opponent could afford to spend just $1,961 on such advertising. Against an equally underfunded 1992 challenger, Eugene F. Slason, Johnson decided to forgo the three television commercials her campaigns generally run. That move sliced her broadcast advertising budget to the $72,569 it cost to produce and air three 60-second radio spots.

Fearing that the negative campaign tactics employed by Helms in his bitter Senate contest with Democrat Harvey B. Gantt would create a general anti-Republican backlash in 1990, Rep. Alex McMillan (R-N.C.) had paid Severin/Aviles Associates of New York $201,685 to create and place television commercials showcasing McMillan's work ethic. A secondary reason for the advertising push was redistricting. "We wanted to make a big push in 1990 to drive up the margin of victory," explained Frank H. Hill, McMillan's chief of staff. "We didn't want to give Democrats in the state legislature a reason to split up the district." The strategy apparently worked, since redistricting gave McMillan a more Republican constituency. With no such worries in 1992, McMillan opted to spend nothing on either television or radio commercials.

As in 1990, the $542,248,774 price tag attached to the 1992 campaigns was attributable in part to the fact that most members of Congress have created their own state-of-the-art, permanent political machines that operate 365 days each year, during off-years as well as election years. Between January 1, 1987, and December 31, 1991, incumbent senators seeking reelection in 1992 spent $30,128,255 to maintain their permanent campaign operations. During 1991, House incumbents spent $39,215,256 to keep their campaign engines humming.

Sen. Alfonse M. D'Amato (R-N.Y.) spent a staggering $3,753,302 to maintain his high-octane permanent campaign during the off-years. This outlay amounted to 32 percent of his total spending. Off-year overhead totaled $1,540,909, including after-tax salaries of $328,240. Fund-raising expenses during this period amounted to $1,352,607.

Direct-mail fund raising cost Sen. Bob Packwood (R-Ore.) $2,216,705 during the off-years, accounting for 69 percent of his total spending during that five-year period. Packwood's off-year expenses represented 40 percent of his total spending.

Still more impressive was the $937,542 Majority Leader Richard A. Gephardt (D-Mo.) invested in his "campaign" operation during 1991. He spent $514,304 on overhead and $222,146 for fund-raising events and direct-mail solicitations. Throughout the election cycle he maintained a Washington, D.C., fund-raising office with a staff of eight, including Richard Sullivan, a national fund-raiser for the Democratic Senatorial Campaign Committee (DSCC) and Donald J. Foley, political director at the DSCC.

Entrenched incumbents were not the only ones pouring money into permanent campaigns. After garnering 67 percent of the vote to win an open seat in 1990, freshman Rep. Jim Ramstad immediately settled into the permanent campaign mode. Off-year expenses totaled $151,776, including monthly rent of $600 on his campaign headquarters. Campaign manager Tim Berkness was hired in May 1991, and Berkness added two part-time staffers four months later.

Ramstad began 1991 with debts of $122,580 and cash reserves of only $2,448. Twenty-four months later he had whittled his debts to $21,793 while increasing his cash-on-hand to $317,719. He raised $486,967 from individual contributors who gave at least $200, $270,772 from donors who gave less than $200, and $260,016 from political action committees (PACs). He accomplished this impressive feat by sinking 41 percent of his $599,672 campaign outlays into fund raising.

While both overhead and fund raising represented smaller proportions of the typical incumbent's budget during the election year itself, spending on these items was by no means insignificant. Senate incumbents spent $85,440,675 during 1992; $27,577,530 of that total, or 32 percent, was invested in overhead and fund raising. Of the $160,181,884 spent by House members in 1992, 33 percent was committed to overhead and raising money.

Even though we refer to it as "campaign overhead," many incumbents spent large sums of their campaign treasuries to enhance their personal lifestyles. During the six years leading up to his 1992 reelection, D'Amato spent $156,729 of his campaign funds to lease and maintain two Lincoln Towncars, one of which was leased for his use in Washington, D.C. Inouye used his campaign funds to finance 403 meals costing less than $200 each, including a $12.50 bill at the

Szechuan Garden in Rockville, Md., and a $22.59 meal at the Wo Fat restaurant in Honolulu.

Together, members of the House and Senate simply gave away $10,653,432 of the money they collected for the 1992 campaigns. Although political party organizations were the chief beneficiaries of this philanthropic spirit, fellow members of Congress, local candidates, charities, local booster groups, and various ideological organizations benefited as well. In a year of turmoil, few incumbents felt they could afford to significantly reduce their political bridge-building efforts. Some significantly increased their giving.

The $66,186 Dellums donated from his treasury to other candidates, civic organizations, ideological groups, and Democratic party organizations represented a 39 percent increase over his 1990 donations. IMPAC 2000, a political action committee devoted to assisting Democrats in state redistricting battles, received $41,688. He donated $5,000 to the Democratic Congressional Campaign Committee. He spent $1,650 on tickets to a Congressional Black Caucus event, $1,315 on tickets to the Black Filmmakers Hall of Fame, and $1,000 on tickets to a dinner sponsored by the Black Women Organized for Educational Development.

Among the most important political bridges to maintain were those that tied incumbents to friendly, visiting constituents. House and Senate incumbents together spent $3,828,682 on constituent gifts and entertainment. Rep. John P. Murtha invested $45,395 of his treasury in constituent stroking. He spent $19,864 on gifts, including baubles from Lenox China and sweets from L&D candies. Tickets to various sporting events cost the campaign $8,513— $3,804 for season tickets to Pittsburgh Steelers football games, $1,176 for season tickets to Washington Redskins games, $1,804 for Pittsburgh Pirates tickets, $1,080 for University of Pittsburgh at Johnstown football tickets, and $649 for tickets to the Johnstown Chiefs, a minor league baseball club. He spent $6,896 on flowers for constituents, $5,300 on year-end holiday cards, and $4,822 on constituent meals and receptions.

Rep. Tom Bevill (D-Ala.) put $18,404 into his constituent stoking efforts during the 1992 election cycle—$2,724 more than in 1990. He spent $1,750 on cookbooks, $4,587 on constituent meals, $3,042 on calendars, $3,131 on year-end holiday cards, and $3,574 for glossy 8 × 10 photos, which he autographed for visitors. Each Christmas

Bevill ran newspaper ads inviting people to drop by his home for coffee and cookies; the parties cost his campaign $1,574.

There were a few incumbents who had no reason to spend freely on their reelection bids and actually chose not to do so, proving it is possible to thrive politically without spending huge sums. As he had since his initial House race in 1953, Rep. William H. Natcher (D-Ky.) paid for his entire campaign—all $6,625 of it—from his own pocket. After refusing to take political contributions of any kind for thirty-nine years, Natcher had no reason to change.

Mirroring his past campaigns, Natcher ran no television commercials. He had no campaign office, no paid or unpaid campaign staff. As the second ranking Democrat and acting chair of the Appropriations Committee, he had no reason to curry favor with fellow House members by contributing to their campaigns.

Instead, Natcher's campaign was a throwback to the 1950s. His office was his Chevrolet Citation, which he drove through all twenty counties in the district. Campaign stops consisted of conversations in coffee shops and drug stores. He spent $6,580 to run fifty small preprimary ads in twenty-seven newspapers. Each ad simply advised readers that he was the incumbent and was seeking reelection. Items listed on his preprimary campaign financial statements as "miscellaneous and postage" amounted to $19.47. Natcher completely ignored his weak general election opponent, filing expenses of only $25.20 after May 27. When Natcher died in March 1994, it truly was an end of an era.

While not quite as frugal as Natcher, Rep. Andrew Jacobs, Jr. (D-Ind.) also has a decidedly different approach to campaigning. "I am willing to lose before I take PAC contributions," Jacobs remarked. "It's obscene that lobbyists are able to make campaign contributions."

Jacobs rarely raises or spends much on his campaigns, and his 1992 rematch with economics professor Janos Horvath proved to be no exception. Jacobs spent just $14,376 to dispatch Horvath, which was $294 less than Jacobs invested to beat him in 1990.

Jacobs raised his funds primarily from a list of 700 "friends" who had responded to past direct-mail solicitations. However, even then, Jacobs set strict limits. When, in September 1992, he realized that his campaign bank account had risen to more than $39,000, the nine-term incumbent mailed out a letter asking his supporters not to send more money. "It's fall and time for a solicitation, but this time we don't need any money, so thank you," Jacobs remembered writing.

Jacobs ran the same radio spots in 1992 that he has run for the past several elections. "Gregory Peck recorded several ads a few years ago that were suitably self-indulgent and said nothing negative about me," Jacobs noted. He added that his ads said nothing negative about Horvath because "I don't do that, and we can't afford it anyway."

With retirements setting a postwar record and redistricting creating twenty-four additional open House seats, open seat candidates accounted for 20 percent of the $542,248,774 spent in 1992. Candidates vying for seventy-seven open seats in the House spent a total of $61,804,805. The average expenditure of $406,611 was more than twice the average outlay reported by those who challenged incumbents. The sixteen candidates contesting eight open Senate seats spent a total of $45,235,336. Their $2,827,209 average exceeded that of Senate challengers by $905,208, or 47 percent (see Tables 1-1 and 1-2). This increased spending translated directly into closer races. The winner in sixty of the seventy-seven House open seat contests received 55 percent of the vote or less in the primary election, the general election, or both. Another seven open seat winners garnered no more than 60 percent at some point on their electoral journey to Washington. In ten cases, the winner cruised through the process with 61 percent or more. In six of the eight Senate open seat races the winner received 55 percent or less.

Yet, even in these hotly contested open seat races, the average House candidate spent just 30 percent of his or her budget on broadcast advertising. The comparable figure for Senate candidates was 44 percent—far less than the long-assumed standard of 50 to 75 percent.

Where did all the money come from to fund these campaigns? PACs contributed $173,939,292 to those candidates who survived the primary process and went on to contest the November general election. PACs donated $1,240,597 to Gephardt; $1,148,438 to Rep. Vic Fazio (D-Calif.); $962,937 to Rostenkowski; $934,613 to Rep. David E. Bonior (D-Mich.); $767,931 to Dingell; and $711,367 to Rep. Steny H. Hoyer (D-Md.). In all, 28 House incumbents collected more than $500,000 from PACs and 189 received between $200,000 and $499,999 over the two-year cycle. Twenty-four senators had PAC donations of at least $1 million, led by Sen. Arlen Specter (R-Pa.), who collected $2,017,041 over the six-year cycle.

To trace Rep. George E. Brown, Jr. (D-Calif.) to his position as chairman of the Committee on Science, Space and Technology, one need look no further than his fund-raisers. In early 1991 Brown held a $1,000-a-head event aimed at PACs representing aerospace companies; in July Lockheed's PAC spent $763 to stage a small reception on his behalf. In May 1992 Brown drew close to 100 contributors to a fund-raiser at Houston's Clear Lake Space Club. One month later he traveled to New York for a fund-raising breakfast thrown for him by the Loral Corporation. In all, PACs representing aerospace, science, and technology interests contributed $115,488 to Brown's reelection effort.

As chairman of the subcommittee on Health and the Environment, Waxman was able to tap PACs representing health care interests for $177,800. In all, 203 PACs contributed a total of $402,915 to Waxman's coffers, which amounted to 64 percent of his donations. Individual contributions of $200 or less accounted for only 6 percent of his total contributions.

Although PACs donated primarily to incumbents, twenty-five candidates who vied for open seats in the House and five House challengers proved they had already mastered the fund-raising game by collecting at least $200,000 from PACs. Among this group were open seat winners Maria Cantwell (D-Wash.), Michael N. Castle (R-Del.), and Karen L. Thurman (D-Fla.), as well as losing challengers Anita Perez Ferguson (D-Calif.), Gwen Margolis (D-Fla.), and Andy Fox (D-Va.). Rep. Rod Chandler (R-Wash.), who gave up his House seat in an unsuccessful bid to succeed retiring Republican Sen. Brock Adams, led all Senate challengers with PAC donations of $1,143,695.

Democratic state representative Cynthia A. McKinney raised $166,642 from PACs for her open seat contest in Georgia's newly created majority-black District 11; this represented 54 percent of her total contributions. The closer she came to victory, the easier it became to raise PAC money. In the primary, PACs accounted for only 11 percent of her contributions. While McKinney failed to secure the 50 percent necessary to avoid a runoff in the five-candidate primary, her opponent was the only white candidate in the race. With McKinney's victory virtually assured, PACs accounted for 61 percent of her donations preceding the runoff. That figure grew to 65 percent in the perfunctory general election campaign.

However, while PACs have been cursed as the source of fund-raising evil—special interest money—they accounted for just 32 percent of the $543,398,701 raised by congressional candidates who contested the November general elections. Fifty-five percent of the money raised by these candidates came from individual contributors.

In 1990 federal records showed that 62 people had violated the $25,000 annual limit on contributions to federal candidates and political committees set in 1974 by Congress. Replicating that study on 1992 contribution data yielded 110 violators, including Angelo Parisi, a chef who at one time owned restaurants in both New York and Huntington Beach, Calif. During 1991 and 1992, Parisi made federal contributions totaling $100,004, of which $66,262 was credited to 1992. In all, seven people donated more than $50,000 during 1992, more than twice the legal limit. Twenty-one others gave at least $40,000 (see Table 1-7).

Reflecting the fact that the Federal Election Commission rarely acts to enforce the law, does so only when violations are brought to its attention, and rarely negotiates anything more than token fines, seven of those on the 1992 list were repeat offenders from 1990, including Corning executive James R. Houghton, the brother of Rep. Amo Houghton (R-N.Y.)

Some violators, including William C. Mow, chairman of Bugle Boy Jeans in Los Angeles, Calif., indicated they were unaware of the law. Julian Klein, a retired New Yorker, explained that he simply responded to requests from Republican campaigns without bothering to keep track of the total amount. "I just kept getting requests in the mail, and when I could I sent money" Klein noted. "I didn't know about any limit." In all, Klein wrote ninety-one checks totaling $28,850 during 1992.

Others blamed their violations on mistakes made by the campaigns. "I requested that those checks be credited to my wife, but the individual campaigns credited all of it to me," complained Michael L. Keiser, a repeat offender from 1990 and president of Recycled Paper Products of Chicago, Ill., the country's fourth-largest greeting card manufacturer. Unfortunately for Keiser, his wife was the only person who could request that contributions be credited to her, and she had to do so in writing at the time the contributions were made. Barring such notice, campaigns are required to credit the contribution to the person whose signature appeared on the check.

Several others, including Thomas D. Barrow of Houston, Texas, had their own interpretation of the law, which they felt justified their violations. "You have failed to recognize that I reside in a community property state. My wife and I have an account that is community property, and therefore all political contributions are made jointly. I cannot vouch for how the Federal Election Commission keeps its records, but all contributions should have been divided in half. You should recognize that we have a $50,000 limit that we clearly did not exceed." Sadly for Barrow, that is not how the law works. Having signed the checks in question, he was under federal law the sole contributor.

Some were simply unrepentant. "Let them come and get me," taunted Charles J. Harrington, a retired Du Pont executive. "I keep getting requests for donations, and I'm going to keep on donating."

Given that PACs can donate no more than $10,000 to any candidate, corporate executives who wish to help have increasingly taken to "bundling" checks from a number of their colleagues, frequently passing them on to candidates in a single envelope. Sen. Patrick J. Leahy (D-Vt.) passed through Beverly Hills on June 4, 1991 and left with $52,250 from movie studio executives and their spouses. Prominent among the attendees were executives from the Walt Disney Company and its various subsidiaries. At that one reception, Disney executives and their spouses gave Leahy forty-three checks totaling $31,750. The Disney PAC did not contribute to Leahy's 1992 campaign.

While the law firm of Skadden, Arps, Slate, Meagher and Flom did not contribute through its PAC to Democrat Robert Abrams's unsuccessful challenge to D'Amato, the firm's members gave individual contributions to Abrams totaling $36,700. Twenty-four checks totaling $9,500 were passed to Abrams on December 31, 1991.

In short, while news reports were filled with talk of change, candidates collected and spent their money much as they had before. Fueled by special-interest money that flowed from individuals and PACs alike, the cost of the 1992 elections was unnecessarily inflated by spending that went far beyond the business of directly appealing for votes. While Congress continues its seemingly endless debate over campaign finance reform, few on Capitol Hill have proposed changes in the way money is spent. Until that issue is addressed, the aggregate cost of campaigns will remain unnecessarily high.

Table 1-1 What Campaign Money Buys in the 1992 Senate Races: Total Expenditures

Major Category	Incumbents in			Challengers in			Open Seats
	Total	Hot Races[a]	Contested Races[b]	Total	Hot Races[a]	Contested Races[b]	
Overhead							
Office furniture/supplies	$ 2,138,579	$ 1,655,100	$ 483,480	$ 959,838	$ 346,126	$ 113,711	$ 689,957
Rent/utilities	1,295,489	1,038,579	256,911	647,697	536,876	110,821	489,631
Salaries	9,062,286	6,968,809	2,093,478	6,124,369	5,446,217	678,152	5,182,451
Taxes	4,744,248	3,532,457	1,211,790	1,447,210	1,253,826	193,383	1,127,419
Bank/investment fees	140,733	114,660	26,074	48,842	46,627	2,214	56,936
Lawyers/accountants	1,520,892	1,150,329	370,563	378,807	372,002	6,805	260,456
Telephone	1,690,864	1,392,283	298,581	1,461,799	1,269,403	192,396	926,505
Campaign automobile	586,888	488,834	98,054	95,674	71,121	24,553	12,872
Computers/office equipment	1,483,906	1,117,387	366,519	817,681	749,928	67,753	450,141
Travel	5,647,008	4,111,695	1,535,313	1,711,246	1,561,675	149,571	1,332,866
Food/meetings	651,655	503,449	148,206	33,475	31,111	2,364	45,820
Total Overhead	**28,962,549**	**22,073,582**	**6,888,968**	**13,726,638**	**12,184,914**	**1,541,724**	**10,575,054**
Fund Raising							
Events	11,953,477	9,342,020	2,611,457	3,533,953	3,300,064	233,890	3,025,578
Direct mail	11,183,186	9,747,584	1,435,602	6,719,959	6,490,685	229,273	5,423,654
Telemarketing	690,252	339,944	350,308	715,069	696,805	18,265	475,225
Total Fund Raising	**23,826,914**	**19,429,548**	**4,397,366**	**10,968,982**	**10,487,554**	**481,428**	**8,924,458**
Polling	**3,452,440**	**2,644,700**	**807,739**	**1,426,095**	**1,253,330**	**172,765**	**1,114,642**

Advertising							
Electronic media	46,141,090	38,338,087	7,803,002	25,576,877	23,657,286	1,919,591	20,071,775
Other media	924,413	696,847	227,566	336,177	251,164	85,014	321,355
Total Advertising	**47,065,503**	**39,034,934**	**8,030,569**	**25,913,054**	**23,908,449**	**2,004,605**	**20,393,130**
Other Campaign Activity							
Persuasion mail/brochures	3,119,520	2,580,865	538,654	1,827,876	1,588,216	239,661	1,062,077
Actual campaigning	5,921,553	4,807,956	1,113,597	3,111,176	2,928,548	182,628	2,756,360
Staff/Volunteers	73,252	47,418	25,834	28,080	27,137	943	18,282
Total Other Campaign Activity	**9,114,325**	**7,436,239**	**1,678,086**	**4,967,132**	**4,543,901**	**423,231**	**3,836,719**
Constituent Gifts/ Entertainment	**834,972**	**530,990**	**303,981**	**31,697**	**31,457**	**239**	**20,484**
Donations to							
Candidates from same state	100,941	37,758	63,183	3,986	3,986	0	4,988
Candidates from other states	170,643	74,581	96,062	1,026	1,026	0	2,000
Civic organizations	330,014	249,969	80,045	4,663	3,674	990	10,910
Ideological groups	70,820	39,087	31,733	5,849	5,579	270	2,712
Political parties	893,828	322,177	571,651	11,437	9,787	1,650	18,671
Total Donations	**1,566,247**	**723,573**	**842,674**	**26,961**	**24,052**	**2,910**	**39,280**
Unitemized Expenses	1,354,599	1,011,801	342,797	599,478	453,917	145,561	331,569
Total Expenditures	**$116,177,549**	**$92,885,368**	**$23,292,181**	**$57,660,036**	**$52,887,574**	**$4,772,463**	**$45,235,336**

Note: Totals are for the entire six-year cycle, including special elections.

[a]Races where incumbent garners 60 percent or less of the vote.
[b]Races where incumbent garners more than 60 percent of the vote.

Table 1-2 What Campaign Money Buys in the 1992 Senate Races: Average Expenditures

Major Category	Incumbents in			Challengers in			
	Total	Hot Races[a]	Contested Races[b]	Total	Hot Races[a]	Contested Races[b]	Open Seats
Overhead							
Office furniture/supplies	$ 76,378	$ 87,111	$ 53,720	$ 31,995	$ 40,292	$ 12,635	$ 43,122
Rent/utilities	46,267	54,662	28,546	21,590	25,566	12,313	30,602
Salaries	323,653	366,779	232,609	204,146	259,344	75,350	323,903
Taxes	169,437	185,919	134,643	48,240	59,706	21,487	70,464
Bank/investment fees	5,026	6,035	2,897	1,628	2,220	246	3,559
Lawyers/accountants	54,318	60,544	41,174	12,627	17,714	756	16,278
Telephone	60,388	73,278	33,176	48,727	60,448	21,377	57,907
Campaign automobile	20,960	25,728	10,895	3,189	3,387	2,728	805
Computers/office equipment	52,997	58,810	40,724	27,256	35,711	7,528	28,134
Travel	201,679	216,405	170,590	57,042	74,365	16,619	83,304
Food/meetings	23,273	26,497	16,467	1,116	1,481	263	2,864
Total Overhead	1,034,377	1,161,767	765,441	457,555	580,234	171,303	660,941
Fund Raising							
Events	426,910	491,685	290,162	117,798	157,146	25,988	189,099
Direct mail	399,399	513,031	159,511	223,999	309,080	25,475	338,978
Telemarketing	24,652	17,892	38,923	23,836	33,181	2,029	29,702
Total Fund Raising	850,961	1,022,608	488,596	365,633	499,407	53,492	557,779
Polling	123,301	139,195	89,749	47,536	59,682	19,196	69,665

Advertising							
Electronic media	1,647,896	2,017,794	867,000	852,563	1,126,537	213,288	1,254,486
Other media	33,015	36,676	25,285	11,206	11,960	9,446	20,085
Total Advertising	**1,680,911**	**2,054,470**	**892,285**	**863,768**	**1,138,498**	**222,734**	**1,274,571**
Other Campaign Activity							
Persuasion mail/brochures	111,411	135,835	59,850	60,929	75,629	26,629	66,380
Actual campaigning	211,484	253,050	123,733	103,706	139,455	20,292	172,272
Staff/Volunteers	2,616	2,496	2,870	936	1,292	105	1,143
Total Other Campaign Activity	**325,512**	**391,381**	**186,454**	**165,571**	**216,376**	**47,026**	**239,795**
Constituent Gifts/Entertainment	**29,820**	**27,947**	**33,776**	**1,057**	**1,498**	**27**	**1,280**
Donations to							
Candidates from same state	3,605	1,987	7,020	133	190	0	312
Candidates from other states	6,094	3,925	10,674	34	49	0	125
Civic organizations	11,786	13,156	8,894	155	175	110	682
Ideological groups	2,529	2,057	3,526	195	266	30	169
Political parties	31,922	16,957	63,517	381	466	183	1,167
Total Donations	**55,937**	**38,083**	**93,630**	**899**	**1,145**	**323**	**2,455**
Unitemized Expenses	**48,379**	**53,253**	**38,089**	**19,983**	**21,615**	**16,173**	**20,723**
Total Expenditures	**$4,149,198**	**$4,888,704**	**$2,588,020**	**$1,922,001**	**$2,518,456**	**$530,274**	**$2,827,209**

Note: Totals are for the entire six-year cycle, including special elections.

[a]Races where incumbent garners 60 percent or less of the vote.
[b]Races where incumbent garners more than 60 percent of the vote.

Table 1-3 What Campaign Money Buys in the 1992 Senate Races: Expenditures, by Percentage

Major Category	Incumbents in			Challengers in			Open Seats
	Total	Hot Races[a]	Contested Races[b]	Total	Hot Races[a]	Contested Races[b]	
Overhead							
Office furniture/supplies	1.84	1.78	2.08	1.66	1.60	2.38	1.53
Rent/utilities	1.12	1.12	1.10	1.12	1.02	2.32	1.08
Salaries	7.80	7.50	8.99	10.62	10.30	14.21	11.46
Taxes	4.08	3.80	5.20	2.51	2.37	4.05	2.49
Bank/investment fees	.12	.12	.11	.08	.09	.05	.13
Lawyers/accountants	1.31	1.24	1.59	.66	.70	.14	.58
Telephone	1.46	1.50	1.28	2.54	2.40	4.03	2.05
Campaign automobile	.51	.53	.42	.17	.13	.51	.03
Computers/office equipment	1.28	1.20	1.57	1.42	1.42	1.42	1.00
Travel	4.86	4.43	6.59	2.97	2.95	3.13	2.95
Food/meetings	.56	.54	.64	.06	.06	.05	.10
Total Overhead	**24.93**	**23.76**	**29.58**	**23.81**	**23.04**	**32.30**	**23.38**
Fund Raising							
Events	10.29	10.06	11.21	6.13	6.24	4.90	6.69
Direct mail	9.63	10.49	6.16	11.65	12.27	4.80	11.99
Telemarketing	.59	.37	1.50	1.24	1.32	.38	1.05
Total Fund Raising	**20.51**	**20.92**	**18.88**	**19.02**	**19.83**	**10.09**	**19.73**
Polling	**2.97**	**2.85**	**3.47**	**2.47**	**2.37**	**3.62**	**2.46**

Advertising						
Electronic media	39.72	41.27	33.50	44.36	44.73	40.22
Other media	.80	.75	.98	.58	.47	1.78
Total Advertising	**40.51**	**42.02**	**34.48**	**44.94**	**45.21**	**42.00**
Other Campaign Activity						
Persuasion mail/brochures	2.69	2.78	2.31	3.17	3.00	5.02
Actual campaigning	5.10	5.18	4.78	5.40	5.54	3.83
Staff/Volunteers	.06	.05	.11	.05	.05	.02
Total Other Campaign Activity	**7.85**	**8.01**	**7.20**	**8.61**	**8.59**	**8.87**
Constituent Gifts/Entertainment	**.72**	**.57**	**1.31**	**.05**	**.06**	**.01**
Donations to						
Candidates from same state	.09	.04	.27	.01	.01	0
Candidates from other states	.15	.08	.41	0	0	0
Civic organizations	.28	.27	.34	.01	.01	.02
Ideological groups	.06	.04	.14	.01	.01	.01
Political parties	.77	.35	2.45	.02	.02	.03
Total Donations	**1.35**	**.78**	**3.62**	**.05**	**.05**	**.06**
Unitemized Expenses	**1.17**	**1.09**	**1.47**	**1.04**	**.86**	**3.05**
Total Expenditures	**100.00**	**100.00**	**100.00**	**100.00**	**100.00**	**100.00**

(additional column)
Electronic media	44.37
Other media	.71
Total Advertising	**45.08**
Persuasion mail/brochures	2.35
Actual campaigning	6.09
Staff/Volunteers	.04
Total Other Campaign Activity	**8.48**
Constituent Gifts/Entertainment	**.05**
Candidates from same state	.01
Candidates from other states	0
Civic organizations	.02
Ideological groups	.01
Political parties	.04
Total Donations	**.09**
Unitemized Expenses	**.73**
Total Expenditures	**100.00**

Note: Totals are for the entire six-year cycle, including special elections.

[a] Races where incumbent garners 60 percent or less of the vote.
[b] Races where incumbent garners more than 60 percent of the vote.

Table 1-4 What Campaign Money Buys in the 1992 House Races: Total Expenditures

Major Category	Incumbents in				Challengers in			
	Total	Hot Races[a]	Contested Races[b]	Unopposed	Total	Hot Races[a]	Contested Races[b]	Open Seats
Overhead								
Office furniture/supplies	$ 3,063,833	$ 1,567,795	$ 1,453,124	$ 42,914	$ 1,157,549	$ 817,953	$ 339,596	$ 972,210
Rent/utilities	3,210,015	1,698,212	1,458,080	53,724	1,107,949	744,741	363,208	968,932
Salaries	17,584,466	9,228,350	8,143,580	212,536	6,574,871	4,706,294	1,868,577	6,692,947
Taxes	5,726,173	2,794,972	2,840,847	90,354	1,021,178	796,484	224,694	1,009,987
Bank/investment fees	456,861	238,690	216,962	1,210	73,489	54,601	18,888	77,877
Lawyers/accountants	3,540,575	1,795,126	1,706,714	38,735	418,806	297,912	120,894	368,575
Telephone	2,987,569	1,647,308	1,280,893	59,369	1,497,218	1,047,122	450,096	1,208,963
Campaign automobile	1,103,064	609,773	444,267	49,024	85,959	55,449	30,510	91,266
Computers/office equipment	3,142,414	1,558,358	1,499,613	84,443	929,400	647,196	282,204	648,237
Travel	7,439,927	3,646,677	3,530,401	262,849	1,380,697	917,275	463,421	1,277,535
Food/meetings	1,250,157	484,878	654,326	110,953	90,338	65,490	24,849	72,742
Total Overhead	**49,505,056**	**25,270,139**	**23,228,807**	**1,006,110**	**14,337,454**	**10,150,517**	**4,186,937**	**13,389,272**
Fund Raising								
Events	22,917,783	10,600,198	11,917,392	400,193	3,287,026	2,480,155	806,872	3,626,302
Direct mail	7,429,739	4,206,801	3,187,778	35,160	1,852,774	1,372,676	480,099	1,356,013
Telemarketing	485,907	279,264	206,643	0	187,809	162,031	25,778	90,475
Total Fund Raising	**30,833,429**	**15,086,262**	**15,311,814**	**435,353**	**5,327,610**	**4,014,862**	**1,312,748**	**5,072,790**
Polling	**6,994,215**	**4,220,705**	**2,754,310**	**19,200**	**2,037,398**	**1,580,163**	**457,235**	**2,061,062**

Advertising								
Electronic media	49,484,954	31,232,428	18,230,545	21,981	20,457,833	16,902,381	3,555,452	18,249,374
Other media	5,236,282	2,374,824	2,840,220	21,238	1,929,805	1,365,950	563,854	1,587,920
Total Advertising	**54,721,236**	**33,607,252**	**21,070,764**	**43,219**	**22,387,638**	**18,268,332**	**4,119,306**	**19,837,294**
Other Campaign Activity								
Persuasion mail/brochures	24,499,213	14,784,542	9,666,302	48,369	10,139,985	7,562,416	2,577,569	13,604,775
Actual campaigning	14,726,433	7,776,335	6,695,385	254,713	6,190,367	4,397,739	1,792,628	6,255,507
Staff/Volunteers	527,244	283,559	237,442	6,243	52,577	36,932	15,646	88,246
Total Other Campaign Activity	**39,752,890**	**22,844,435**	**16,599,129**	**309,326**	**16,382,929**	**11,997,086**	**4,385,843**	**19,948,528**
Constituent Gifts/ Entertainment	**2,993,710**	**1,183,217**	**1,692,677**	**117,816**	**34,236**	**24,660**	**9,576**	**71,280**
Donations to								
Candidates from same state	1,816,962	372,727	1,278,550	165,685	17,123	10,597	6,525	28,692
Candidates from other states	1,356,449	311,972	1,007,476	37,001	2,385	2,360	25	5,850
Civic organizations	1,146,242	384,273	729,685	32,284	49,982	36,894	13,088	61,124
Ideological groups	534,750	222,122	309,112	3,515	10,630	5,013	5,617	17,501
Political parties	4,232,783	1,502,895	2,661,971	67,916	58,766	39,510	19,255	61,447
Total Donations	**9,087,185**	**2,793,989**	**5,986,795**	**306,402**	**138,885**	**94,375**	**44,511**	**174,613**
Unitemized Expenses	**5,422,418**	**2,497,737**	**2,746,014**	**178,667**	**1,414,758**	**920,600**	**494,158**	**1,249,966**
Total Expenditures	**$199,310,139**	**$107,503,735**	**$89,390,309**	**$2,416,095**	**$62,060,908**	**$47,050,594**	**$15,010,313**	**$61,804,805**

Note: Totals are for the entire two-year cycle, including special elections.

[a] Races where incumbent garners 60 percent or less of the vote.
[b] Races where incumbent garners more than 60 percent of the vote.

Table 1-5 What Campaign Money Buys in the 1992 House Races: Average Expenditures

Major Category	Incumbents in				Challengers in			
	Total	Hot Races[a]	Contested Races[b]	Unopposed	Total	Hot Races[a]	Contested Races[b]	Open Seats
Overhead								
Office furniture/supplies	$ 8,779	$ 10,452	$ 7,608	$ 5,364	$ 3,233	$ 5,018	$ 1,742	$ 6,396
Rent/utilities	9,198	11,321	7,634	6,715	3,095	4,569	1,863	6,375
Salaries	50,385	61,522	42,637	26,567	18,366	28,873	9,582	44,033
Taxes	16,407	18,633	14,874	11,294	2,852	4,886	1,152	6,645
Bank/investment fees	1,309	1,591	1,136	151	205	335	97	512
Lawyers/accountants	10,145	11,968	8,936	4,842	1,170	1,828	620	2,425
Telephone	8,560	10,982	6,706	7,421	4,182	6,424	2,308	7,954
Campaign automobile	3,161	4,065	2,326	6,128	240	340	156	600
Computers/office equipment	9,004	10,389	7,851	10,555	2,596	3,971	1,447	4,265
Travel	21,318	24,311	18,484	32,856	3,857	5,627	2,377	8,405
Food/meetings	3,582	3,233	3,426	13,869	252	402	127	479
Total Overhead	**141,848**	**168,468**	**121,617**	**125,764**	**40,049**	**62,273**	**21,471**	**88,087**
Fund Raising								
Events	65,667	70,668	62,395	50,024	9,182	15,216	4,138	23,857
Direct mail	21,289	28,045	16,690	4,395	5,175	8,421	2,462	8,921
Telemarketing	1,392	1,862	1,082	0	525	994	132	595
Total Fund Raising	**88,348**	**100,575**	**80,167**	**54,419**	**14,882**	**24,631**	**6,732**	**33,374**
Polling	**20,041**	**28,138**	**14,420**	**2,400**	**5,691**	**9,694**	**2,345**	**13,560**

Advertising							
Electronic media	141,791	208,216	95,448	2,748	57,145	103,696	18,233	120,062
Other media	15,004	15,832	14,870	2,655	5,391	8,380	2,892	10,447
Total Advertising	**156,794**	**224,048**	**110,318**	**5,402**	**62,535**	**112,076**	**21,125**	**130,509**
Other Campaign Activity							
Persuasion mail/brochures	70,198	98,564	50,609	6,046	28,324	46,395	13,218	89,505
Actual campaigning	42,196	51,842	35,054	31,839	17,292	26,980	9,193	41,155
Staff/Volunteers	1,511	1,890	1,243	780	147	227	80	581
Total Other Campaign Activity	**113,905**	**152,296**	**86,906**	**38,666**	**45,762**	**73,602**	**22,492**	**131,240**
Constituent Gifts/ Entertainment	**8,578**	**7,888**	**8,862**	**14,727**	**96**	**151**	**49**	**469**
Donations to							
Candidates from same state	5,206	2,485	6,694	20,711	48	65	33	189
Candidates from other states	3,887	2,080	5,275	4,625	7	14	0	38
Civic organizations	3,284	2,562	3,820	4,035	140	226	67	402
Ideological groups	1,532	1,481	1,618	439	30	31	29	115
Political parties	12,128	10,019	13,937	8,490	164	242	99	404
Total Donations	**26,038**	**18,627**	**31,344**	**38,300**	**388**	**579**	**228**	**1,149**
Unitemized Expenses	**15,537**	**16,652**	**14,377**	**22,333**	**3,952**	**5,648**	**2,534**	**8,223**
Total Expenditures	**$571,089**	**$716,692**	**$468,012**	**$302,012**	**$173,354**	**$288,654**	**$76,976**	**$406,611**

Note: Totals are for the entire two-year cycle, including special elections.

[a] Races where incumbent garners 60 percent or less of the vote.
[b] Races where incumbent garners more than 60 percent of the vote.

Table 1-6 What Campaign Money Buys in the 1992 House Races: Expenditures, by Percentage

Major Category	Incumbents in				Challengers in			
	Total	Hot Races[a]	Contested Races[b]	Unopposed	Total	Hot Races[a]	Contested Races[b]	Open Seats
Overhead								
Office furniture/supplies	1.54	1.46	1.63	1.78	1.87	1.74	2.26	1.57
Rent/utilities	1.61	1.58	1.63	2.22	1.79	1.58	2.42	1.57
Salaries	8.82	8.58	9.11	8.80	10.59	10.00	12.45	10.83
Taxes	2.87	2.60	3.18	3.74	1.65	1.69	1.50	1.63
Bank/investment fees	.23	.22	.24	.05	.12	.12	.13	.13
Lawyers/accountants	1.78	1.67	1.91	1.60	.67	.63	.81	.60
Telephone	1.50	1.53	1.43	2.46	2.41	2.23	3.00	1.96
Campaign automobile	.55	.57	.50	2.03	.14	.12	.20	.15
Computers/office equipment	1.58	1.45	1.68	3.50	1.50	1.38	1.88	1.05
Travel	3.73	3.39	3.95	10.88	2.22	1.95	3.09	2.07
Food/meetings	.63	.45	.73	4.59	.15	.14	.17	.12
Total Overhead	**24.84**	**23.51**	**25.99**	**41.64**	**23.10**	**21.57**	**27.89**	**21.66**
Fund Raising								
Events	11.50	9.86	13.33	16.56	5.30	5.27	5.38	5.87
Direct mail	3.73	3.91	3.57	1.46	2.99	2.92	3.20	2.19
Telemarketing	.24	.26	.23	0	.30	.34	.17	.15
Total Fund Raising	**15.47**	**14.03**	**17.13**	**18.02**	**8.58**	**8.53**	**8.75**	**8.21**
Polling	**3.51**	**3.93**	**3.08**	**.79**	**3.28**	**3.36**	**3.05**	**3.33**

Advertising								
Electronic media	24.83	29.05	20.39	.91	32.96	35.92	23.69	29.53
Other media	2.63	2.21	3.18	.88	3.11	2.90	3.76	2.57
Total Advertising	**27.46**	**31.26**	**23.57**	**1.79**	**36.07**	**38.83**	**27.44**	**32.10**
Other Campaign Activity								
Persuasion mail/brochures	12.29	13.75	10.81	2.00	16.34	16.07	17.17	22.01
Actual campaigning	7.39	7.23	7.49	10.54	9.97	9.35	11.94	10.12
Staff/Volunteers	.26	.26	.27	.26	.08	.08	.10	.14
Total Other Campaign Activity	**19.95**	**21.25**	**18.57**	**12.80**	**26.40**	**25.50**	**29.22**	**32.28**
Constituent Gifts/Entertainment	**1.50**	**1.10**	**1.89**	**4.88**	**.06**	**.05**	**.06**	**.12**
Donations to								
Candidates from same state	.91	.35	1.43	6.86	.03	.02	.04	.05
Candidates from other states	.68	.29	1.13	1.53	.00	.01	.00	.01
Civic organizations	.58	.36	.82	1.34	.08	.08	.09	.10
Ideological groups	.27	.21	.35	.15	.02	.01	.04	.03
Political parties	2.12	1.40	2.98	2.81	.09	.08	.13	.10
Total Donations	**4.56**	**2.60**	**6.70**	**12.68**	**.22**	**.20**	**.30**	**.28**
Unitemized Expenses	**2.72**	**2.32**	**3.07**	**7.39**	**2.28**	**1.96**	**3.29**	**2.02**
Total Expenditures	**100.00**	**100.00**	**100.00**	**100.00**	**100.00**	**100.00**	**100.00**	**100.00**

Note: Totals are for the entire two-year cycle, including special elections.

[a]Races where incumbent garners 60 percent or less of the vote.
[b]Races where incumbent garners more than 60 percent of the vote.

Table 1-7 Individuals in Violation of Federal Election Campaign Contribution Laws: 1992 Election Cycle

#		City	1991	1992	#		City	1991	1992
1	Angelo Parisi	New Rochelle, N.Y.	$33,742	$66,262	56	Robert Gumbiner	Long Beach, Calif.	$33,000	$24,450
2	William C. Mow	Los Angeles	18,285	65,350	57	Eugene Dinsmore	Omaha, Neb.	11,356	32,985
3	D. Lloyd Wilson	Cozad, N.M.	6,815	52,500	58	William Lerach[a]	San Diego	3,000	32,468
4	David Packard	Los Altos, Calif.	4,805	50,950	59	Thomas F. Kranz	Los Angeles	18,500	32,183
5	John D. Murchinson	Dallas	1,000	50,500	60	Bruce C. Gottwald	Richmond, Va.	8,250	31,500
6	Edmund A. Stanley, Jr.	Oxford, Md.	19,250	50,450	61	Mary M. Ashmore	Boynton Beach, Fla.	14,850	31,000
7	Abe Pollin	Landover, Md.	3,500	50,250	62	Elinor Goodspeed[a]	Washington, D.C.	14,900	30,700
8	John A. Gabriel	Sante Fe Springs, Calif.	1,640	49,840	63	Candace Straight	Bloomfield, N.J.	18,500	30,540
9	Thomas A. Kershaw	Boston	19,000	49,144	64	Ray B. Auel	Sherwood, Ore.	17,000	30,500
10	Joseph W. Cotchett	Burlingame, Calif.	5,000	48,000	65	Ian Cumming	Salt Lake City	10,500	30,302
11	Richard B. Cray	Kansas City, Mo.	13,000	47,750	66	Michael Keiser[a]	Chicago	20,700	30,250
12	Charles Intriago	Miami	0	47,500	67	Elsie H. Hillman[a]	Pittsburgh	13,250	30,150
13	Charles White	San Diego	22,440	46,641	68	Stanley C. Gault	Wooster, Ohio	0	30,100
14	Grover Connell	Westfield, N.J.	2,000	46,319	69	Peter M. Flanigan	New York	18,250	30,050
15	William Hambrecht	San Francisco	21,000	46,250	70	William M. Keck II	Los Angeles	10,000	30,000
16	Ann Cox Chambers	Atlanta, GA	1,500	44,750	71	Mary M. Newman	Corona Del Mar, Calif.	14,750	30,000
17	Henry Salvatori	Los Angeles	13,410	43,900	72	Harriet Stimson Bullitt	Seattle	0	29,750
18	Don Henley	Beverly Hills	3,500	43,850	73	Irwin M. Rosenthal	New York	0	29,750
19	Edgar Uihlein	Northbrook, Ill.	17,000	43,700	74	Arthur B. Belfer	New York	24,430	29,645
20	Glenn E. Stinson	Naples, Fla.	17,000	43,300	75	Howard Gilman	New York	10,000	29,500
21	Peter C. Cook	Grand Rapids, Mich.	24,000	43,110	76	Lawrence Lewis Jr	Richmond, Va.	23,000	29,475
22	John P. Manning	Boston	21,000	42,800	77	Paul J. Meyer	Dallas	29,300	20,000
23	Herbert F. Collins	Boston	17,000	42,000	78	Thomas D. Barrow	Houston	22,000	29,000
24	Thomas Hansberger	Ft. Lauderdale, Fla.	24,000	40,650	79	James E. Davis	Jacksonville, Fla.	10,000	29,000
25	C. Thomas Clagett, Jr.	Washington, D.C.	18,250	40,392	80	Julian Klein	New York	13,700	28,850
26	Don Gray Angell, Jr.	Pompano Beach, Fla.	0	40,000	81	Gary David Goldberg	Los Angeles	2,750	28,750
27	Robert Coates	Dallas	0	40,000	82	Zora Charles	Beverly Hills	0	28,500

#	Name	Location		
28	David Rosenberg	Exton, Pa.	20,000	**40,000**
29	Laurence W. Levine	New York	1,297	**39,500**
30	Patricia Connell	Westfield, N.J.	2,000	**39,319**
31	Chesley Pruet	El Dorado, Ark.	17,250	**39,200**
32	Norman V. Kinsey[a]	Shreveport, La.	**28,000**	**38,750**
33	Eugene Applebaum	Troy, Mich.	15,250	**38,000**
34	S. Daniel Abraham	New York	14,000	**38,000**
35	Robert Day	New York	22,000	**38,000**
36	Stephen C. Swid	New York	0	**38,000**
37	Bruce D. Benson	Denver	4,000	**37,625**
38	Henry L. Hillman	Pittsburgh	7,000	**37,500**
39	Jonathan Tisch	New York	1,250	**36,750**
40	Phillip B. Rooney Sr.	Hinsdale, Ill.	10,000	**36,250**
41	John K. Funk	Houston	12,530	**35,660**
42	Henry J. Smith	Dallas	10,500	**35,500**
43	W. Clement Stone	Lake Forest, Ill.	11,500	**35,500**
44	Charles J. Harrington	Wilmington, Del.	**35,430**	**28,735**
45	John F. Hotchkis	Los Angeles	16,000	**35,000**
46	Susan Quinn Keck	Los Angeles	10,000	**35,000**
47	Jerome S. Moss	Hollywood	10,000	**34,750**
48	James Bronce Henderson	Detroit	22,797	**34,500**
49	Frederick A. Klingenstein	New York	18,000	**34,500**
50	Edward Lozick	Highland Heights, Ohio	17,000	**34,500**
51	Robert A. Daly	Los Angeles	5,500	**33,718**
52	Robert J. Stein	Washington, D.C.	17,500	**33,605**
53	J. Weldon Granger	Houston	8,000	**33,575**
54	James A. Elkins Jr.	Houston	21,000	**33,250**
55	James R. Houghton[a]	Corning, N.Y.	6,000	**33,150**

#	Name	Location		
83	Andrew Athens	Chicago	13,500	**28,475**
84	Stanley Hirch[a]	Studio City, Calif.	23,500	**28,300**
85	Sheldon Silverston	New York	15,510	**28,245**
86	James A. Ortenzio	New York	10,000	**28,000**
87	John N. Irwin, II	New York	**27,500**	24,000
88	Joshua L. Mailman	New York	21,000	**27,500**
89	Clifford L. Michel	Gladstone, N.J.	**27,500**	14,750
90	William W. Harris	Cambridge, Mass.	23,000	**27,250**
91	George Argyros	Costa Mesa, Calif.	17,500	**27,000**
92	Thomas Klutznick	Chicago	1,000	**27,000**
93	John N. Palmer	Jackson, Miss.	13,000	**27,000**
94	Andrew A. Kiss	Washington, D.C.	23,791	**26,956**
95	Allan C. Greenberg	New York	1,000	**26,775**
96	Cynthia Friedman	Washington, D.C.	14,750	**26,750**
97	Albert Abramson	Bethesda, Md.	16,000	**26,500**
98	David S. Steiner	West Orange, N.J.	**26,500**	23,140
99	Karl M. Samuelian	Los Angeles	21,360	**26,500**
100	Anita Hirsh	Studio City	6,500	**26,500**
101	H. Wayne Huizenga	Ft. Lauderdale, Fla.	15,000	**26,000**
102	Charles M. Pigott	Bellevue, Wash.	17,000	**26,000**
103	Steven J. Ross	New York	**26,000**	13,500
104	Paul J. Elston	New York	4,500	**25,850**
105	Bernard Rapoport	Waco, Texas	**25,750**	24,211
106	Frederick W. Field	Beverly Hills	24,500	**25,500**
107	Sylvia Steiner	West Orange, N.J.	7,000	**25,500**
108	William W. Boeschstein	Toledo, Ohio	20,000	**25,250**
109	John H. Lindsey	Houston	16,000	**25,250**
110	Peter L. Buttenwieser	Pittsburgh	19,000	**25,106**

Note: Totals in bold indicate contributors in excess of the $25,000 limit established in 1974 by Congress.

[a]Also exceeded the federal $25,000 contribution limit in 1990.

CHAPTER 2

What Campaign Money *Still* Buys
The Gold-Plated, Permanent Campaign Revisited

> I maintain a campaign headquarters year-round, and I have
> done so since I first came to Congress.
>
> *Rep. James H. Quillen (R-Tenn.),*
> *first elected to the House in 1962*

To understand why the cost of modern campaigns rises with each election, one need look no further than the permanent campaign organization devised by Rep. Richard A. Gephardt (D-Mo.), the House majority leader. Gephardt had won 57 percent of the general election vote in 1990, marking the first time in eight House campaigns that his winning percentage had fallen below 60 percent. While pundits pointed to his $1,448,831 effort as evidence that an anti-incumbent groundswell was building, few noticed that only 40 percent of his massive treasury had been spent on direct appeals for votes. Fifty-three percent of his spending had been pumped into overhead and fund raising.

The 1992 campaign proved to be no different. Courtesy of a redistricting deal he struck with incumbents in neighboring districts prior to the 1990 election, Gephardt was assured of a more Democratic constituency in 1992. Although one of the deal's participants, Republican Rep. Jack Buechner, lost his 1990 reelection bid, Gephardt refused to cede back to Buechner's successor, Democratic Rep. Joan Kelly Horn, any of the Democratic voters he had been promised.

Yet, despite his strengthened position, Gephardt sank $937,542 into his permanent campaign during 1991. Gephardt's off-year spending amounted to more than five times what the typical challenger had to spend on his or her entire campaign. It was nearly three times what his Republican challenger, Malcolm L. Holekamp, spent during 1992. As impressive as those numbers are, they do not include the $112,313 Gephardt transferred from his House campaign treasury to the Gephardt for President Committee to repay debts accumulated during his unsuccessful 1988 presidential bid.

Gephardt began 1991 with $193,486 in his campaign bank account. One year later, he had increased his cash reserves to $1,055,609. He accomplished that astounding feat by pouring $190,584 into fund-raising events and $31,562 into direct-mail solicitations. Gephardt's fund-raising itinerary took him to the Regency Hotel in New York City; the Commerce Club in Atlanta, Ga.; the Sterling Hotel in Sacramento, Calif.; the Park Hyatt in San Francisco, Calif.; and the Decathlon Club in Santa Clara, Calif. He traveled to Houston, Texas; Minneapolis, Minn.; and New Orleans, La., where the law firm of Barham & Markle sponsored a reception. In Washington, D.C., the American Council of Life Insurance organized a reception, as did CAREPAC, the political action committee (PAC) established by Blue Cross and Blue Shield, and the Realtors Political Action Committee. In all, Gephardt collected $1,851,589 during 1991, including $727,309 from PACs.

To support his off-year fund-raising operation, Gephardt spent $10,976 to lease office space in Washington, D.C. The Washington operation employed seven people who drew after-tax salaries totaling $106,310. Telephone bills, parking fees, and office supplies totaled $3,314, $2,060 and $1,033, respectively.

Gephardt also maintained an off-year headquarters in St. Louis, where rent and utilities amounted to $24,200. His campaign manager, Joyce Aboussie, collected $44,392 during 1991, and eight other employees collected after-tax salaries totaling $61,100. Off-year telephone bills for the St. Louis office totaled $25,126. He paid $3,996 to Federal Express, bought $1,988 in office supplies from Bizmart Office Supplies in St. Louis, and spent $2,114 to have his photocopier repaired, $1,785 to have the office cleaned, and $1,863 for a telephone answering service.

Between his hectic fund-raising schedule and his work as House majority leader, Gephardt accumulated off-year campaign travel bills of $99,806, including a total of $21,407 paid to eighteen corporations for the use of their private jets. Among those corporations putting their aircraft at Gephardt's disposal were Federal Express of Memphis, Tenn.; the Perot Company of Dallas, Texas; Healthsouth Rehabilitation Corp. of Birmingham, Ala.; Syntex Communication of San Jose, Calif.; Ren Corp. of Nashville, Tenn.; and Hospital Investors Management of Englewood Cliffs, N.J.

Over the two-year election cycle, overhead and fund-raising expenses accounted for half of Gephardt's $3,065,439 campaign outlays. With a staff that never dropped below fifteen, Gephardt's permanent campaign was nothing less than a thriving small business dedicated to his reelection.

While Gephardt's was the Cadillac of permanent campaigns, it was by no means unique (see Table 2-1). Off-year expenses reported by the 349 House incumbents who contested the November general election totaled $39,128,255, or 20 percent of the money spent by these incumbents during the two-year election cycle. Rep. Robert K. Dornan (R-Calif.) spent $463,777 during 1991, including $403,929 on his nationwide direct-mail fund-raising effort. Minority Whip Newt Gingrich (R-Ga.) invested $461,636 in his off-year effort, including $169,514 in overhead and $139,273 in fund raising. Rep. Martin Frost (D-Texas) spent $406,199 in 1991, including $195,982 on overhead and $106,350 on fund raising. Rep. Ronald V. Dellums (D-Calif.) invested $385,644 to keep his permanent campaign operation humming, $186,018 of which was spent on direct-mail solicitations. Excluding four 1991 special election victors, 47 incumbents spent more during the off-year than the typical challenger spent on his or her entire campaign.

Similarly, the 28 senators who won renomination reported spending a total of $30,736,874 during the five-year period between January 1, 1987, and December 31, 1991, an average of $1,097,746. Overhead costs during this period amounted to $12,839,612, including $3,323,953 for after-tax salaries, $2,172,519 for payroll and income taxes, $2,634,013 for travel, and $1,008,747 for office furniture and supplies. Fund-raising outlays added $12,372,322, of which $6,176,246 was invested in events, $5,923,807 was spent on direct-mail solicitations, and $272,270 was put into telemarketing. Off-year expenses represented 26 percent of the money spent by Senate incumbents. Those with the largest off-year budgets were Alfonse M. D'Amato (R-N.Y.), $3,753,302; Bob Packwood (R-Ore.), $3,190,034; Arlen Specter (R-Pa.), 2,288,367; John Seymour (R-Calif.), $1,856,709; and Bob Kasten (R-Wis.), $1,687,704 (see Table 2-1).

This heavy investment in the "bricks and mortar" of politics continued into the election year. During 1992, House incumbents who won renomination reported spending $34,570,993 on office overhead and $19,049,546 on fund raising, which together accounted for 33 percent of their spending for the year. Senate incumbents spent $16,122,938 on overhead and $11,454,592 on fund raising, or 32 percent of their election-year outlays.

Put simply, in an age of entrepreneurial politics, the candidate's own organization has virtually replaced the local political party as the vehicle to electoral success. Whereas the local parties once supplied candidates with fund-raising assistance, office space, campaign literature and other campaign paraphernalia, and an army of eager volunteers who worked the phones and knocked on doors to turn out supporters on election day, candidates must now largely provide these things for themselves. Once elected, candidates have no reason to disband the campaign apparatus and every reason to maintain it. If anything, the real or imagined anti-incumbent fears that rippled through the 1992 elections served to increase many incumbents' investment in their permanent campaigns.

The 1992 versions of these modern political machines tended to have:

- *Well-appointed offices.* While some members opened additional offices as the election neared, most members have replaced the temporary storefront campaign headquarters with permanent offices to house their computers and other equipment. During the 1992 election cycle, rent and utilities payments reported by the 349 House members who contested the November general elections amounted to $3,210,015. Over the six-year Senate election cycle, the 28 incumbents who won renomination spent a total of $1,295,489 on rent and utilities.
- *Well-paid professional staffs.* During the 1992 election cycle, salaries, benefits, and payroll taxes represented 12 percent of the average House incumbent's budget, the same percentage as in 1990. In the Senate, the average outlay for these items climbed from 11 percent in 1990 to 12 percent in 1992. Many incumbent's leaned heavily on their congressional staffs to run their campaigns.
- *Lawyers and accountants.* Many members of Congress kept a lawyer, an accountant, or both on retainer. Incumbents with

legal difficulties invariably used campaign funds to pay their legal bills, even when the matter had absolutely nothing to do with the election. During the 1992 cycle, House members paid $3,540,575 in legal and accounting fees; Senate incumbents spent $1,520,892.

- *Large travel budgets.* During 1991 and 1992, House incumbents reported spending a total of $7,439,927 on travel, an average of $21,318. In 1990 the average expenditure for travel among House incumbents was $16,247. Senate incumbents, all of whom traveled extensively to raise money, reported travel expenses totaling $5,647,008 during the six-year election cycle. The average outlay of $201,679 was $37,729 higher than the average travel expenses reported by senators who ran in 1990.

- *A year-round fund-raising operation.* Most members of Congress raise money continuously. The typical senator raised more than $14,000 a week during his or her six-year term, while the average House member raised more than $5,000 each week. That nonstop fund-raising effort had a high price tag: $54,660,343. The average House incumbent sank 15 percent of his or her budget into raising money; the comparable figure for senators was 21 percent.

- *Large entertainment budgets.* Most incumbents invested some of their campaign funds in constituent stroking. Some did nothing more than send year-end holiday cards, but many members also used campaign funds to purchase gifts, send flowers, and treat their supporters to lunch or dinner. On average, House incumbents spent $8,578 to stoke their constituents; the typical senator spent $29,820 over the six-year cycle. Comparable figures for House and Senate incumbents in 1990 were $6,741 and $30,038, respectively.

- *Sizable donations.* To build political bridges with constituents and other politicians, House members donated $9,087,185 to other candidates, political party committees, ideological groups, and civic organizations during the 1992 election cycle. The 28 Senators seeking reelection in 1992 collectively gave away $1,566,247 of their campaign funds during their six-year cycle.

- *Political consultants.* To one degree or another, most candidates depended on consultants to mold their campaign. Some candidates simply turned over their day-to-day campaign operations to general consultants. Others used consultants for specific tasks—to help orchestrate the nonstop fund-raising activities, design persuasion mailers, or create an advertising campaign. During the 1992 election cycle, House candidates paid these braintrusts a total of $126,335,527; Senate candidates paid their consultants $121,258,601. In all, payments to consultants accounted for 46 percent of total spending.

- *Investments.* Members of Congress earned substantial income by investing their campaign cash reserves. D'Amato collected $575,115 in interest on his cash reserves over the six-year Senate cycle. Rep. David Dreier (R-Calif.) collected $245,083 in investment income on his $2 million campaign treasury; this accounted for 38 percent of his total receipts during 1991 and 1992. Dreier's investment income was more than ten times as much as his Democratic opponent, Al Wachtel, managed to scrape together for his token challenge. Rep. Dan Rostenkowski (D-Ill.) reported investment income of $212,723. However, in Rostenkowski's case, not all his investments proved to be money-makers. He reported investment expenses and losses with Prudential Securities totaling $60,314. He also paid Salomon Brothers $18,942 for what he termed "decreased bond value."

As in the 1990 election cycle, these permanent campaign organizations were built almost entirely without regard to the strength of real or anticipated political opposition. Of the $80,338,485 House incumbents spent on overhead and fund raising, 50 percent was spent by members whose reelection was never really in doubt. The 130 incumbents who received between 61 percent and 70 percent of the vote in both their primary and general elections spent an average of $511,838. The average expenditure reported by the 69 incumbents who received 71 percent of the vote or more was $366,194. On average, the 9 Senate incumbents who garnered more than 60 percent of the vote reported spending $2,588,020.

First elected in 1986, Rep. Mike Espy (D-Miss.) won reelection with 65 percent of the vote in 1988 and 84 percent in 1990. He had no

Democratic primary opposition in 1992 and garnered 76 percent in the general election. Nevertheless, Espy spent $256,309 on his 1992 campaign. His off-year overhead expenses of $49,656 actually exceeded his election year outlays for overhead by $28,319. The $18,728 he spent to raise money in 1992 was $16,813 less than he invested in fund raising during 1991.

Rep. Dan Burton (R-Ind.) had received 63 percent of the vote or better in each of his five previous House races, and redistricting made his solidly Republican district even more Republican. Even so, Burton invested $399,952 in his 1992 reelection effort—nearly fifteen times as much as his Democrat challenger, Natalie M. Bruner, was able to spend. Burton spent $123,484 in 1991 alone to keep his permanent campaign operation running smoothly, including $73,298 on overhead and $24,809 on fund raising. He spent $11,743 in 1991 on meals apparently unrelated to his fund-raising efforts or constituent entertainment, which amounted to 44 percent of Bruner's entire campaign budget. Burton prevailed with 72 percent of the vote.

Rep. Tom Lantos (D-Calif.) ran the quintessential permanent campaign. Having received two-thirds of the vote or more in four successive contests and having been helped, if anything, by redistricting, Lantos spent $600,660 during the 1992 election cycle. In the off-year, Lantos spent $216,505 to keep his campaign machinery well oiled, including $73,025 on overhead and $112,934 on fund raising. His Republican opponent, realtor Jim Tomlin, spent a total of $5,555.

In a district where registered Republicans comprised 52 percent of the electorate and registered Democrats accounted for only slightly more than 30 percent, Republican Rep. John Kyl (Ariz.) outspent his Democratic challenger, Walter R. Mybeck, by one hundred to one. Needless to say, most of Kyl's efforts were directed at maintaining his political machine, not at defeating the underfunded Mybeck. In 1991 Kyl spent $104,785, including $60,219 on overhead, $29,321 on fund raising, and $3,989 on year-end holiday cards and constituent gifts. Over the two-year election cycle, such expenditures accounted for 65 percent of Kyl's spending.

Having garnered 70 percent of the vote in winning his fourth term in 1986 and facing a 1992 challenger who spent $331,513 to attract 31 percent of the votes, Sen. Bob Dole (R-Kan.) put $2,177,754 into his reelection effort. Off-year spending accounted for 31 percent of Dole's investment.

Kentucky's senior senator, Democrat Wendell H. Ford, had won 65 percent of the vote or more in his two previous reelection bids. His 1992 Republican opponent, David L. Williams, had just $353,805 to invest in the campaign. Nevertheless, Ford spent $2,283,638, in part because he invested $716,151 to keep his permanent campaign running during the off-years.

As these examples illustrate, the permanent, high-octane campaign was a bipartisan phenomenon. It could be found in every state. It has become a hallmark of modern politics. While the House ethics committee has ruled that campaign funds should not be used for any purpose that is not "exclusively and solely" for the benefit of the campaign, some members routinely treat their campaign treasuries as slush funds, paying for a host of purchases that fall well outside even a loose interpretation of that rule.

Campaign Headquarters

There is perhaps no greater misnomer in the political lexicon than "campaign headquarters." While candidates once opened their offices a few months before the election and closed them the day after the campaign ended, those days are long gone. Discouraged by House and Senate rules from using their taxpayer-funded congressional offices for purely political purposes and largely robbed of an effective local political party structure, most incumbents maintain a "political office," which is dedicated to a host of activities that further their political fortunes.

During the 1992 election cycle, House and Senate incumbents spent a total of $19,014,669 on their most basic political office expenses: $4,505,504 on rent and utilities, $5,204,412 on office furniture and supplies, $4,678,433 on telephone service, and $4,626,320 on computers and other office equipment. Over the two-year cycle, the typical House member reported spending $35,541 on such items; the comparable figure for senators was $236,030 over the six-year cycle. Thirty-five percent of this spending on political infrastructure, or $6,705,619, was spent during the off-years. During 1991, the average House incumbent spent $11,060 on such items. Between January 1, 1987, and December 31, 1991, these items cost the average senator seeking reelection $102,422.

Taken at face value, these numbers would suggest considerable change between the 1990 and 1992 election cycles. Compared with 1990, average reported spending in 1992 on infrastructure was up 22 percent among House incumbents and down 12 percent among Senate incumbents. However, when such payments are examined as a proportion of total spending, these shifts appear much less dramatic.

In the 1990 cycle, rent, utilities, office furniture, supplies, telephone service, computers, and other office equipment accounted for 7.47 percent of the typical House incumbent's budget; for 1992 the comparable figure was 6.23 percent. The average senator committed 6.57 percent of his or her budget to such items during the 1990 cycle; in 1992 the average was 5.70 percent. What had been considered a political necessity in 1990 remained a political necessity in 1992. This marginal decline in the proportion of the average budget devoted to these basic items was as much a function of the record number of retirements by entrenched incumbents as it was evidence of a fundamental change in politics.

D'Amato set the pace for Senate incumbents, with outlays of $792,772, including $217,716 for rent and utilities (see Table 2-2). Over the six-year cycle, his campaign paid $278,180 for office furniture and supplies and $118,648 for computer hardware, software, and other office equipment. Telephone service cost $178,228, including $52,253 for the use of cellular telephones and $3,963 for beepers. Sixty percent of these outlays were made between January 1, 1987, and December 31, 1991.

Other incumbent senators who invested heavily in their most basic campaign overhead were Specter, $634,367; Kasten, $420,380; Daniel K. Inouye (D-Hawaii), $379,225; Christopher J. Dodd (D-Conn.), $327,718; and Seymour, $311,292. The biggest off-year spenders on infrastructure were D'Amato, $472,634; Specter, $342,662; Kasten $215,507; Tom Daschle (D-S.D.), $191,616; Terry Sanford (D-N.C.), $122,767; and Daniel R. Coats (R-Ind.), $108,392.

In the House, those who invested most heavily in basic office overhead were Reps. Gephardt, $249,832; Gingrich, $156,461; Thomas J. Downey (D-N.Y.), $131,366; Tom McMillen (D-Md.), $129,882; Frost, $122,378; and Sam Gejdenson (D-Conn.), $118,315 (see Table 2-2). The heaviest off-year spenders were Gephardt, $95,509; Downey, $63,897; Gejdenson, $55,937; Helen Delich Bentley (D-Md.),

$52,226; Joe L. Barton (R-Texas), $50,751; and Joseph P. Kennedy II (D-Mass.), $48,231.

In some cases, these outlays benefited members of Congress personally, as well as politically. During the 1992 election cycle, Rostenkowski's campaign paid $30,000 to rent space in a building he and his sisters owned. Rostenkowski's campaign had rented the space continuously since 1986, and during that time its monthly rent had risen from $500 to $1,250—a steeper rise than justified by market conditions, according to local real estate analysts. The campaign paid $1,642 for cable television service, which included several premium movie channels, for the office space. The space was connected by a hallway to Rostenkowski's home in an adjacent building and, according to local press reports, no cable service was provided to his residence.

Rostenkowski was not alone. The permanent campaign office of Rep. Lamar Smith (R-Texas) was located on the bottom floor of a condominium he owns. Smith charged his campaign monthly rent of $857 for the first thirteen months of the election cycle; in February 1992 he raised the rent to $926. The campaign also paid for upkeep on the property, including $314 to Orkin Pest Control, $221 for the repair of an air conditioning unit, $194 to repair an alarm system for the building, $169 for service on a heat pump, $50 for a furnace checkup, and $203 for unspecified office repairs.

Sen. Dale Bumpers (D-Ark.) used campaign funds to rent an apartment in Little Rock where he stayed whenever he traveled home to Arkansas. By the end of 1992, the apartment rent cost the campaign $530 a month.

CAMPAIGN STAFF

As Gephardt's permanent campaign illustrates, year-round campaign offices do not run themselves. During the 1992 election cycle, incumbents who contested the November general elections paid their full-time and part-time employees a total of $26,646,752, an 11 percent increase over 1990. Given the fact that many fewer incumbents sought reelection in 1992—349 in 1992 versus 405 in 1990—this increase is particularly astounding. Off-year payroll expenses amounted to $7,599,342.

In the Senate, Specter paid after-tax salaries and benefits totaling $994,312, of which $507,704 was paid out during the off-years. D'Amato's payroll reached $716,721 by the end of 1992, with off-year salaries totaling $328,240. Daschle's employees received $686,475 over the six-year cycle, $409,327 of which was collected in the off-years. Total and off-year payrolls for Sen. Ernest F. Hollings (D-S.C.) were $563,941 and $246,064, respectively (see Table 2-3).

Among House incumbents, Gephardt's $413,335 payroll was the largest by far. It was more than twice what he spent on salaries and benefits in 1990. Others who invested heavily in staff were Joe Moakley (D-Mass.), $247,780; Gingrich, $229,477; Bentley, $218,190; Rep. Sam M. Gibbons (D-Fla.), $189,218; Downey, $188,203; John Bryant (D-Texas), $163,639; Dave Nagle (D-Iowa), $162,436; and Gerry E. Studds (D-Mass.), $162,371 (see Table 2-3).

Incumbents were not the only ones building sizable campaign staffs. During her nonstop two-year Senate campaign to succeed retiring Sen. Alan Cranston, Rep. Barbara Boxer (D-Calif.) incurred the largest payroll of any Senate candidate—$1,165,444. While she was in the race for considerably less than two years, Carol Moseley-Braun ran up the second highest payroll among Senate candidates. A hefty 14 percent of Moseley-Braun's $1,038,949 payroll, or $144,550, was paid to her campaign manager, Z. Kgosie Matthews, who was also her fiancee at one point. Matthews made considerably more during his brief tenure than any other campaign manager.

California Republican Michael Huffington, who knocked off Rep. Robert J. Lagomarsino in the primary, led all House candidates by paying out $424,215 in salaries. More than fifty people drew payroll checks from Huffington's campaign during 1992. Democrat Jane Harman, who prevailed in one of California's fifteen open seat contests, ranked sixth among all House candidates, spending $205,990 on salary payments.

Many campaigns referred to members of their staff as "consultants," despite the fact that they worked regular hours under the supervision of the candidate or another senior staff member. By labeling their employees consultants, candidates avoided paying payroll taxes and other benefits. Ordinary entrepreneurs have been routinely called to task by the Internal Revenue Service for this practice, but since campaigns are rarely audited, few candidates have ever been fined or even questioned.

Nagle paid no taxes on his $162,436 payroll. Republican Joan Milke Flores, who was defeated by Harman in California's District 36, dispensed payroll checks totaling $135,173 without paying any taxes. Pennsylvania Republican Jon D. Fox, who lost to Democrat Marjorie Margolies-Mezvinsky, paid no taxes on his $127,510 payroll. Bob Filner (D-Calif.) paid no taxes, yet his payroll amounted to $124,414. In all, forty House candidates had payrolls in excess of $50,000 and opted not to pay taxes (see box, page 45).

Although congressional staffers are forbidden from doing campaign work on government time, they are not prohibited from donating their own time to their boss's reelection efforts. Some members of Congress take full advantage of this caveat, leaning heavily on their congressional staffs to manage the day-to-day operations of their campaigns.

At $99,041, the payroll of Rep. Nancy L. Johnson (R-Conn.) was not one of the fifty highest, but 89 percent of what she paid out in salaries went to members of her congressional staff. Rep. Bob Carr (D-Mich.) invested $128,968, or about 10 percent of his $1.3 million campaign, in salaries. Carr's congressional staff collected 66 percent, or $85,640, of those payments. Downey paid $84,631 of his $188,203 payroll to congressional staffers. Rep. Peter H. Kostmayer (D-Pa.) paid 63 percent of his $117,601 payroll to congressional staffers in his loss to Republican James C. Greenwood. In Maryland, McMillen, who lost to Republican Rep. Wayne T. Gilchrest, sank $119,391 of his $1,527,903 treasury into salaries, $63,761 of which went to congressional staffers. In all, eleven House incumbents paid members of their congressional staffs salaries totaling more than $50,000 (see Table 2-4).

Of the $80,776 Lantos paid out in campaign salaries, $29,500 went to fifteen members of his congressional staff. These payments included $20,500 in bonuses, which ranged from $500 to $5,000. Nine of the staffers receiving bonuses had not been paid by the campaign previously.

As in 1990, one of the more interesting examples of this double-dipping involved Rep. Bill McCollum (R-Fla.). Staff salaries accounted for a hefty 15 percent of McCollum's campaign budget, largely because he paid two of his congressional staffers a total of $56,815. McCollum's chief of staff, Vaughn S. Forrest, drew large, lump-sum payments from the 1992 campaign for "consulting," as he

The Top Fifteen Spenders in the 1992 House Races: Payrolls Without Taxes

Rank	Candidate	Expenditures
1	Dave Nagle, D-Iowa	$162,436
2	Joan Milke Flores,[a] R-Calif.	135,173
3	Jon D. Fox,[a] R-Pa.	127,510
4	Bob Filner,[a] D-Calif.	124,414
5	Bill Filante,[a] R-Calif.	122,312
6	Hamilton Fish, Jr., R-N.Y.	118,433
7	Peter Torkildsen,[a] R-Mass.	98,912
8	Jim McCrery, R-La.	98,227
9	Ken Calvert,[a] R-Calif.	97,308
10	Terry Everett,[a] R-Ala.	95,715
11	Cathey Steinberg,[a] D-Ga.	94,900
12	Lamar Smith, R-Texas	90,964
13	Jay C. Kim,[a] R-Calif.	82,012
14	Charles Wilson, D-Texas	81,284
15	John Linder,[a] R-Ga.	77,974

Note: Totals are for the entire two-year cycle.

[a]Nonincumbent or special election candidate.

had in the 1990 campaign. Forrest received four campaign checks totaling $38,190 between April 16, 1991, and June 1, 1992. Forrest's last check from the McCollum campaign came just months before his request that he be allowed to remain on the congressional payroll while campaigning for the District 7 House race against John L. Mica, which he ultimately lost."I am not a millionaire. Millionaires quit to run," Forrest told a local newspaper.

Over the six-year Senate election cycle, seventeen members of Daschle's staff received salary payments totaling $243,472 from the campaign, 80 percent of which went to three staffers. State director Richard P. Weiland collected $87,850 to augment his government salary. Staff assistant Rita Lewis and special assistant Peter Stavrianos received campaign salaries totaling $66,879 and $39,172 respectively. On December 21, 1992, the campaign issued checks ranging from $1,500 to $4,000 to fourteen Senate staffers for what appeared to be year-end bonuses (see Table 2-4).

Specter was also heavily dependent upon his congressional staff to keep his campaign on an even keel. Eighteen of his Senate staffers drew payroll checks totaling $237,075. Mark Meyer, a caseworker in Specter's Pittsburgh office, collected $64,362. Other staffers drawing sizable checks were staff assistant Tom Bowman, $42,393; legislative assistant Charles D. Brooks, $27,539; press secretary Daniel J. Mc-Kenna, $18,799; executive director Patrick L. Meehan, $18,255; executive director Steve Dunkle, $14,334; and legislative assistant Anne Pizzoli, $13,809.

Packwood paid eleven Senate employees a total of $163,058, with $87,428 of it going to Elaine Franklin, his chief of staff. Press and community liaison Matt Evans and staff assistant Laura Fetuuaho collected $27,182 and $16,790, respectively.

D'Amato paid special assistant Kieran Mahoney and public affairs director Zenia Mucha campaign salaries of $73,826 and $44,173, respectively. Susan LaBombard, the Washington, D.C., congressional office manager for Sen. Christopher S. Bond (R-Mo.), collected campaign payroll checks totaling $53,471.

In all, thirty Senate staffers collected campaign checks of $20,000 or more.

While some members are extremely careful to separate their official government business from the business of campaigning, others are not.The gray area that has been established between the two staff functions has opened the door to ethical abuses. Take, for example, the case of Rep. Carroll Hubbard, Jr. (D-Ky.), who lost to Tom Barlow in the Democratic primary.

In April 1994 Hubbard plead guilty to federal charges that he had misappropriated more than $50,000 in campaign funds and had ordered members of his congressional staff to work on his and his wife's 1992 House campaigns while on the government payroll. According to Hubbard's statement, his staff members arranged campaign schedules, solicited campaign contributions, and campaigned in Kentucky under assumed names, all at taxpayer expense.

Although it was fairly common practice for members of Congress to rely heavily on spouses or other family members to run their campaigns, some members took the opportunity to pay their relatives handsomely for their time. Most incumbents who opted to pay family members had done so in 1990, as well.

In his final campaign before joining the new Clinton administration as secretary of agriculture, Espy reached out to his brother Tom. Payments to his brother and to his brother's firm, Reliance Consultants, amounted to $66,369, or 26 percent of Espy's total spending. Neither of the Espys returned calls to clarify precisely what services Tom Espy performed for the campaign, although in 1990 Reliance had collected $24,608 for fund raising and get-out-the-vote efforts.

Fund raising, in particular, proved to be a family affair. Rep. Gary A. Franks (R-Conn.) paid his wife Donna $23,890 for serving as his principal fund-raiser. Robin Dornan Griffin, Dornan's daughter and chief creative consultant on his direct-mail fund-raising program, received $55,353 for her efforts. Rep. Donald M. Payne (D-N.J.) paid his brother William $68,024 for serving as his campaign's fund-raising consultant. Rep. Jolene Unsoeld paid her daughter, Terres Unsoeld, $18,637 to stage events in Los Angeles.

Rep. Steve Gunderson (R-Wis.) paid his brother Matthew $26,400 for serving as his campaign manager. His sister, Naomi Bodway, served as the campaign's general consultant. Her firm, KaestnerBodway of Middleton, Wis., collected $31,585 for that advice, as well as for supplying yard signs, campaign buttons, and bumper stickers.

As he had in 1990, California Democratic Rep. Esteban E. Torres chose to leave the management of his permanent campaign to his daughter, Carmen Garcia. Payments to Garcia, who also coordinated fund-raising events, crafted the persuasion mail, and wrote the campaign's fund-raising solicitations, amounted to $66,990, or more than one-quarter of Torres's $256,596 budget for the two-year election cycle.

Others who put their relatives on the campaign payroll included Rep. Sander M. Levin (D-Mich.), who paid his son Matthew $13,426 for work on the campaign during the off-year. As in 1990, Lantos paid his daughter, Katrina Lantos-Swett, $22,600 for serving as his campaign treasurer. Rep. Ralph M. Hall (D-Texas) had only one permanent employee, his daughter-in-law, Jody Hall, who collected $39,644 in salary payments.

LEGAL SERVICES

The 1992 election cycle produced its share of high-profile legal and ethical investigations involving members of Congress. While House and Senate rules allow members to establish separate committees to raise money to cover the legal bills incurred during such investigations, most members tap their campaign treasuries to cover at least part of the cost.

In the House, Rostenkowski found himself under federal scrutiny for possible misuse of both his campaign and congressional office accounts. During 1992 he spent $156,953 of his campaign treasury on his legal defense (see box, page 49). The Washington, D.C., law firms of Brand & Lowell and Katten, Muchin, Zavis & Dombroff collected $71,892 and $10,132, respectively. Chicago attorney Thomas A. Jaconetty received $3,018. Rostenkowski also tapped his campaign for $71,911 to cover legal bills incurred by his administrative assistant, Virginia C. Fletcher, and one of his staff assistants, Mary Lesinski. In all, bills associated with his well-publicized legal problems accounted for 11 percent of Rostenkowski's campaign outlays.

The target of a federal investigation that led to his indictment on bribery charges in May 1992, Rep. Joseph M. McDade (R-Pa.) tapped his campaign treasury to cover $97,217 in legal fees associated with his defense. Two Washington, D.C., law firms, Brand & Lowell and McCamish, Martin & Loeffler, received $50,000 and $10,000, respectively. Sal Cognetti, Jr., of Scranton, Pa., collected $37,000.

Rep. Nicholas Mavroules (D-Mass.) was indicted by a federal grand jury in August 1992 on seventeen counts of racketeering, bribery, and income tax evasion. He spent $78,148 of his campaign treasury to defray the cost of his defense. Following his November loss to Republican Peter G. Torkildsen, Mavroules was convicted and sent to prison.

Heading into the 1992 campaign, Rep. Harold E. Ford (D-Tenn.) was facing a second trial on federal mail, bank, and tax fraud charges. Between January 1, 1987, and December 31, 1991, he had spent $393,976 from his campaign treasury to pay legal bills associated with his defense. At the beginning of 1992, he began paying for all such expenses out of a separate legal defense committee, which allowed him to reduce campaign outlays for his defense from $172,000

The Top Twenty-Five Spenders in the
1992 House Races: Legal Services

Rank	Candidate	Expenditures
1	Dan Rostenkowski, D-Ill.	$156,953
2	Joseph M. McDade, R-Pa.	97,217
3	Jerry F. Costello, D-Ill.	84,000
4	Nicholas Mavroules, D-Mass.	78,148
5	Michael Huffington,[a] R-Calif.	72,501
6	Gene Green,[a] D-Texas	63,499
7	Joe L. Barton, R-Texas	56,322
8	Martin Frost, D-Texas	56,290
9	Harold E. Ford, D-Tenn.	51,413
10	Nita M. Lowey, D-N.Y.	47,347
11	Albert G. Bustamante, D-Texas	46,380
12	Joe Moakley, D-Mass.	45,885
13	Bill Green, R-N.Y.	44,069
14	Gary A. Condit, D-Calif.	40,422
15	Bill Zeliff, R-N.H.	40,250
16	Tom Lantos, D-Calif.	39,898
17	Vic Fazio, D-Calif.	37,563
18	Robert T. Matsui, D-Calif.	35,168
19	Sonny Callahan, R-Ala.	35,000
20	John D. Dingell, D-Mich.	33,900
21	Cardiss Collins, D-Ill.	32,863
22	Sander M. Levin, D-Mich.	32,721
23	Peter Hoagland, D-Neb.	31,340
24	Eliot L. Engel, D-N.Y.	30,332
25	Mary Rose Oakar, D-Ohio	28,960

Note: Totals are for the entire two-year cycle.
[a]Nonincumbent or special election candidate.

in 1990 to $51,413 in the 1992 cycle. On April 9, 1993 Ford was acquitted on all charges.

Under the cloud of a grand jury investigation that would ultimately lead to his indictment and conviction on federal bribery and racketeering charges, Rep. Albert G. Bustamante (D-Texas) diverted $46,380 of his campaign funds to his legal defense.

In the Senate, members set up separate legal defense committees, which have not been included as part of their campaign outlays. In August 1991 the Senate ethics committee dropped a two-year probe of D'Amato, who had been accused, among other things, of allowing his brother to use his Senate office facilities for personal business. Rather than tapping his campaign funds to repay more than $400,000 in legal bills, D'Amato established a "Legal Expense Trust Fund" in December 1991.

Criminal and ethical investigations were not the only reasons for incurring large legal bills. Once it became clear that Illinois would lose two House seats, Democratic Rep. Jerry F. Costello paid $84,000 to his attorney, Grey Chatham of Belleville, to make sure his interests in the redistricting process would be well taken care of.

State senator Gene Green (D-Texas) appeared to win his run-off election by a mere 180 votes, after finishing second to Houston City Council member Ben Reyes in the five-candidate Democratic primary. However, the results were overturned by a state district judge when it was discovered that several hundred people who had voted in the Republican primary illegally crossed over to vote in the Democratic runoff. That necessitated a third campaign, which Green won by 1,132 votes. Green's legal bills and court costs associated with the case amounted to $63,499 and $17,555, respectively.

Following the 1990 campaign, New Hampshire Democrat Joseph F. Keefe filed a nuisance complaint with the Federal Election Commision (FEC), charging that Republican Bill Zeliff had made an improper $150,000 loan to his campaign. Since the loan was made using proceeds from the sale of property Zeliff and his wife jointly owned, Keefe argued that half the loan was really an illegal campaign contribution made by Zeliff's wife. Zeliff paid the Washington, D.C., law firm Wiley, Rein & Fielding $40,250 from his 1992 campaign treasury for its work on the complaint.

Other candidates relied on their attorneys to make certain that campaign financial statements were filed correctly with the FEC. In all, House and Senate candidates paid their attorneys $2,646,921.

TRAVEL

Travel is a fact of life for members of Congress (see Table 2-5). Many House members return to their districts several times a month, if not every weekend. In addition to trips home, Senators scour the country for money. With far more money than they need to campaign, many incumbents choose to travel in a style reserved only for the very wealthy. In the more than 7,000 campaign financial reports we examined, we found thousands of expenditures for chartered airplanes, expensive hotels, and fine restaurants. In many instances, the travel clearly had nothing to do with their campaigns.

Rep. Louis Stokes tapped his campaign treasury in January 1991 for $1,841 to pay the bill at the Washington Hilton and Towers for "candidate and family hotel accommodations." He spent $1,285 of his campaign funds to pay for him and his family to participate in "the New York Congressional Tour" in March 1991. The campaign picked up another $1,861 tab in September 1991 at the Washington Hilton and Towers for "candidate and family hotel accommodations." In April 1992 his campaign paid $351 for his family's hotel accommodations at Walt Disney World Resorts in Orlando, Fla., and $2,385 for "candidate's family air fare." He spent $2,343 of his treasury to take his family to New York for the Democratic National Convention in July 1992, and there was another $555 expense in October for his family's air fare and a $3,199 hotel bill at the Washington Hilton and Towers, where he and his family stayed during the Congressional Black Caucus's annual weekend bash. Stokes closed out the election cycle with December payments of $682 to cover "candidate and family hotel accommodations" at the Marriott Hotel in Cleveland and $4,270 for "candidate's family air fare."

Rep. Henry A. Waxman (D-Calif.) spent $47,294 on travel unrelated to his fund-raising efforts. He used $4,500 of his campaign funds to defray the costs of a trip he and his wife took to Jerusalem in March 1991, including $753 for lodging at the King David Hotel and $3,699 for air fare. While there, Waxman attended a conference of Jewish parliamentarians from around the world. He justified using his campaign funds to pay for the trip by saying that he met with constituents and monitored the airlift of Ethiopian Jews, an issue of importance to his West Hollywood constituency.

During the four-day 1992 Democratic National Convention in New York, Moseley-Braun spent $22,445, including a hefty $15,367 bill at the Le Parker Meridian Hotel. No other Senate candidate, Democrat or Republican, diverted as much of their campaign funds to cover convention expenses.

After the election but before she was sworn in, Moseley-Braun used $4,028 from her treasury to pay lodging expenses at the Four Seasons Hotel in Maui, Hawaii. When first queried about the trip, a spokeswoman for Moseley-Braun said the Hawaiian trip was envisioned as a fund-raising excursion, but when that did not work out as planned, Moseley-Braun did not seek compensation for an equal amount of personal expenses. After a story on the trip appeared in the *Los Angeles Times* in January 1994, the spokeswoman said that the money had been repaid to the campaign, referring us to the senator's mid-year 1993 report, which showed these "off-sets to loan" payments. However, the three "payments"—dated January 1, February 4, and March 11, 1993—amounted to $3,877, or $151 less than the hotel bill. No connection between the offsets and the hotel bill were specifically noted.

Hawaii was not a lucrative destination for anyone outside Hawaii who might have been looking for campaign contributions. Moseley-Braun collected only one Hawaiian contribution—a $1,075 donation from a Honolulu resident on November 2, 1992. Having paid four professional event planners a total of $68,498 for their fund-raising advice, Moseley-Braun would have been ill-advised to have considered a serious fund-raising trip to Hawaii.

Among all challengers, 433 House members, and 98 senators who do not call Hawaii home, including those who lost in primaries, only Rep. William Lehman (D-Fla.) appeared to have ventured to Hawaii for a major-donor event. On December 31, 1991, prior to his decision to retire, Lehman picked up $11,750 in contributions of $200 or more from Honolulu residents. While 37 other House and Senate candidates from the mainland collected at least one contribution of $200 or more from Hawaii, only Sen. Ford collected more than five such contributions. Maui, a vacationer's paradise, was not a fund-raising destination for any member of Congress from the mainland.

At the time Moseley-Braun tapped her treasury to cover her stay in Maui, her campaign was reporting debts of nearly $550,000, including $46,990 owed to campaign employees and contract workers.

This was not the first time Moseley-Braun had commingled her personal and campaign funds. In July 1992 she had "borrowed" $10,000 from her campaign to pay for a new home computer, fax machine, and cellular telephone. When queried by the local press, her campaign spokesman said she had tapped her treasury to cover these blatantly personal expenses because she was "a single mother with a fourteen-year-old son and a mother in a nursing home." The spokesman also noted that Moseley-Braun had made the purchases to help her "stay in touch with her family." Moseley-Braun's attorney, Lou Vitullo, said he would not comment on the $10,000 "loan." The FEC is currently auditing Moseley-Braun's campaign.

As the travel outlays by Stokes and Moseley-Braun illustrate, many candidates tapped their campaign treasuries to pay their expenses at the 1992 national conventions. In all, House candidates spent a total of $479,940 while attending their national party conventions; Senate candidates spent $131,613.

Among House candidates, Rep. Thomas S. Foley (D-Wash.) easily led the way, spending $29,206 of his campaign funds during the four-day 1992 Democratic National Convention in New York. His campaign paid an astounding $25,000 in expenses at the New York Hilton for Foley and his staff.

Before leaving for New York, Bustamante spent $7,123 of his campaign funds on a "pre-convention kickoff party" at the National Democratic Club. While in New York, he spent another $8,444, including $390 on tickets to *Miss Saigon,* $390 on tickets to the *Phantom of the Opera,* and $240 on tickets to *Les Miserables.* During their four-day stay in New York, Democratic Reps. Pelosi, Harold Ford, John Lewis (Ga.), and Dave McCurdy (Okla.) tapped their campaigns for $11,371, $10,328, $10,168, and $10,023, respectively. Among House candidates who used campaign money to pay for convention expenses, only four Republicans ranked in the top twenty-five. During their stay in Houston, Reps. Franks, Tom DeLay (Texas), Tom Ridge (Pa.), and Bud Shuster (Pa.) spent $8,989, $7,035, $5,579, and $4,855, respectively. Other Senate candidates who spent liberally from their campaign funds to cover convention expenses were incumbents Dodd, $21,706; Bumpers, $11,276; Dole, $10,496; and Glenn, $7,407.

While members are forbidden by law from soliciting campaign contributions or anything else of value from corporations, congressional leaders such as Gephardt were all too happy to accept the use of jets owned by companies that routinely lobby them. Indeed, flying aboard corporate jets amounted to nothing less than a thinly disguised corporate contribution, which has been illegal since 1907. In the 1992 election cycle, members were required to reimburse their corporate benefactors for no more than the equivalent of first-class commercial airfare, usually far less than the cost incurred by the corporation for supplying the plane, pilot, and fuel.

Over the two-year House election cycle, Gephardt reimbursed twenty-eight different corporations a total of $38,877—an amount that exceeds what 135 challengers spent on their entire campaigns. As the health care reform debate was heating up, Gephardt paid six corporations with interests in health care legislation a total of $16,669 for the use of their jets. None of the firms are headquartered in Gephardt's district.

Gephardt paid Ren Corp.-U.S.A. of Nashville, Tenn., which specializes in dialysis patient treatment, $4,940 for seven trips. For making its aircraft available on four occasions, Hospital Investors Management of Englewood Cliffs, N.J., received $2,770. Syntex of San Jose, Calif., and Pfizer Inc. of New York, both pharmaceutical manufacturers, collected single charter reimbursements of $3,782 and $880, respectively. Gephardt paid HealthSouth Rehabilitation Corp. of Birmingham, Ala., $1,985 for two flights. AFLAC, a health and life insurance company headquartered in Columbus, Ga., was reimbursed a total of $2,312 for two trips.

Throughout the six-year Senate election cycle, Dole also made frequent use of corporate jets. Among others, Dole paid reimbursements to Archer, Daniels, Midland for $52,834; ConAgra, $24,991; Torchmark Corp., $24,495; Federal Express, $14,635; Chambers Development Co., $10,725; and U.S. Tobacco, $7,383.

While politicians routinely object to the inference of a quid pro quo relationship between contributions and votes, the development of these special relationships creates the impression of a potential conflict of interest.

Candidates were not the only ones traveling. Field workers were routinely reimbursed for mileage and gasoline for their trips around the district. However, in D'Amato's case, even these clearly legitimate expenses took on the smell of excess. Over the six-year Senate election cycle, D'Amato spent $23,645 on limousine services, $16,002 of which was spent to ferry members of his staff around New York City. "There are parts of New York you don't want to be out hailing a yellow cab in," explained staffer Kieran Mahoney.

CAMPAIGN CARS

Just as corporations often provide their chief executive officers with luxury automobiles as a perquisite of employment, 110 members of Congress tapped their campaign treasuries for a total of $1,689,952 to pay for campaign cars (see Table 2-6). Although some would argue that such automobiles are a legitimate political expense when used to ferry members around their districts, it is debatable whether a Lincoln Continental or Cadillac is necessary. There is certainly some question as to whether members restrict their use of campaign cars to campaigning or use them regularly for personal errands. This is particularly true for those who purchase, license, repair, and fuel their "campaign cars" in the greater Washington, D.C., metropolitan area.

During the six years leading up to his reelection, D'Amato spent $156,729 to lease and maintain various automobiles, the most recent of which were a 1992 Lincoln Towncar, which was kept in New York, and a 1990 Lincoln Towncar, which was kept in Washington, D.C. The 1992 Lincoln cost the campaign $647 each month; the 1990 Lincoln used by D'Amato in Washington cost his campaign $927 each month. Repairs to his campaign cars totaled $20,315, including $10,022 paid to Dave Pyle's Lincoln Mercury in Annandale, Va. Insurance, registration, and licensing fees added $28,217. He spent $31,495 on gasoline over the six-year cycle. D'Amato's investment accounted for 27 percent of the $586,888 spent on campaign cars by the fifteen Senate incumbents who leased or purchased automobiles during the cycle.

Dodd spent $90,024 on his campaign car over the six-year cycle— $60,701 on lease payments; $10,682 to insure, register, and license it; $5,648 to repair it; and $12,993 to fill it with gas. Inouye spent $15,773 of his campaign treasury to purchase a van from Avis Rent-A-Car and $20,691 to lease an Acura. Insurance and registration fees added $22,132. Repairs and gasoline cost $5,335. Sen. John B. Breaux (D-La.) spent $62,274 to lease and maintain two campaign automobiles: a van for hauling campaign paraphernalia and a sedan driven by Breaux.

In the House, the leading spenders on campaign cars were John P. Murtha (D-Pa.), $46,177; William D. Ford (D-Mich.), $40,778; Charlie Rose (D-N.C.), $31,201; Gary L. Ackerman (D-N.Y.), $31,131; Glenn English (D-Okla.), $30,796; W. G. "Bill" Hefner (D-N.C.), $30,373: Ron Marlenee (R-Mont.), $28,507; and John T. Myers (R-Ind.), $28,250. In all, ninety-five House incumbents reported spending a total of $1,103,064 on their campaign cars.

Murtha's campaign leased a 1989 Ford Crown Victoria from Central Transportation in Edensburg, Pa., for the first seventeen months of the cycle. In May 1992 Murtha's campaign treasury paid $7,000 to buy out the lease. He began leasing a second car in September 1991 from Jim Dewar Olds Leasing in Johnstown, Pa. Total lease and purchase payments were $28,180. The campaign spent $8,103 to repair the cars, $5,886 to license and register them, and $4,008 to fuel them.

In February 1991 Ford's campaign made its last $411 payment on a car he used in Washington, D.C. That same month, his campaign made a $2,603 down payment on a new car from Dave Pyle's, the same Lincoln Mercury dealership frequented by D'Amato, and began making monthly loan payments of $732. The campaign also spent $16,416 on a new car in Michigan.

Rose had spent $8,288 of his 1990 campaign treasury to purchase a car, but apparently it proved insufficient. In June 1992 the campaign bought a $13,821 car from Fair Bluff Motors in Fair Bluff, N.C. Six months later, the campaign shelled out $10,594 to Valley Motors in Fayetteville, N.C., for another car. The $6,786 he spent to insure, maintain, and fuel the automobiles included a $272 bill at Precision Tune in Alexandria, Va.

Ackerman tapped his campaign funds for $14,608 to lease a Lincoln Towncar. Insurance and registration cost the campaign $10,224. Maintenance and gasoline added $3,205 and $3,094, respectively.

In October 1991 English spent $26,140 of his campaign treasury to purchase a new Buick. Together with registration and licensing fees, English's campaign car accounted for 40 percent of his off-year spending.

Hefner drove a Cadillac at campaign expense. Lease payments over the two-year cycle amounted to $23,643. Insurance, registration, and repairs to the car cost the campaign $3,483. Gasoline added $3,247.

Myers invested $19,635 of his campaign treasury in a new Chrysler LeBaron convertible. In addition to the registration and license fees for the LeBaron, the campaign also picked up the tab for insurance premiums and upkeep on three other cars—a 1970 white Impala convertible, a 1989 Plymouth Sundance, and a 1984 Chrysler.

FUND RAISING

Permanent campaigns require a constant cash flow. The typical House incumbent invested $88,348 in his or her fund-raising operation, $33,959 of which was spent during 1991. The average Senate incumbent spent $850,961 to raise money, with an average of $441,869 being spent between January 1, 1987, and December 31, 1991. In all, the 377 House and Senate incumbents who contested the 1992 general election spent $54,660,343 to raise money, of which $24,156,205 was spent during years in which they did not face the voters.

Although one might assume that the goal is to collect as much money as possible while spending as little as possible to raise it, that is frequently not the case. Fund-raising activities often serve a broad range of political goals beyond the immediate campaign. In fact, many members of Congress organized their campaigns around their fund-raising operations. Some focused on direct mail because it freed them from the demands of PACs and "fat cats," who frequently expect access in return for their large contributions. Others used events of various types to regularly bring together their most ardent supporters and to engage more people in the political process.

As he had in 1990, Dornan spent far more than any other House candidate to raise money during the 1992 election cycle—$1,151,338 (see Table 2-7). This staggering total represented 74 percent of his spending, and with contributions totaling $1,407,922, Dornan collected only $1.22 for each dollar he invested.

Driving this inefficient fund-raising operation were his outlays for direct-mail solicitations, which amounted to $1,121,604, of which $403,929 was spent during 1991. Each month Dornan's consultants fired off a letter to approximately 7,500 regular contributors. Four to six times each year the campaign mailed prospecting letters in an effort to expand the donor base. Dornan paid Response Dynamics of Alexandria, Va., $967,650 for list rental, production, postage, and caging services. His daughter said the average contribution was only $11.50.

On the other side of the political spectrum, Rep. Bernard Sanders (I-Vt.), the only socialist in the House, also relied primarily on direct mail to fund his campaign. However, unlike Dornan, Sanders's direct-mail operation was handled entirely in-house. As a result, he got to keep far more of what he collected. Over the two-year election cycle, Sanders spent $119,596 on his direct-mail program and $5,023 on events, including $1,000 directed at raising money from PACs. Sanders's efforts to raise money from individual donors yielded $3.43 for each dollar invested. "Bernie has been associated with certain issues since he was mayor [of Burlington]—labor, education, and women's issues—and that's how people around the country have gotten to know him," noted Sanders's wife Jane. "We have one of the best mailing lists in the country, and we got at least one contribution from every state."

Many permanent campaigns were built around "congressional clubs," which confer special benefits to those who donate. Rep. Dennis Hastert (R-Ill.) treated his congressional club members to three or four events each year, as well as a trip to the nation's capital. The Hastert campaign spent $3,908 in 1991 on the Washington excursion, including $817 for part of the tab at the J. W. Marriott, $827 for dinner at Gadsby's Tavern in Alexandria, Va., and another $641 for food at the House restaurant. Expenses for the 1992 Washington briefing totaled $3,852, including $1,630 for lodging at the Mount Vernon Inn and $625 at the House restaurant. The congressional club members also received $2,887 in gifts.

Gunderson operated a two-tiered congressional club. For a $1,000 donation, supporters became members of his "Executive Club," which entitled them to a lapel pin; a special gift, such as a pen-and-pencil set; and invitations to all his major fund-raising events. Among these events was the annual "brat party," which was held in his parent's back yard and featured sausage, beer, and ice cream. A more formal reception featured Vice President Dan Quayle. The campaign also held seven more intimate dinners for congressional club members. For a $250 donation, Gunderson provided members with a reduced package of these same benefits.

As in past campaign's, the fund-raising operation of Rep. Dean A. Gallo (R-N.J.) was inefficient by design. While he held an annual high-yield reception for PACs in Washington, D.C., and staged both periodic dinners and an annual Christmas party for his $1,000 donors, many of Gallo's events were designed primarily to get more people involved in the campaign and to maintain contact with loyal supporters. One low-dollar event was an annual golf outing, which cost the campaign $11,863 in 1991 and $11,552 in 1992. Each year Gallo rented a luxury box at the Meadowlands Racetrack and invited supporters to join him for an evening of harness racing. The two catered events cost the campaign $18,261 and raised little more than they cost. An afternoon of professional football at Giants Stadium cost $1,802 in 1991 and $2,501 in 1992. He spent $3,651 on souvenir shirts and mugs, which he gave away at these events.

For some House candidates and virtually all Senate candidates, the fund-raising focus was more global, either by choice or by necessity. The 1992 campaigns of 248 successful congressional candidates, most of them incumbents, were financed primarily with PAC donations and contributions of $200 or more from individuals who lived beyond the borders of the states they sought to represent. In the House, thirty-eight incumbents and two open seat candidates relied on PACs and out-of-state contributors for at least 75 percent of their campaign funds. In the Senate, thirteen incumbents and five open seat candidates collected at least 50 percent of their cash from PACs and out-of-state donors.

Having been appointed in May 1991 to succeed Sen. John Heinz, a three-term Republican who had been killed in a plane crash, Democratic Sen. Harris Wofford was initially given little chance of winning the November 1991 special election against Republican Dick Thornburgh, a former two-term governor and U.S. attorney general. With just six months to prove the pun-dits wrong, Wofford launched a nationwide search for money. The campaign employed four professional fund-raisers, who together were paid $86,744, which accounted for 70 percent of Wofford's event costs.

Only 5 percent of Wofford's total spending was invested in fund-raising events and direct mail, but a substantial proportion of his overhead was directly related to raising money. After his appointment he immediately opened a Washington fund-raising office that employed twenty people throughout much of the six-month campaign.

Rent for the office cost $17,000. The campaign also employed four-teen people across the country to raise money, including four in Massachusetts, two in New York, and others in California, Connecticut, New Jersey, North Carolina, South Carolina, Texas, Virginia, and West Virginia. These efforts enabled Wofford to raise more than $3.3 million, 61 percent of which came from PACs and out-of-state donors who gave $200 or more.

Sen. Charles E. Grassley (R-Iowa) collected 56 percent of his $2,456,091 in nonparty contributions from PACs and large out-of-state contributors. Campaign manager Bob Hauss said Grassley made a concerted effort to raise his national profile by holding events aimed at pro-Israel supporters in Illinois, Florida, and California.

McCurdy spent considerable time and money exploring a possible presidential bid, at on point devoting a month to visiting swing districts around the country. Although he opted not to enter the race, McCurdy continued to travel extensively for Democratic presidential nominee Bill Clinton. As long as he was making the trips, McCurdy decided he should expand his own fund-raising network. He paid Tim Phillips of Washington, D.C., $48,053 to serve as a one-man advance team. Phillips planned the travel, set up meetings with like-minded supporters, and introduced McCurdy to people that his chief of staff, Stephen K. Patterson, described as "potential contributors and people who could help us down the road." In addition to Phillips, McCurdy hired three professional fund-raisers to help fill his coffers. They collected a total of $115,852 for their work. Together, Phillips and these three firms helped raise $270,250 from PACs and $115,950 from out-of-state donors who gave $200 or more. Large donations from in-state residents amounted to $93,700. McCurdy raised no more than 28 percent of his contributions from individual donors in Oklahoma.

Upon hearing that Democratic Rep. Byron L. Dorgan (D-N.D.) would be seeking the open Senate seat created by the temporary retirement of fellow Democrat Kent Conrad, state insurance commissioner Earl Pomeroy announced plans to seek Dorgan's House seat. Having served as president of the National Association of Insurance Commissioners, Pomeroy knew who to ask for the money he needed.

Pomeroy traveled to Washington, D.C., where the Independent Insurance Agents of America's PAC, INSUR PAC, spent $1,238 to sponsor a fund-raiser on his behalf. During the six-month campaign, PACs representing MetLife, Continental Insurance, the Principal

Group, the American International Group, and the Alliance of American Insurers also sponsored in-kind fund-raising events for Pomeroy. These six insurance PACs together picked up $9,112 of Pomeroy's event costs, which represented 35 percent of his total event expenses.

Less than one month after opening his Bismarck headquarters, Pomeroy opened a Washington, D.C., fund-raising office to make certain that a steady stream of PAC dollars continued to flow into the campaign. Rent of the Washington office and payments to the staff who ran it amounted to $29,071. With PACs accounting for 69 percent of his total receipts, the office proved well worth the expense. Pomeroy raised $61,904 from individuals who gave at least $200, but only $7,077 was collected from North Dakotans. Donors from twenty-three states anted up $54,827, with at least $15,900 coming from insurance company executives. At most, Pomeroy raised 15 percent of his money in-state.

CONSTITUENT STROKING

In the absence of a strong political party structure, members of Congress must build and maintain a network of contacts and supporters who can be called upon at a moment's notice to help fend off any strong electoral challenge that may arise. For most members, that network is established over time through the expenditure of thousands of dollars on year-end holiday cards, gifts, and entertainment. During the 1992 election cycle, members of Congress spent $3,828,682 on constituent stroking, including $1,482,174 on cards; $863,084 on parties, including inaugural festivities; $527,329 on meals with constituents; $456,081 on gifts; $233,939 on flowers; $106,078 on calendars; $71,718 on awards and commemorative plaques; $70,683 on sports and theater tickets; and $17,596 on the congressional art contest.

As in 1990, Rep. Charles Wilson (D-Texas) led all House incumbents in expenditures on constituent entertainment and gifts (see Table 2-8). His annual dominoes tournament, which drew about 400 people in 1986, swelled to approximately 1,600 constituents in both 1991 and 1992. These two events cost a total of $54,681, including $37,323 for the dominoes, $2,967 to engrave them with "Vote for Charles Wilson," $1,135 for trophies, and $9,166 for fried chicken and biscuits. Wilson also spent $21,948 on constituent meals and other entertainment, $7,484 on various gifts, and $2,113 on flowers.

Rep. Kweisi Mfume (D-Md.) spent $10,798 to host a free open house for district residents in the spring of 1991 and 1992. He rented tents, tables, and chairs and set them up in a parking lot near his main congressional office in Baltimore. The campaign hired magicians and supplied face painting and balloons for the children. Adults received a picture of Mfume. Attendees were fed by local caterers and entertained by musicians from Morgan State University.

Mfume's campaign hosted an annual year-end holiday reception at the Walters Art Gallery in Baltimore, where local elected officials and other invited guests celebrated the season. No one paid to attend the affairs, which together cost $7,566. He spent $6,286 of his treasury on holiday cards. Plaques given in recognition of various constituent achievements cost the campaign $1,155. He spent $1,364 on lunches with visiting constituents, primarily at the House restaurant. Assorted gifts added $4,883.

As in past years, Mfume used campaign funds to frame the winning entry in the district's congressional art contest. In 1991 the campaign also gave cash awards of $500 to the winner, $200 to the runner-up, and $100 to the third-place entrant. A catered party to celebrate the winners cost the campaign $200. Mfume increased the prizes in 1992 for finishing second and third to $300 and $200, respectively. The party to toast the winners cost $180.

Rep. John D. Dingell (D-Mich.), elected to his nineteenth term in 1992, spent $34,730 of his campaign treasury to send year-end holiday cards (see Table 2-9). Constituent gifts cost his campaign $8,127, including $3,680 for calendars from the Capitol Historical Society. He spent $7,881 on flowers and $3,968 on meals and other entertainment.

Rep. Cardiss Collins (D-Ill.) invested $50,201 of her treasury in constituent gifts and entertainment, a 68 percent increase over 1990. Her annual picnic for senior citizens cost $3,750 in 1991 and $11,336 in 1992; half the difference in cost was accounted for by a $3,870 expenditures for aprons she passed out in 1992. She spent a total of $25,634 on four bingo events, and a brunch for local ministers cost the campaign $3,869. Collins spent $1,810 on Easter cards and $2,554 on year-end holiday cards.

Rep. Ike Skelton (D-Mo.) tapped his campaign treasury for $24,600 to pay for constituent meals, including $3,683 for meals at the House dining room and $2,228 for seven dinners at Maison Blanche near the White House. He reported spending $5,371 on dinners with constituents at restaurants near his home in McLean, Va., including a $1,414 Turkish feast at Kazan Restaurant. Various constituent gifts cost the campaign $11,939, including $1,272 for congressional club cookbooks, $350 for Christmas ornaments from the White House Historical Society, and $327 for edibles from Burger's Smokehouse in California, Mo. Holiday greeting cards and various parties cost the campaign $4,221 and $6,229, respectively.

Expenditures on "meals for supporters" by Rep. Solomon P. Ortiz (D-Texas) totaled $18,601 over the course of the 1992 election cycle. Ortiz paid $7,033 for such meals at restaurants in Washington, D.C., including a $612 dinner at Mr. K's and a $153 dinner at Le Rivage. Back home, he spent $7,406 to dine with constituents, including a $14 repast at Whataburger and a $15 meal at a local Denny's restaurant. He also billed the campaign for $1,028 for dinners with constituents in Matamoros, Mexico, as well as $2,372 in constituent meals consumed at unspecified locations. "He tries to see constituents outside the office," press secretary Cathy A. Travis explained. "There are too many distractions in the office—phone calls, staff people wanting to see him. It's better if they leave."

Ortiz's annual Christmas party for constituents and volunteers cost his campaign $9,530. Year-end holiday cards added $4,686. His treasury was tapped for $1,000 to help pay for the funeral of a constituent killed in Operation Desert Storm. Continental Airlines was paid $2,500 to ferry the Robstown, Texas, High School band to and from Washington. Flowers and other gifts cost $1,506 and $1,281 was invested in the congressional art contest for high school students.

Rep. William Ford increased his expenditures for constituent stroking from $5,771 in 1990 to $13,461 in 1992. He spent $1,364 on trees, which were donated to local schools on Arbor Day. He sent poinsettias to volunteers and local elected officials each Christmas, at a total cost of $2,562. Annual Christmas parties catered by the Culinary Arts Department at the William D. Ford Vocational Tech Center cost a total of $3,192. Year-end holiday cards cost the campaign $4,388.

Some members liked to reward supporters with tickets to athletic events. Rep. James H. Quillen (R-Tenn.) spent $10,801 of his campaign treasury to purchase tickets to various sporting events, including $1,800 for Super Bowl tickets, $1,814 for tickets to the Kentucky Derby, $5,395 for tickets to University of Tennessee football games, and $1,792 for Washington Redskins tickets. Quillen said he preferred to give the tickets to lucky supporters, rather than attend. "I haven't been to a Redskins game in twenty-five years," Quillen explained. "The last time I went, it was a night game and I fell asleep."

Myers tapped his campaign treasury in both 1991 and 1992 to pay for sixteen season tickets to Indianapolis Colts football games and four season tickets to Purdue University football games. Unlike Quillen, Myers and his wife personally used the tickets to entertain constituents, campaign volunteers, and county party chairs. Total cost: $10,153.

Among Senate incumbents, Bond topped the list for constituent stroking, spending $92,083 over the six-year cycle, $89,540 of which was spent on year-end holiday cards. Others who spent liberally on their constituents included Bob Graham (D-Fla.), $86,965; Dodd, $81,730; D'Amato, $53,446; Specter, $50,770; and Ford, $50,364 (see Table 2-8).

Over the course of the six-year cycle, Graham spent $58,722 on various constituent events and $10,993 on holiday cards. The campaign paid $4,633 for tickets to sporting events, including $3,905 for tickets to the 1991 Super Bowl in Tampa. Press secretary Ken Klein said the tickets were passed out to the senator's friends. Graham also used $4,156 in campaign money to buy gifts, including boxes of pecans and "Florida Ties," which were given at Christmas to fellow senators and employees of the congressional barbershop and shoeshine stand.

Each year Graham gathered together his long-time friends and supporters for a weekend of golf, tennis, and political seminars. According to Klein, these weekends were not a pitch for money but, rather, were a way to stay in touch. The 150 to 200 guests paid their own transportation and hotel expenses, as well as any golf and tennis fees, but the campaign paid for some of the meals and entertainment. For instance, in 1991 the campaign paid $12,989 for food at the Senate restaurant and $5,500 to hire the Capitol Steps, who entertained Graham's guests with political satire and song.

Dodd invested $33,536 in constituent meals, regularly hosting receptions in the Senate restaurant for groups such as the Connecticut Senior Intern Program. The program sponsored an annual week-long trip to Washington for one hundred high school seniors from across the state. A similar reception for members of the Peace Corps cost the Dodd campaign $1,088. He spent $30,998 on year-end holiday cards, $5,225 on flowers for constituents, and $3,111 on miscellaneous gifts. To celebrate his victory and that of the Democratic presidential ticket, Dodd spent $8,861 of his campaign treasury on inaugural festivities.

Whatever the method, the extravagant gifts and entertainment have the same intent—to build a strong base of support from which to run, either for reelection or for higher office. Few but the richest challengers can compete in such a system.

OTHER MEALS AND ENTERTAINMENT

Members of Congress routinely spent campaign funds for meals and entertainment that had absolutely nothing to do with campaigning. Once again, D'Amato had the dubious distinction of spending significantly more than any of his Senate colleagues (see Table 2-10). Over the six-year Senate election cycle, he spent $163,098 on meals and entertainment that had no apparent connection to his constituent entertainment or fund-raising activities. This spending averaged $523 for each of the 312 weeks in the cycle. D'Amato spent $35,252 of his campaign treasury at Gandel's Gourmet, a delicatessen on Capitol Hill. The campaign also spent thousands of dollars at the Senate restaurant for meals that were not campaign related, including a $4,439 harvest day celebration of New York agriculture products, to which senators and their staffs were invited.

Inouye spent $106,894 on meals that had no apparent connection to fund raising or constituent entertainment. For example, Inouye reported PAC and individual contributions totaling only $4,100 for 1989, but he billed the campaign $1,250 that year for one meal at Germaine's restaurant in Washington, D.C. Inouye also reported "campaign meals" totaling $545 at the Borobudur Intercontinental Hotel in Jakarta, Indonesia, and $349 at the Sherwood in Taipei, Taiwan. Over the six-year cycle, the campaign paid $26,120 for 403 meals that cost less than $200—183 in Hawaii, 168 in Washington, D.C., 46 near his Maryland home, and 6 in Virginia. Total cost to the campaign: $26,120.

As in 1990, no one in the House could compete with Shuster when it came to dining out on the campaign. Over the two-year cycle, Shuster spent $70,913 on meals that were unrelated to fund raising, including $25,163 in unitemized credit card bills. He spent $11,355 of his treasury on meals in Washington, D.C., including $7,218 for seventeen meals at Tortilla Coast and $428 for two meals at the Willard Hotel. Across the river in suburban Virginia, Shuster spent $17,308 on meals, including $8,054 for twenty-four meals from Sutton Place Gourmet in Alexandria and $1,288 for ten meals at the Ritz Carlton Hotel in Arlington. To satisfy his sweet tooth, Shuster spent $1,731 at Alexandria Pastry.

While the heart of Shuster's Pennsylvania district was a two-hour drive from Washington, $5,543 of his Washington, D.C, and Virginia meal expenses were listed as "food for volunteers." His Washington volunteers ate $2,462 worth of food from Tortilla Coast, $513 in chicken from Popeye's, and $845 in food from Peking Duck Gourmet. One "happy hour" visit to the Crowbar cost the campaign $226. Shuster billed the campaign for $11,848 in itemized meals in his home state, and none of these meals were listed as "meals for volunteers."

Between January 1, 1991, and December 31, 1992, Rostenkowski charged his campaign $28,734 for seventy-four meals—an average of $388 each time he dined out at campaign expense. His favorite haunt when the campaign was picking up the tab was Gibson's in Chicago, where he dined twelve times at a total cost of $5,943. Seven meals at Morton's in Chicago cost the campaign $3,304. Four meals at the Big Foot Country Club in Fontana, Wis., and a dinner at Lake Benedict Manor in Genoa City, Wis.—both of which are near his summer vacation home—cost the campaign $1,839 and $1,465, respectively.

Rep. Jerry Lewis (R-Calif.) paid out nearly $26,000 from his campaign coffers for meals that were unrelated to his fund-raising activities, many at posh restaurants on Capitol Hill. During the first six months of 1991, contributions to Lewis's campaign totaled only $4,810. During that same period, meals at the Monocle amounted to $2,072, meals at La Brasserie came to $1,214, and a single dinner at Le Mistral cost the campaign $1,097. Bills at Gandel's delicatessen totaled $405. Press secretary David M. LesStrang could not provide details on any specific meal, but said they were for both business and constituent entertainment.

Rep. Douglas Applegate (D-Ohio) consumed 171 meals at campaign expense, or an average of one meal every four days for the entire two-year cycle. He spent $2,094 on 83 meals in Ohio. Forty-five meals in Washington, D.C., and its suburbs cost the campaign $1,785. He spent $466 at restaurants in Pennsylvania, including a $6.98 meal at a Red Lobster in Pittsburgh. Meals in West Virginia cost the campaign $617. According to James R. Hart, Applegate's administrative assistant, most of these meals were in connection with speaking engagements when Applegate "can't use his official House account."

In all, members of Congress spent $1,901,812 on meals, an average of $3,582 for House members and $23,273 for Senate incumbents.

DONATIONS

Rep. Waxman had far more money than he needed to defeat his opponent, so he simply gave away $338,803 of his treasury, which accounted for 47 percent of his "campaign" spending for the 1992 cycle. This modern-day Robin Hood took from rich PACs and gave to poor candidates and party organizations. As chairman of the subcommittee on Health and Environment, Waxman was able to tap PACs representing health care interests for $177,800. In all, 203 PACs donated $402,915 to Waxman's campaign coffers, which amounted to 64 percent of his contributions.

Waxman bestowed $67,688 on IMPAC 2000, the PAC established to assist Democrats in redistricting. He gave $55,000 to the Democratic Congressional Campaign Committee, $40,000 to the United Democratic Fund of Minnesota, $20,000 to the Democratic Senatorial Campaign Committee, and $5,000 to the California Democratic party.

State senator Herschel Rosenthal received a $50,000 check from Waxman's campaign just four days before Rosenthal lost his primary contest to California state representative Tom Hayden. California state representative Terry B. Friedman received $10,000 for his race. Six House colleagues with whom he shared committee assignments each collected $2,000; another six received $1,000 donations. His donations to other candidates totaled $123,500.

Waxman's reasons for sharing his wealth with other candidates were simple. "First of all, they vote for or fight for the issues I care about," he noted. "Secondly, when you help somebody you develop a good working relationship with them."

Waxman was by no means alone (see Table 2-11). Representing one of the safest Democratic seats in the country, Rep. Howard L. Berman devoted only 15 percent of the $720,810 he spent in 1992 to direct appeals for votes. He gave $353,428, or 49 percent of his total campaign outlays, to other candidates, party organizations, and civic groups. He donated $90,001 to Rosenthal's state senate campaign. Other Californians benefiting from Berman's largess included state representatives Friedman and Dave Elder, who received $25,000 and $22,000, respectively. State representative Teresa Hughes picked up $12,000 for her successful state senate bid. To assist Democratic redistricting efforts, Berman donated $65,688 to IMPAC 2000. He gave $11,500 to the Democratic Congressional Campaign Committee and $1,500 to the Democratic National Committee. Sixty-one House and Senate candidates received donations ranging from $250 to $2,000.

For many members of Congress, donations to other candidates, political organizations, and civic groups serve as a cornerstone of political success. During the 1992 cycle, House and Senate incumbents gave away $10,653,432. The typical House member gave away $26,038, only $454 less on average than they donated in 1990. On average, Senate incumbents gave away $55,937, or $4,071 less than their 1990 counterparts.

Those involved in leadership battles invariably use their campaign treasuries to build bridges to other members whose votes they need or to demonstrate to their peers that they possess the proper party spirit. For example, Rep. Dick Armey (R-Texas) spent $277,198 more on his 1992 campaign than he had in 1990, but his underfunded opponent had nothing to do with it. The 1992 contest Armey worried most about was his successful fight to wrest the chairmanship of the Republican Conference away from Rep. Jerry Lewis.

To win that fight, Armey liberally distributed his campaign funds to a host of fellow Republicans. He made $1,000 donations to twenty-three candidates, $950 contributions to thirty-four candidates, and $500 donations to fourteen others. Most of his $1,000 gifts went to incumbents in hotly contested races, such as Gingrich, Gilchrest, Frank Riggs of California, Marlenee, and Iowans Jim Nussle and Jim Ross Lightfoot. His largest donation, $1,450, went to Michael D.

Crapo of Idaho, who won the District 2 seat vacated by Richard Stallings. He donated $900 to Texan David Hobbs, who lost to Rep. Pete Geren.

Armey also sent "issue mailers" valued at $25 each to 159 challengers and open seat contestants. These unsolicited mailings dispensed helpful hints on how to successfully campaign against their Democratic opponents. Armey spent $816 on travel related to campaign appearances he made on behalf of four Republican challengers.

Lewis countered Armey's monetary onslaught by giving $110,864 to Republican House and Senate candidates. He also spent a total of $3,519 to attend campaign "schools" in Fair Oaks, Va., and Los Angeles, lending his expertise to Republican hopefuls from around the country. Unfortunately for Lewis, many of those he backed were not around to vote for him in December 1992, when he lost the leadership battle to Armey. Lewis donated $40,500 to challengers and open seat candidates who lost their House bids; he also gave $5,000 to House incumbents who lost.

As the list of donations dispensed by Berman and Waxman suggests, national, state, and local party organizations depended at least as much upon incumbents as incumbents depended upon them. Over the two-year election cycle, House incumbents who won renomination donated $4,232,783 to party coffers. Those contributing most heavily were Waxman, $189,903; Robert T. Matsui (D-Calif.), $93,983; Vic Fazio (D-Calif.), $92,075; Berman, $88,688; Nancy Pelosi (D-Calif.), $85,338; Bruce F. Vento (D-Minn.), $73,400; James L. Oberstar (D-Minn.), $68,322; and Joe L. Barton (R-Texas), $65,773 (see Table 2-12).

California Democrats dominated the list primarily because of their large donations to IMPAC 2000, which totaled $683,040. In addition to collecting $67,688 from Waxman and $65,688 from Berman, the redistricting PAC received $66,688 from Matsui, $47,168 from Julian C. Dixon, and $41,688 each from Pelosi, Dellums, Don Edwards, and Norman Y. Minetta (see box, page 70).

Senate incumbents who gave freely to party organizations included Daschle, $221,382; Kent Conrad (D-N.D.), $149,079; Patrick J. Leahy (D-Vt.), $85,171; John McCain (R-Ariz.), $57,051; Ford, $55,550; Dole, $52,995; and Richard C. Shelby (D-Ala.), $40,055. Together, the twenty-eight incumbents who contested the November

Donations by California Democrats to IMPAC 2000

Representative	Donation
Henry A. Waxman	$ 67,688
Robert T. Matsui	66,688
Howard L. Berman	65,688
Julian C. Dixon	47,168
Ronald V. Dellums	41,688
Don Edwards	41,688
Norman Y. Mineta	41,688
Nancy Pelosi	41,688
Calvin Dooley	38,188
Anthony C. Beilenson	35,000
Richard H. Lehman	35,000
Vic Fazio	34,000
Leon E. Panetta	29,000
Matthew G. Martinez	23,000
George Miller	22,688
George E. Brown, Jr.	19,180
Esteban E. Torres	13,000
Gary Condit	12,500
Pete Stark	7,000
Maxine Waters	500
Total	**$683,040**

general election gave $893,828 to help various party organizations (see Table 2-12).

Elected in 1986 with only 52 percent of the vote, Daschle had anticipated a strong challenge in 1992, so he never stopped running. Between January 1, 1987, and December 31, 1991, he invested nearly $1.7 million in his permanent campaign, including $988,002 for staff, travel, and other overhead; $368,504 for fund raising; $42,128 for polling; $20,402 for constituent gifts and entertainment; and $125,632 for advertising. However, once Daschle realized that no strong challenge was coming, he began to give his campaign funds away. Between October 15 and October 30, 1992, Daschle's campaign contributed $210,000 to the South Dakota Democratic party for its efforts on behalf of state and local candidates.

Freshman Sen. Kent Conrad announced on April 2, 1992, that he would not seek a second term, citing his 1986 campaign pledge to serve only six years if the federal budget and trade deficits had not been brought under control. Five months later, Conrad reversed course and announced he would seek the Senate seat left vacant by the death of Sen. Quentin Burdick. In the interim, Conrad had dispatched a letter to those who had already contributed to his general election fund asking them whether they wanted their money refunded or donated to the North Dakota Democratic party. As a result of that letter, Conrad funneled $52,336 to the state party during his brief retirement. This accounted for 35 percent of his total party donations.

While most members of Congress used donations to build political influence within their own parties, Rep. David E. Bonior (D-Mich.) spent $94,319 of his campaign treasury on television advertising in support of a proposed ballot initiative that would have mandated a $500 property tax cut for middle income homeowners. The initiative was sponsored by the Michigan Homeowners Tax Break Committee, which Bonior cochaired.

As a way to foster goodwill in their communities, House and Senate incumbents dipped into their campaign funds for $1,476,256 to satisfy an almost continuous stream of requests from charities and booster organizations. Rep. Jim McDermott (D-Wash.), one of two physicians in the House, spent $3,696 of his campaign treasury to print materials for the international AIDS conference held in June 1992. He spent $4,000 of his campaign funds to help defray the costs of an AIDS cartoon exhibit displayed at that same convention. Most of his other charitable contributions were more modest, such as his $35 gift to Girls Inc. of Puget Sound and his $30 donation to the Union Gospel Mission.

Over his six-year election cycle, Inouye donated $171,686 of his campaign treasury to various charities and booster groups. In April 1988 he gave $150,000 to the Hawaii Education Foundation, an organization he founded that provides college scholarships to Hawaiian high school students.

Some members gave for much more personal reasons. Looking only at his campaign financial statements, it would be difficult to tell whether Lantos represented California or New Hampshire. While he contributed $16,296 to candidates and party organizations in California, he donated $33,500 to candidates and party organizations in New Hampshire. He gave $12,500 to the New Hampshire Democratic party. He contributed to three of New Hampshire's gubernatorial candidates—$5,000 each to Ned Helms, Norman E. D'Amours, and the eventual nominee, Deborah Arnesen. He even contributed to both Democratic candidates for mayor of Nashua. Not coincidentally, Lantos's son-in-law, Rep. Dick Swett, represents New Hampshire's District 2, which includes Nashua.

In Ohio, Republican Rep. Paul E. Gillmor essentially used his campaign as an auxiliary fund for his wife Karen, who waged a successful campaign for the state senate. Gillmor's campaign donated $72,000 to his wife's campaign, including a $22,000 loan he later forgave. He spent $13,198 of his treasury on postage, which he then gave to his wife's campaign as an in-kind contribution.

In 1988 Rep. Pete Stark (D-Calif.) made an interest-free loan of $88,645 from his campaign funds to his son Jeff, who used it to make an unsuccessful bid for Alameda county supervisor. In 1992 that loan was forgiven, although it was not included in his contributions for the 1992 election cycle, since he had "spent" the money four years earlier.

SEEKING HIGHER OFFICE

Rep. Arthur Ravenel, Jr. (R-S.C.) was seeking a fourth term in 1992, but he was already running for governor in 1994. Having spent just $3,522 on fund raising during his virtually uncontested 1990 campaign, Ravenel sank $22,088 into a single event in March 1992. The dinner, held to coincide with Ravenel's sixty-fifth birthday, netted roughly $50,000. "We made a bigger effort for the birthday party in 1992 because we knew we were running for governor," noted Sharon H. Chellis, Ravenel's administrative assistant. Such fundraising efforts and the lack of strong opposition allowed Ravenel to increase his cash reserves from $284,458 to $430,586. On December 28, 1992, less than two months after winning reelection, Ravenel transferred those reserves into his gubernatorial campaign account.

Ravenel was not alone. Like entrepreneurs everywhere, many members of Congress are eager to expand their horizons. In 1991 and 1992 thirteen House members decided to relinquish their seats to seek Senate seats or wage gubernatorial campaigns. Many others used their 1992 campaign treasuries to explore the possibilities open to them in 1994.

Rep. Don Sundquist (R-Tenn.) spent $995,922 during the 1992 election cycle—more than twice what he spent on his 1990 reelection effort. That massively increased spending was partly the result of a redistricting plan that increased Democratic strength in his district. It also reflected the fact that Sundquist's 1990 Democratic opponent had put less than $5,000 into his token challenge, while his 1992 Democratic challenger, retired minister David R. Davis, had $93,582 to spend. However, much of the increased spending related more to Sundquist's plans to run for governor in 1994 than to his 1992 reelection effort.

Sundquist began airing his television and radio commercials in July, despite being unopposed in the August 8 primary. During July and August he spent $17,090 for air time on Memphis television stations, $18,319 for radio spots, and $3,252 for time on local cable television outlets. With an eye toward the 1994 gubernatorial campaign, he also spent $27,914 to buy time on Nashville television, which reached only a small portion of his constituents but allowed him to reach large numbers of voters crucial to any statewide bid. Testimonial ads featuring former senator Howard Baker and former governor Lamar Alexander focused on Sundquist's integrity and his commitment to Tennessee, not simply the parochial interests of his district.

In 1991 Rep. Matsui transferred $437,448 from his House committee to the Matsui for Senate Committee, which he intended to use to run for the seat vacated by Democratic Sen. Alan Cranston. At the end of 1991, Matsui abruptly withdrew from the crowded field, opting to remain in his safe House seat.

Seriously considering a 1994 gubernatorial bid, Rep. Bob Clement (D-Tenn.) asked his media adviser, Morgan/Fletcher & Co. of Nashville, to develop a two-minute biographical television commercial. The spot highlighted the Clement family's political history, pointing to his father's three terms as governor and his aunt's service in the state senate. Morgan/Fletcher produced several hundred copies of an eight-minute video, which were given to key supporters.

Fortunately for Rep. John Conyers, Jr. (D-Mich.), the contest for mayor of Detroit takes place every four years during the off-year for congressional candidates. Having unsuccessfully challenged Mayor Coleman A. Young in the 1989 Democratic primary, Conyers transferred $92,660 of his excess 1992 funds into a mayoral campaign fund he established for another unsuccessful bid in 1993.

Facing only token challenges or having the ability to raise far more than they needed for their campaigns, some members used their 1992 war chests to pay off campaign debts accumulated during previous, unsuccessful campaigns for higher office. Over the six-year Senate election cycle, Dole transferred more than $1.3 million from his campaign treasury to repay debts from his 1988 presidential bid and still found nearly $2.2 million to spend on his Senate campaign. His opponent managed to scrape together less than $332,000 for her token challenge.

Between 1987 and 1992, Sen. John Glenn (D-Ohio) used $958,945 from his Senate campaign account to repay debts from his failed 1984 presidential campaign. The fact that he did not use more of his treasury for that purpose fueled a blistering television ad campaign by his Republican opponent, Lt. Gov. Mike DeWine. "He's got a condo in Vail, a million-dollar home, and a fifty-three foot yacht. But John Glenn still owes $3 million." In a takeoff on the Energizer bunny commercials, the ad ended with a toy astronaut breaking through the on-screen graphics, pounding on a drum with the Glenn campaign logo on it. "John Glenn. He keeps owing, and owing, and owing," intoned the voice-over.

Over the two-year House cycle, Gephardt spent $244,999 of his treasury to pay off debts accumulated during his short-lived 1988 presidential campaign. Rep. W. J. "Billy" Tauzin (D-La.) spent a much more modest $15,922 to repay the last of his debts from a failed gubernatorial bid in 1987. Tauzin had previously tapped his 1990 House campaign for $275,600 to reduce that debt.

In short, while the cost of political campaigns is rising rapidly, that cost is only partially related to the increased cost of things most people think of as campaigning—appealing to constituents for votes. Modern campaign funds are, in fact, political funds that provide many of the same services that local party organizations once supplied. For some members of Congress, their campaign treasuries are little more than private slush funds that enable them to live a lifestyle not afforded by their congressional paycheck.

Table 2-1 The Top Twenty-Five Spenders in the 1992 Congressional Races: Off-Year Spending

	House		Senate	
Rank	Candidate	Expenditures	Candidate	Expenditures
1	Richard A. Gephardt, D-Mo.	$937,542	Dick Thornburgh,[a] R-Pa.	$4,261,596
2	John W. Olver,[a] D-Mass.	817,878	Alfonse M. D'Amato, R-N.Y.	3,753,302
3	Ed Pastor,[a] D-Ariz.	661,337	Harris Wofford,[a] D-Pa.	3,257,485
4	Sam Johnson,[a] R-Texas	500,880	Bob Packwood, R-Ore.	3,190,034
5	Robert K. Dornan, R-Calif.	463,777	Arlen Specter, R-Pa.	2,288,367
6	Newt Gingrich, R-Ga.	461,636	John Seymour, R-Calif.	1,856,709
7	Martin Frost, D-Texas	406,199	Bob Kasten, R-Wis.	1,687,704
8	Ronald V. Dellums, D-Calif.	385,644	Tom Daschle, D-S.D.	1,669,963
9	John P. Murtha, D-Pa.	377,282	Barbara Boxer,[a] D-Calif.	1,586,179
10	John D. Dingell, D-Mich.	364,960	Terry Sanford, D-N.C.	1,488,679
11	Joseph P. Kennedy II, D-Mass.	355,317	Dianne Feinstein,[a] D-Calif.	1,244,805
12	David E. Bonior, D-Mich.	339,097	Wyche Fowler, Jr., D-Ga.	1,218,666
13	Thomas W. Ewing,[a] R-Ill.	328,294	Barbara A. Mikulski, D-Md.	1,194,782
14	Robert T. Matsui, D-Calif.	320,895	Christopher S. Bond, R-Mo.	1,111,859
15	Helen Delich Bentley, R-Md.	308,352	Robert Abrams, D-N.Y.	1,036,036
16	Ron Marlenee, D-Mont.	307,797	Christopher J. Dodd, D-Conn.	977,286
17	Jerry F. Costello, D-Ill.	307,505	Bruce Herschensohn, R-Calif.	926,863
18	Tom McMillen, D-Md.	306,273	Daniel K. Inouye, D-Hawaii	886,842
19	Thomas J. Downey, D-N.Y.	282,725	Ernest F. Hollings, D-S.C.	881,100
20	Norman Y. Mineta, D-Calif.	280,393	John McCain, R-Ariz.	875,064
21	Les Aspin, D-Wis.	270,167	Daniel R. Coats, R-Ind.	816,501
22	Sam M. Gibbons, D-Fla.	262,265	Harry Reid, D-Nev.	716,617
23	Howard L. Berman, D-Calif.	258,958	Wendell H. Ford, D-Ky.	716,151
24	Charles B. Rangel, D-N.Y.	253,237	Bob Dole, R-Kan.	680,274
25	Bud Shuster, R-Pa.	252,110	John B. Breaux, D-La.	647,257

Note: Totals are for entire two-year House and six-year Senate cycles; both include special election expenditures.

[a]Nonincumbent or special election candidate.

Table 2-2 The Top Twenty-Five Spenders in the 1992 Congressional Races: Campaign Office Basics

	House		Senate	
Rank	Candidate	Expenditures	Candidate	Expenditures
1	Michael Huffington,[a] R-Calif.	$261,749	Alfonse M. D'Amato, R-N.Y.	$792,772
2	Richard A. Gephardt, D-Mo.	249,832	Carol Moseley-Braun,[a] D-Ill.	702,201
3	Newt Gingrich, R-Ga.	156,461	Barbara Boxer,[a] D-Calif.	636,649
4	Thomas J. Downey, D-N.Y.	131,366	Arlen Specter, R-Pa.	634,367
5	Tom McMillen, D-Md.	129,882	Dianne Feinstein,[a] D-Calif.	425,521
6	Martin Frost, D-Texas	122,378	Bob Kasten, R-Wis.	420,380
7	Sam Gejdenson, D-Conn.	118,315	Bruce Herschensohn,[a] R-Calif.	388,305
8	Joe Moakley, D-Mass.	110,174	Daniel K. Inouye, D-Hawaii	379,225
9	Helen Delich Bentley, R-Md.	109,902	Lynn Yeakel,[a] D-Pa.	360,622
10	Pete Geren, D-Texas	108,051	Christopher J. Dodd, D-Conn.	327,718
11	Elton Gallegly, R-Calif	106,898	John Seymour, R-Calif.	311,292
12	Joseph P. Kennedy II, D-Mass.	105,607	Robert Abrams, D-N.Y.	310,722
13	Joe L. Barton, R-Texas	103,969	Tom Daschle, D-S.D.	302,616
14	Ron Marlenee, D-Mont.	98,876	Terry Sanford, D-N.C.	252,811
15	Richard H. Baker, R-La.	96,968	Ernest F. Hollings, D-S.C.	242,196
16	John P. Murtha, D-Pa.	95,480	John McCain, R-Ariz.	241,612
17	Steny H. Hoyer, D-Md.	88,523	Les AuCoin,[a] D-Ore.	239,103
18	Michael A. Andrews, D-Texas	88,184	Daniel R. Coats, R-Ind.	237,314
19	Bob Carr, D-Mich.	86,009	Robert F. Bennett, R-Utah	231,313
20	Jane Harman,[a] D-Calif.	85,918	Wyche Fowler, Jr., D-Ga.	228,748
21	Vic Fazio, D-Calif.	85,758	Christopher S. Bond, R-Mo.	221,875
22	Sam M. Gibbons, D-Fla.	85,729	Bob Graham, D-Fla.	179,948
23	Jack Fields, R-Texas	84,789	Russell D. Feingold,[a] D-Wis.	179,284
24	John W. Olver,[a] D-Mass.	81,709	Harris Wofford,[a] D-Pa.	170,600
25	Joseph J. DioGuardi,[a] R-N.Y.	79,547	Wendell H. Ford, D-Ky.	166,715

Note: Totals are for entire two-year House and six-year Senate cycles; both include special election expenditures.

[a]Nonincumbent or special election candidate.

Table 2-3 The Top Twenty-Five Spenders in the 1992 Congressional Races: Salaries

	House		Senate	
Rank	Candidate	Expenditures	Candidate	Expenditures
1	Michael Huffington,[a] R-Calif.	$424,215	Barbara Boxer,[a] D-Calif.	$1,165,444
2	Richard A. Gephardt, D-Mo.	413,335	Carol Moseley-Braun,[a] D-Ill.	1,038,949
3	Joe Moakley, D-Mass.	247,780	Arlen Specter, R-Pa.	994,312
4	Newt Gingrich, R-Ga.	229,477	Bruce Herschensohn,[a] R-Calif.	973,918
5	Helen Delich Bentley, R-Md.	218,190	Alfonse M. D'Amato, R-N.Y.	716,721
6	Jane Harman,[a] D-Calif.	205,990	Tom Daschle, D-S.D.	686,475
7	Sam M. Gibbons, D-Fla.	189,218	Dianne Feinstein,[a] D-Calif.	669,526
8	Thomas J. Downey, D-N.Y.	188,203	Lynn Yeakel,[a] D-Pa.	574,358
9	John W. Olver,[a] D-Mass.	167,419	Ernest F. Hollings, D-S.C.	563,941
10	John Bryant, D-Texas	163,639	Bob Kasten, R-Wis.	550,284
11	Dave Nagle, D-Iowa	162,436	Robert F. Bennett,[a] R-Utah	503,326
12	Gerry E. Studds, D-Mass.	162,371	Robert Abrams,[a] D-N.Y.	495,344
13	Martin Frost, D-Texas	154,438	John Seymour, R-Calif.	491,765
14	Pat Williams, D-Mont.	154,365	Christopher J. Dodd, D-Conn.	467,713
15	Jack Reed, D-R.I.	153,485	Terry Sanford, D-N.C.	453,870
16	Thomas J. Bliley, Jr., R-Va.	152,971	Les AuCoin,[a] D-Ore.	439,190
17	Les Aspin, D-Wis.	152,786	Paul Coverdell,[a] R-Ga.	419,091
18	Bill Green, R-N.Y.	152,322	Daniel R. Coats, R-Ind.	369,179
19	Ron Marlenee, D-Mont.	148,620	Rod Chandler,[a] R-Wash.	328,441
20	Frank Pallone, Jr., D-N.J.	146,855	Richard Williamson,[a] R-Ill.	322,458
21	Marjorie Margolies-Mezvinsky,[a] D-Pa.	140,261	Bob Packwood, R-Ore.	318,469
22	Dick Chrysler,[a] R-Mich.	135,889	Harris Wofford,[a] D-Pa.	309,474
23	Joan Milke Flores,[a] R-Calif.	135,173	John Glenn, D-Ohio	306,395
24	Jack Fields, R-Texas	134,718	Christopher S. Bond, R-Mo.	294,603
25	Sander M. Levin, D-Mich.	132,854	Don Nickles, R-Okla.	290,731

Note: Totals are for entire two-year House and six-year Senate cycles; both include special election expenditures.

[a] Nonincumbent or special election candidate.

Table 2-4 The Top Fifteen Spenders in the 1992 Congressional Races: Congressional Staff Payroll

Rank	House		Senate	
	Candidate	Expenditures	Candidate	Expenditures
1	Nancy L. Johnson, R-Conn.	$87,823	Tom Daschle, D-S.D.	$243,472
2	Bob Carr, D-Mich.	85,640	Arlen Specter, R-Pa.	237,075
3	Thomas J. Downey, D-N.Y.	84,631	Bob Packwood, R-Ore.	163,058
4	Peter H. Kostmayer, D-Pa.	73,579	Harry Reid, D-Nev.	139,689
5	Tom McMillen, D-Md.	63,761	Kent Conrad, D-N.D.	134,130
6	David E. Bonior, D-Mich.	62,707	Alfonse M. D'Amato, R-N.Y.	129,089
7	Jim McCrery, R-La.	60,292	Rod Chandler, R-Wash.	110,825
8	Pat Williams, D-Mont.	59,154	Christopher S. Bond, R-Mo.	108,950
9	Steny H. Hoyer, D-Md.	59,099	Don Nickles, R-Okla.	98,488
10	Joe Moakley, D-Mass.	57,986	Terry Sanford, D-N.C.	92,759
11	Bill McCollum, R-Fla.	56,815	Barbara A. Mikulski, D-Md.	69,743
12	Michael A. Andrews, D-Texas	48,684	John McCain, R-Ariz.	65,511
13	Frank Pallone, Jr., D-N.J.	47,458	Wyche Fowler, Jr., D-Ga.	59,278
14	Bernard Sanders, I-Vt.	46,825	Ernest F. Hollings, D-S.C.	45,335
15	E. Clay Shaw, Jr., R-Fla.	44,802	Dale Bumpers, D-Ark.	40,992

Note: Totals are for entire two-year House and six-year Senate cycles; both include special election expenditures.

Table 2-5 The Top Twenty-Five Spenders in the 1992 Congressional Races: Travel

	House		Senate	
Rank	Candidate	Expenditures	Candidate	Expenditures
1	Richard A. Gephardt, D-Mo.	$191,711	Bob Kasten, R-Wis.	$462,716
2	Ron Marlenee, D-Mont.	119,392	Daniel K. Inouye, D-Hawaii	442,292
3	Bud Shuster, R-Pa.	102,561	Carol Moseley-Braun,[a] D-Ill.	401,492
4	Bill Richardson, D-N.M.	96,788	Arlen Specter, R-Pa.	372,297
5	Jim Ross Lightfoot, R-Iowa	91,407	Bob Dole, R-Kan.	368,244
6	Albert G. Bustamante, D-Texas	89,884	Alfonse M. D'Amato, R-N.Y.	340,733
7	Don Sundquist, R-Tenn.	88,576	Ernest F. Hollings, D-S.C.	323,769
8	Thomas S. Foley, D-Wash.	82,659	John Seymour, R-Calif.	310,522
9	Don Young, R-Alaska	76,232	Christopher S. Bond, R-Mo.	270,041
10	Pat Williams, D-Mont.	74,306	Tom Daschle, D-S.D.	267,654
11	Martin Frost, D-Texas	73,541	Barbara Boxer,[a] D-Calif.	250,390
12	Michael A. Andrews, D-Texas	71,912	Richard C. Shelby, D-Ala.	237,154
13	Tom Ridge, R-Pa.	68,561	Harry Reid, D-Nev.	225,279
14	Bob McEwen, R-Ohio	68,268	Frank H. Murkowski, R-Alaska	211,085
15	Tom Bevill, D-Ala.	67,965	John B. Breaux, D-La.	179,242
16	Charles Wilson, D-Texas	66,709	Terry Sanford, D-N.C.	176,413
17	Newt Gingrich, R-Ga.	66,547	Dianne Feinstein,[a] D-Calif.	167,327
18	Dave McCurdy, D-Okla.	61,390	Lynn Yeakel,[a] D-Pa.	166,949
19	Joseph P. Kennedy II, D-Mass.	60,402	Dick Thornburgh,[a] R-Pa.	165,742
20	Barbara F. Vucanovich, R-Nev.	58,981	Bruce Herschensohn,[a] R-Calif.	157,510
21	John P. Murtha, D-Pa.	58,638	Christopher J. Dodd, D-Conn.	157,323
22	Tom McMillen, D-Md.	58,558	Wendell H. Ford, D-Ky.	157,284
23	Ronald V. Dellums, D-Calif.	58,416	Wyche Fowler, Jr., D-Ga.	153,601
24	Clark Kent Ervin,[a] R-Texas	58,088	Harris Wofford,[a] D-Pa.	129,946
25	Norm Dicks, D-Wash.	57,656	John McCain, R-Ariz.	126,023

Note: Totals are for entire two-year House and six-year Senate cycles; both include special election expenditures.

[a]Nonincumbent or special election candidate.

Table 2-6 The Top Fifteen Spenders in the 1992 Congressional Races: Campaign Cars

Rank	House		Senate	
	Candidate	*Expenditures*	*Candidate*	*Expenditures*
1	John P. Murtha, D-Pa.	$46,177	Alfonse M. D'Amato, R-N.Y.	$156,729
2	William D. Ford, D-Mich.	40,778	Christopher J. Dodd, D-Conn.	90,024
3	Charlie Rose, D-N.C.	31,201	Daniel K. Inouye, D-Hawaii	63,931
4	Gary L. Ackerman, D-N.Y.	31,131	John B. Breaux, D-La.	62,274
5	Glenn English, D-Okla.	30,796	Terry Sanford, D-N.C.	55,874
6	W. G. "Bill" Hefner, D-N.C.	30,373	Patrick J. Leahy, D-Vt.	52,531
7	Ron Marlenee, R-Mont.	28,507	Carol Moseley-Braun,[a] D-Ill.	33,920
8	John T. Myers, R-Ind.	28,250	Wyche Fowler, Jr., D-Ga.	23,597
9	Bob Stump, R-Ariz.	24,784	Arlen Specter, R-Pa.	23,421
10	Joseph D. Early, D-Mass.	24,214	Wendell H. Ford, D-Ky.	15,637
11	Thomas J. Downey, D-N.Y.	23,698	Frank H. Murkowski, R-Alaska	15,627
12	Richard Ray, D-Ga.	23,091	Charlene Haar,[a] R-S.D.	13,163
13	Don Sundquist, R-Tenn.	22,211	Steve Lewis,[a] D-Okla.	10,940
14	Floyd H. Flake, D-N.Y.	21,899	Russell D. Feingold,[a] D-Wis.	10,785
15	Robert E. "Bud" Cramer, D-Ala.	20,878	Mike DeWine,[a] R-Ohio	9,273

Note: Totals are for entire two-year House and six-year Senate cycles; both include special election expenditures.

[a]Nonincumbent or special election candidate.

Table 2-7 The Top Twenty-Five Spenders in the 1992 Congressional Races: Fund Raising

	House		Senate	
Rank	Candidate	Expenditures	Candidate	Expenditures
1	Robert K. Dornan, R-Calif.	$1,151,338	Bob Packwood, R-Ore.	$3,189,922
2	Randy "Duke" Cunningham, R-Calif.	435,252	Barbara Boxer,[a] D-Calif.	2,938,393
3	Richard A. Gephardt, D-Mo.	433,500	Dianne Feinstein,[a] D-Calif.	2,727,505
4	Gerry E. Studds, D-Mass.	338,709	John Seymour, R-Calif.	2,726,687
5	Ronald V. Dellums, D-Calif.	325,649	Bruce Herschensohn,[a] R-Calif.	2,712,734
6	Frank Riggs, R-Calif.	323,986	Carol Moseley-Braun,[a] D-Ill.	2,340,023
7	Newt Gingrich, R-Ga.	317,409	Alfonse M. D'Amato, R-N.Y.	2,268,931
8	Steny H. Hoyer, D-Md.	275,483	Arlen Specter, R-Pa.	1,855,639
9	Les Aspin, D-Wis.	265,828	John McCain, R-Ariz.	1,476,090
10	Dean A. Gallo, R-N.J.	247,603	Barbara A. Mikulski, D-Md.	1,403,752
11	Dick Zimmer, R-N.J.	246,516	Terry Sanford, D-N.C.	1,135,533
12	Ron Marlenee, R-Mont.	246,018	Bob Kasten, R-Wis.	1,069,644
13	Tom Lantos, D-Calif.	245,960	Robert Abrams,[a] D-N.Y.	1,045,544
14	Jim Ramstad, R-Minn.	245,583	Christopher S. Bond, R-Mo.	971,604
15	Joseph P. Kennedy II, D-Mass.	239,646	Dick Thornburgh,[a] R-Pa.	935,866
16	Tom McMillen, D-Md.	231,757	Wyche Fowler, Jr., D-Ga.	935,194
17	Dave McCurdy, D-Okla.	231,613	John Glenn, D-Ohio	753,173
18	Sam Johnson,[a] R-Texas	226,796	Daniel R. Coats, R-Ind.	725,587
19	Joseph D. Early, D-Mass.	221,066	Tom Daschle, D-S.D.	673,775
20	James P. Moran, Jr., D-Va.	215,148	Richard Williamson,[a] R-Ill.	651,735
21	Vic Fazio, D-Calif.	210,731	Lynn Yeakel,[a] D-Pa.	651,726
22	Sander M. Levin, D-Mich.	208,992	Charles E. Grassley, R-Iowa	629,171
23	Martin Frost, D-Texas	205,691	Lauch Faircloth,[a] R-N.C.	556,161
24	Pat Williams, D-Mont.	194,607	Christopher J. Dodd, D-Conn.	502,485
25	H. L. "Bill" Richardson, R-Calif.	193,037	Daniel K. Inouye, D-Hawaii	471,769

Note: Totals are for entire two-year House and six-year Senate cycles; both include special election expenditures.

[a]Nonincumbent or special election candidate.

Table 2-8 The Top Twenty-Five Spenders in the 1992 Congressional Races: Constituent Entertainment and Gifts

Rank	House		Senate	
	Candidate	Expenditures	Candidate	Expenditures
1	Charles Wilson, D-Texas	$86,226	Christopher S. Bond, R-Mo.	$92,083
2	John D. Dingell, D-Mich.	54,707	Bob Graham, D-Fla.	86,965
3	Cardiss Collins, D-Ill.	50,201	Christopher J. Dodd, D-Conn.	81,730
4	Ike Skelton, D-Mo.	46,989	Alfonse M. D'Amato, R-N.Y.	53,446
5	Don Sundquist, R-Tenn.	46,871	Arlen Specter, R-Pa.	50,770
6	John P. Murtha, D-Pa.	45,395	Wendell H. Ford, D-Ky.	50,364
7	Norman Y. Mineta, D-Calif.	44,575	Bob Dole, R-Kan.	49,765
8	Thomas J. Manton, D-N.Y.	42,911	Wyche Fowler, Jr., D-Ga.	40,089
9	Barbara-Rose Collins, D-Mich.	40,772	Harry Reid, D-Nev.	37,047
10	Solomon P. Ortiz, D-Texas	39,104	Patrick J. Leahy, D-Vt.	36,711
11	Robert T. Matsui, D-Calif.	35,673	Ernest F. Hollings, D-S.C.	29,932
12	Jerry Huckaby, D-La.	34,382	Tom Daschle, D-S.D.	27,402
13	Don Young, R-Alaska	34,296	Bob Kasten, R-Wis.	25,768
14	Kweisi Mfume, D-Md.	34,231	Kent Conrad, D-N.D.	25,310
15	Joseph D. Early, D-Mass.	31,963	Frank H. Murkowski, R-Alaska	24,745
16	Edolphus Towns, D-N.Y.	30,738	Dianne Feinstein,[a] D-Calif.	24,520
17	Leon E. Panetta, D-Calif.	30,390	John B. Breaux, D-La.	20,184
18	Sherwood Boehlert, R-N.Y.	30,146	Barbara A. Mikulski, D-Md.	19,246
19	Michael Bilirakis, R-Fla.	29,123	Don Nickles, R-Okla.	18,241
20	James H. Quillen, R-Tenn.	28,032	John McCain, R-Ariz.	14,875
21	Robert H. Michel, R-Ill.	26,643	John Seymour, R-Calif.	13,792
22	Toby Roth, R-Wis.	24,697	Terry Sanford, D-N.C.	12,662
23	Duncan Hunter, R-Calif.	24,649	Wayne Owens,[a] D-Utah	9,882
24	Mary Rose Oakar, D-Ohio	23,493	Dale Bumpers, D-Ark.	7,932
25	Tim Valentine, D-N.C.	23,424	Daniel R. Coats, R-Ind.	6,839

Note: Totals are for entire two-year House and six-year Senate cycles; both include special election expenditures.

[a] Nonincumbent or special election candidate.

Table 2-9 The Top Fifteen Spenders in the 1992 Congressional Races: Holiday Cards

	House		Senate	
Rank	Candidate	Expenditures	Candidate	Expenditures
1	John D. Dingell, D-Mich.	$34,730	Christopher S. Bond, R-Mo.	$89,540
2	Norman Y. Mineta, D-Calif.	22,592	Wyche Fowler, Jr., D-Ga.	34,438
3	Toby Roth, R-Wis.	21,572	Arlen Specter, R-Pa.	31,359
4	Harold Rogers, R-Ky.	19,793	Christopher J. Dodd, D-Conn.	30,998
5	Don Sundquist, R-Tenn.	19,110	Alfonse M. D'Amato, R-N.Y.	27,219
6	Robert H. Michel, R-Ill.	17,799	Patrick J. Leahy, D-Vt.	21,530
7	Patricia Schroeder, D-Colo.	16,573	Bob Kasten, R-Wis.	16,475
8	George Miller, D-Calif.	16,435	Kent Conrad, D-N.D.	13,391
9	Bob McEwen, R-Ohio	16,319	Bob Graham, D-Fla.	10,993
10	Bill Archer, R-Texas	16,152	Ernest F. Hollings, D-S.C.	9,936
11	Robert T. Matsui, D-Calif.	14,264	Frank H. Murkowski, R-Alaska	7,925
12	Benjamin A. Gilman, R-N.Y.	13,609	Daniel R. Coats, R-Ind.	4,455
13	Tom Lantos, D-Calif.	12,822	John B. Breaux, D-La.	3,944
14	Leon E. Panetta, D-Calif.	12,387	John McCain, R-Ariz.	3,500
15	Paul E. Kanjorski, D-Pa.	11,771	Harry Reid, D-Nev.	3,185

Note: Totals are for entire two-year House and six-year Senate cycles; both include special election expenditures.

Table 2-10 The Top Fifteen Spenders in the 1992 Congressional Races: Restaurants/Meetings

| | House | | Senate | |
Rank	Candidate	Expenditures	Candidate	Expenditures
1	Bud Shuster, R-Pa.	$70,913	Alfonse M. D'Amato, R-N.Y.	$163,098
2	Dan Rostenkowski, D-Ill.	28,734	Daniel K. Inouye, D-Hawaii	106,894
3	Jerry Lewis, R-Calif.	25,840	Christopher J. Dodd, D-Conn.	36,210
4	Dan Burton, R-Ind.	24,154	Christopher S. Bond, R-Mo.	33,564
5	John D. Dingell, D-Mich.	23,666	Frank H. Murkowski, R-Alaska	28,963
6	Kweisi Mfume, D-Md.	22,181	Bob Graham, D-Fla.	26,222
7	John P. Murtha, D-Pa.	19,281	Barbara A. Mikulski, D-Md.	26,161
8	Robert T. Matsui, D-Calif.	16,519	John B. Breaux, D-La.	25,198
9	Edolphus Towns, D-N.Y.	15,336	Ernest F. Hollings, D-S.C.	22,170
10	Barbara B. Kennelly, D-Conn.	15,189	Arlen Specter, R-Pa.	21,831
11	Albert G. Bustamante, D-Texas	14,686	Terry Sanford, D-N.C.	21,696
12	Michael Huffington,[a] R-Calif.	14,539	Patrick J. Leahy, D-Vt.	17,258
13	Charles Wilson, D-Texas	14,293	Harry Reid, D-Nev.	16,936
14	Dale E. Kildee, D-Mich.	13,208	Tom Daschle, D-S.D.	14,264
15	Joseph D. Early, D-Mass.	13,133	Wyche Fowler, Jr., D-Ga.	12,773

Note: Totals are for entire two-year House and six-year Senate cycles; both include special election expenditures.

[a]Nonincumbent or special election candidate.

Table 2-11 The Top Twenty-Five Spenders in the 1992 Congressional Races: Donations

	House		Senate	
Rank	Candidate	Expenditures	Candidate	Expenditures
1	Howard L. Berman, D-Calif.	$353,428	Tom Daschle, D-S.D.	$263,721
2	Henry A. Waxman, D-Calif.	338,803	Daniel K. Inouye, D-Hawaii	189,707
3	Charles B. Rangel, D-N.Y.	197,018	Kent Conrad, D-N.D.	178,888
4	Robert T. Matsui, D-Calif.	185,092	Bob Dole, R-Kan.	95,570
5	Nancy Pelosi, D-Calif.	173,308	Patrick J. Leahy, D-Vt.	94,270
6	David E. Bonior, D-Mich.	150,979	Barbara A. Mikulski, D-Md.	76,119
7	Jerry Lewis, R-Calif.	128,564	John McCain, R-Ariz.	75,909
8	Vic Fazio, D-Calif.	120,754	Wendell H. Ford, D-Ky.	75,295
9	Edolphus Towns, D-N.Y.	117,158	Alfonse M. D'Amato, R-N.Y.	74,024
10	Joe L. Barton, R-Texas	115,939	John B. Breaux, D-La.	59,711
11	George Miller, D-Calif.	109,229	Bob Graham, D-Fla.	58,222
12	Paul E. Gillmor, R-Ohio	95,285	Christopher J. Dodd, D-Conn.	54,219
13	Norman Y. Mineta, D-Calif.	94,435	Richard C. Shelby, D-Ala.	48,352
14	John D. Dingell, D-Mich.	94,099	Harry Reid, D-Nev.	45,879
15	Thomas M. Foglietta, D-Pa.	91,605	Don Nickles, R-Okla.	30,502
16	James L. Oberstar, D-Minn.	86,541	Frank H. Murkowski, R-Alaska	23,203
17	Julian C. Dixon, D-Calif.	85,437	Bob Packwood, R-Ore.	21,450
18	Bill Richardson, D-N.M.	84,523	Wyche Fowler, Jr., D-Ga.	16,315
19	Dick Armey, R-Texas	83,451	Dale Bumpers, D-Ark.	15,832
20	Thomas J. Manton, D-N.Y.	82,860	Ernest F. Hollings, D-S.C.	15,020
21	Charles E. Schumer, D-N.Y.	82,304	Terry Sanford, D-N.C.	12,046
22	John P. Murtha, D-Pa.	80,782	Charles E. Grassley, R-Iowa	11,946
23	Michael R. McNulty, D-N.Y.	80,291	Robert F. Bennett, R-Utah	11,403
24	Jim McDermott, D-Wash.	79,580	Arlen Specter, R-Pa.	10,352
25	Tom Lantos, D-Calif.	78,952	Byron L. Dorgan,[a] D-N.D.	7,015

Note: Totals are for entire two-year House and six-year Senate cycles; both include special election expenditures.

[a] Nonincumbent or special election candidate.

Table 2-12 The Top Twenty-Five Spenders in the 1992 Congressional Races: Donations to Party Organizations

	House		Senate	
Rank	Candidate	Expenditures	Candidate	Expenditures
1	Henry A. Waxman, D-Calif.	$189,903	Tom Daschle, D-S.D.	$221,382
2	Robert T. Matsui, D-Calif.	93,983	Kent Conrad, D-N.D.	149,079
3	Vic Fazio, D-Calif.	92,075	Patrick J. Leahy, D-Vt.	85,171
4	Howard L. Berman, D-Calif.	88,688	John McCain, R-Ariz.	57,051
5	Nancy Pelosi, D-Calif.	85,338	Wendell H. Ford, D-Ky.	55,550
6	Bruce F. Vento, D-Minn.	73,400	Bob Dole, R-Kan.	52,995
7	James L. Oberstar, D-Minn.	68,322	Richard C. Shelby, D-Ala.	40,055
8	Joe L. Barton, R-Texas	65,773	Christopher J. Dodd, D-Conn.	37,135
9	Norman Y. Mineta, D-Calif.	63,831	Barbara A. Mikulski, D-Md.	36,274
10	Edolphus Towns, D-N.Y.	59,390	Harry Reid, D-Nev.	32,399
11	Julian C. Dixon, D-Calif.	49,167	Bob Graham, D-Fla.	32,000
12	Thomas S. Foley, D-Wash.	48,865	Alfonse M. D'Amato, R-N.Y.	21,874
13	Ronald V. Dellums, D-Calif.	48,589	John B. Breaux, D-La.	18,669
14	Don Edwards, D-Calif.	47,538	Dale Bumpers, D-Ark.	13,690
15	George Miller, D-Calif.	45,289	Ernest F. Hollings, D-S.C.	10,195
16	Leon E. Panetta, D-Calif.	39,941	Arlen Specter, R-Pa.	8,225
17	Richard H. Lehman, D-Calif.	39,550	Robert F. Bennett,[a] R-Utah	5,642
18	Michael G. Oxley, R-Ohio	39,404	Byron L. Dorgan,[a] D-N.D.	5,500
19	Robert S. Walker, R-Pa.	39,245	Daniel K. Inouye, D-Hawaii	4,868
20	Calvin Dooley, D-Calif.	38,688	Frank H. Murkowski, R-Alaska	3,366
21	Jack Brooks, D-Texas	38,400	John Glenn, D-Ohio	3,250
22	John D. Dingell, D-Mich.	36,901	Les AuCoin,[a] D-Ore.	2,850
23	Thomas J. Manton, D-N.Y.	36,861	Terry Sanford, D-N.C.	2,739
24	David Dreier, R-Calif.	35,500	Wyche Fowler, Jr., D-Ga.	2,500
25	Anthony C. Beilenson, D-Calif.	35,000	Charles E. Grassley, R-Iowa	2,336

Note: Totals are for entire two-year House and six-year Senate cycles; both include special election expenditures.

[a] Nonincumbent or special election candidate.

CHAPTER 3

House Freshmen
Settling In

Members have 730 days to get reelected.
1990 Freshman Rep. Mike Kopetski (D-Ore.)

Freshman Rep. Scott L. Klug (R-Wis.) had beaten long odds to win his seat in 1990, upsetting fifteen-term Democratic incumbent Robert W. Kastenmeier. A well-known television reporter and news anchor in Madison, Klug had entered the race with one big advantage—60 percent of the voters already knew his name. However, like most challengers, Klug had struggled to overcome one big disadvantage—a shortage of money. While Kastenmeier had pumped $184,753 into advertising, Klug had spent $184,315 on his entire campaign, $64,041 of which was invested in advertising. Klug emerged with a 6-point victory by convincing voters that Kastenmeier was an entrenched incumbent who had been in Congress too long.

Once in office, Klug quickly embraced the monetary advantages of incumbency. During the 1992 election cycle he spent $153,815 to raise money—more than five times what he spent on fund raising in 1990. As a challenger, Klug had raised only $32,800 from political action committees (PACs). During the 1992 cycle, his change in status allowed him to tap that same PAC community for $226,266. Incumbency opened the spigot on large individual donations, as well. With events such as a Mother's Day reception featuring First Lady Barbara Bush that grossed $100,000 and his Team '92 congressional club, Klug raised $300,096 from individuals who gave at least $200—$236,999 more than he had raised from such donors in 1990. A $48,699 investment in direct-mail solicitations helped push his receipts from smaller donors to $311,971, a $243,282 increase over 1990.

During the off-year, Klug spent $106,294 to keep his permanent campaign operation running smoothly. While he closed his campaign office, he still managed to spend $38,673 on overhead and $57,762 on fund raising. When Democratic activist Ada Deer spent $443,644 to challenge Klug in 1992, his new-found fund-raising prowess allowed him to counter with an additional $717,738 election-year splurge— nearly four times as much as he had invested in the 1990 effort.

While Deer invested $176,951 in advertising, Klug poured $321,406 into his ad campaign. Strapped for cash in 1990, Klug had spent $62,584 on a series of ten-second commercials, but in 1992 he pumped $261,689 into producing and airing both fifteen-second and standard thirty-second spots. His tight budget in 1990 had allowed for only $1,457 in other advertising, but in 1992 he had sufficient resources to invest $26,435 in billboards and $32,103 in newspaper advertising.

In 1990 Klug had been unable to afford persuasion mailings, but in 1992 he spent $86,069 on brochures and persuasion mail that targeted farmers, veterans, and undecided voters. A four-page tabloid-style brochure was dropped on doorsteps throughout the district, and volunteers swept through the district with door-hangers on the campaign's final weekend. Unable to afford a phonebank operation in 1990, Klug paid Payco Teleservices of Herndon, Va., $45,119 for such services in 1992. As Brandon R. Scholz, Klug's chief of staff, put it, "You have a level of comfort with more money."

That level of comfort was perhaps best illustrated by the campaign's final weekend. "We knew one of the local newspapers was going to profile the race on the Sunday before the election," recalled Scholz. "So we hired a helicopter to fly us around the district to eight prearranged rallies on the Saturday before the election. We took a reporter and a photographer with us, and the next morning they ran aerial photos of 200 people waiting for Scott, of him in the helicopter, and of him on a wooden box addressing the crowd. They ran a file photo of Ada Deer. That's what having money enabled us to do."

On election day, Klug steamrolled Deer, collecting 63 percent of the vote.

If anything, Klug's experience was somewhat unusual because he prevailed in 1990 with relatively limited resources. While most challengers struggled mightily to raise money, most successful challengers had no such problems. The forty-two freshmen who contested the

1992 general elections had spent a total of $23,837,306 on their 1990 bids, an average of $567,555. That was $177,168 more than the typical incumbent spent that year and even $10,410 higher than the average outlay reported by incumbents involved in hotly contested races.

The principal difference between these successful outsiders and well-heeled incumbents in 1990 was resource allocation. Challengers and open seat candidates elected in 1990 invested 59 percent of their money in direct appeals to voters, while the typical incumbent invested only 40 percent of his or her budget in communicating with the electorate. However, by 1992 this spending difference had virtually disappeared.

Just two years removed from their initial campaigns, the freshman class pumped a total of $22,474,819 into their reelection bids, an average of $535,115. Their investment in direct appeals for votes dropped from 59 in 1990 to 49 percent in 1992. Conversely, concerned over redistricting and anti-incumbent sentiment, those elected prior to 1990 allocated a larger percentage of their 1992 budgets to direct appeals for votes. On average, these longer-term incumbents reported spending $572,555, and 47 percent of that was spent on direct appeals for votes—a 7-point increase (see Tables 3-1 and 3-2).

Although many had run outsider campaigns, most members of the 1990 freshman class quickly adopted the permanent campaign mode in preparing for their reelection. Led by Rep. Jack Reed (D-R.I.), who spent $213,068, and by Randy "Duke" Cunningham (R-Calif.), who spent $167,664, the forty-two freshmen who won renomination spent a total of $3,770,056 during the off-year to lay the groundwork for their reelection bids, an average of $89,763. The typical freshman sank $32,577 into overhead and $38,413 into fund raising, which together accounted for 79 percent of their off-year spending (see box, page 90). Twenty of these newly elected members opted to maintain permanent campaign offices throughout their first term.

The heavy investment in campaign infrastructure continued into 1992. Of the $18,704,763 spent by freshmen during 1992, 36 percent was devoted to overhead and fund raising. The comparable figure for those elected prior to 1990 was 33 percent.

While they reported spending an average of $32,440 less on their first reelection bids than they had invested in winning their seats, the typical freshman reduced his or her investment in advertising by $55,090. Outlays for persuasion mail and other grass-roots appeals

Off-Year Expenditures by 1990 Freshmen

Major Category	Total	Average	Percent
Overhead			
Office furniture/supplies	$ 96,813	$ 2,305	2.57
Rent/utilities	90,494	2,155	2.40
Salaries	378,163	9,004	10.03
Taxes	96,089	2,288	2.55
Bank/investment fees	95,689	2,278	2.54
Lawyers/accountants	159,091	3,788	4.22
Telephone	104,584	2,490	2.77
Campaign automobile	23,522	560	.62
Computers/office equipment	116,975	2,785	3.10
Travel	190,860	4,544	5.06
Food/meetings	15,954	380	.42
Total Overhead	**1,368,234**	**32,577**	**36.29**
Fund Raising			
Events	1,266,912	30,165	33.60
Direct mail	323,310	7,698	8.58
Telemarketing	23,104	550	.61
Total Fund Raising	**1,613,326**	**38,413**	**42.79**
Polling	**40,685**	**969**	**1.08**
Advertising			
Electronic media	63,463	1,511	1.68
Other media	28,628	682	.76
Total Advertising	**92,091**	**2,193**	**2.44**
Other Campaign Activity			
Persuasion mail/brochures	69,496	1,655	1.84
Actual campaigning	185,364	4,413	4.92
Staff/Volunteers	4,748	113	.13
Total Other Campaign Activity	**259,608**	**6,181**	**6.89**
Constituent Gifts/Entertainment	**114,699**	**2,731**	**3.04**
Donations to			
Candidates from same state	12,489	297	.33
Candidates from other states	5,385	128	.14
Civic organizations	22,340	532	.59
Ideological groups	8,592	205	.23
Political parties	85,033	2,025	2.26
Total Donations	**133,839**	**3,187**	**3.55**
Unitemized Expenses	**147,572**	**3,514**	**3.91**
Total Expenditures	**$3,770,056**	**$89,763**	**100.00**

Note: Totals are for the entire two-year cycle.

for votes dropped an average of $19,282. On the other hand, average fund-raising expenses more than doubled from $54,347 to $111,761. As challengers in 1990, these forty-two candidates had given away an average of only $2,159. Running as incumbents in 1992, these same candidates donated an average of $10,336. While constituent entertainment had been an unaffordable luxury in 1990, by 1992 the typical freshman found enough room in his or her budget to spend $4,817 on constituent stroking (see Table 3-3).

To pay for their nonstop campaigns, the new freshmen quickly adopted the fund-raising style of their Capitol Hill brethren. As successful challengers and open seat candidates in 1990, the forty-two freshmen had raised a very respectable $7,994,740 from PACs. During the 1992 election cycle, their PAC receipts jumped 45 percent, to $11,568,763.

Rep. Calvin Dooley (D-Calif.) discovered that PACs were suddenly looking for him and were willing to give him more money than he was asking for. Tickets to his 1991 Washington, D.C., PAC events were $350; by 1992 PACs were encouraging Dooley to raise his prices to $500. "PACs were telling us that they were willing to give us that much, so we said great," explained chief of staff Lisa Quigley. Dooley held three PAC events during the two-year cycle, helping to push his PAC donations to $242,583, a 42 percent increase over 1990.

With cash reserves of only $9,233 at the beginning of 1991 and 1990 campaign debts of $79,406, Rep. Collin C. Peterson (D-Minn.) put considerable emphasis on his off-year fund-raising efforts. During 1991, 55 percent of the $53,942 spent to maintain his permanent campaign was invested in raising money. Those efforts yielded contributions totaling $197,677, including PAC donations of $154,985. By January 1992, Peterson had eliminated his debts and increased his cash-on-hand to $100,431. Over the two-year cycle, he raised $321,507 from PACs, an increase of $135,909 over 1990. In all, contributions from PACs accounted for 70 percent of his total contributions for the 1992 cycle.

Following his 1990 triumph, Rep. Bill Zeliff (R-N.H.) had told us he would actively work to increase contributions from PACs to help repay both the $263,000 he had loaned the campaign and the $112,000 in bank loans the campaign had been forced to take out. He made good on that promise, more than doubling his PAC contributions, from $130,601 in 1990 to $325,915 in 1992.

As a group, freshmen raised 6 percent less in the 1992 election cycle than they had in 1990 from individuals who gave at least $200. Given his debt load, Zeliff could not afford to be one of those who scaled back his fund-raising efforts in any way. During the 1992 cycle, Zeliff raised $309,837 in large individual donations, a 41 percent increase over 1990. He raised $86,599 from out-of-state contributors who gave $200 or more—twice what he raised from such donors in 1990. Zeliff was so pleased with the results of his increased fund-raising efforts that he threw his major donors a thank-you party after the election. The party, held at his Christmas tree farm in Jackson, N.H., cost $6,439.

Arguably, freshmen might be expected to run permanent campaigns because of their potentially tenuous electoral positions. Few could blame these new members for doing everything possible to hold onto their seats, having just spent considerable energy and money to win them. That certainly was the case with Frank Riggs (R-Calif.).

Riggs had pulled off one of the biggest upsets of 1990 by defeating Democratic Rep. Douglas H. Bosco by 3,314 votes, despite being outspent by $175,732. Riggs owed his victory, at least in part, to the candidacy of Darlene G. Comingore, a Peace and Freedom party candidate who garnered 15 percent of the vote. Having won the seat while only capturing 43 percent of the vote, Riggs could not afford to stop running.

Riggs's initial victory had cost $262,809. During 1991 alone, he spent $149,448 to keep his campaign running smoothly. Although he decided not to maintain a permanent campaign headquarters, he spent $43,332 on overhead, including $21,942 on legal and accounting fees. For his initial campaign, Riggs had invested $23,553 in fund raising; during 1991 he spent $85,581 to raise money.

Ultimately, Riggs spent $668,438 on his unsuccessful attempt to hold onto his seat—well over twice what he spent to win it in the first place. Unfortunately for him, 48 percent of his money was invested in raising money, and another 19 percent was put into overhead. Only about 26 percent of his treasury was invested in direct appeals for votes. Without a strong third-party candidate to dilute Democratic strength in the district, he lost by 6,410 votes.

Rep. Gary A. Franks (R-Conn.), the first black Republican elected to the House since 1934, also had good reason to worry. Franks had spent $621,499 during his successful 1990 campaign and had emerged with 52 percent of the general election votes. After a shaky first term in which he was plagued by high staff turnover, sued by a savings and loan for defaulting on loans totaling $471,000, and sued by his 1990 campaign manager for back wages, it looked like Franks would need a minor miracle to win a second term.

Franks never closed his campaign office following the 1990 election, and rent and utilities on that space amounted to $4,315 during 1991. Off-year salaries and taxes added $26,397 and $7,316, respectively, helping to push his overhead for the year to $61,112. With fund-raising costs of $60,225 and miscellaneous expenses of $13,279, Franks's total investment in his off-year campaign totaled $134,616, or 23 percent of the $589,991 he spent during the two-year election cycle.

Even with this substantial preliminary effort, Franks would have probably lost the 1992 election to Democrat James J. Lawlor had it not been for Lynn H. Taborsak, who ran as an independent following her defeat in a bitter Democratic primary. With Taborsak attracting 23 percent and Lawlor 31 percent of the general election votes, Franks slipped through with a 44 percent plurality.

Reapportionment cost Iowa one of its five House seats, and freshman Republican Rep. Jim Nussle found himself locked in a battle for political survival against Democratic Rep. Dave Nagle. To prepare for that 1992 fight, Nussle invested $117,665 in his off-year campaign, including $43,672 in overhead and $56,115 in fund raising. With the help of a $737,077 election-year push, Nussle emerged with a razor-thin 2,966-vote victory.

However, not all freshmen were faced with such difficult circumstances in their first reelection contests. Nine of the freshman class received 70 percent of the vote or better in both the primary and general elections, and fifteen collected at least 60 percent of the vote at each stage of the reelection process. Nineteen of these twenty-four easy winners were already so safely ensconced that they drew no primary opposition.

Most of these lopsided races were financially uncompetitive, as well. Rep. David L. Hobson (R-Ohio) spent $266,760 in garnering 71 percent of the votes in his contest with Democrat Clifford S. Heskett, a retired teacher who spent less than $5,000. Rep. Bill Brewster (D-Okla.) invested $351,147 in his initial reelection bid and collected 75 percent of the vote against Republican Robert W. Stokes, a teaching assistant who scraped together $5,723 for the race. Rep. Jim Ramstad (R-Minn.) spent $599,672 in collecting 64 percent of the general election vote; his opponent, Democrat Paul Mandell, spent $18,166. None of these three freshmen faced primary opposition.

In all, freshmen who won reelection with 60 percent of the vote or more spent $11,661,997 on their 1992 bids, while their opponents spent only $3,576,109. Excluding the $1,441,694 spent by Republican Linda Bean (Maine), who unsuccessfully challenged Democratic Rep. Thomas H. Andrews, challengers in these lopsided races spent only $2,134,415. Although their reelections were never really in doubt, spending by the twenty-four freshmen in these contests accounted for 52 percent of the money spent by members of the 1990 freshman class (see Table 3-4).

Rep. Bill Barrett (R-Neb.) had few worries in his first reelection campaign, even though he had won his 1990 open seat contest by only 4,373 votes. Barrett's predecessor, Republican Virginia Smith, had held the seat from 1974 until her retirement in 1990. President George Bush had carried the district by a two-to-one margin in 1988. Bush ultimately carried District 3 by 23 points in 1992, with independent presidential candidate Ross Perot finishing second. Barrett's 1992 Democratic opponent, farmer Lowell Fisher, had little money and no prior political experience. On election day, Barrett captured 72 percent of the votes.

Reflecting his easy path to reelection, Barrett spent $242,768 less on his 1992 campaign than he had in 1990, a decrease of 39 percent. He spent $85,276 less on advertising and $82,064 less on other direct appeals for votes. Barrett had invested $34,041 in polls during the 1990 campaign; with the 1992 race never in doubt, he spent just $9,700 on polls. Overhead expenses dropped from $165,640 in 1990 to $81,919 in 1992.

Yet, at a time when Barrett was slashing his spending on many aspects of his campaign operation, he significantly increased his investment in fund raising. Having emerged from the 1990 campaign with debts of $70,000 and campaign cash reserves of only $19,982, raising money became a top priority. During 1991, fund-raising expenses accounted for 57 percent of the $67,768 he spent to keep his permanent campaign running smoothly. These efforts reaped individual contributions totaling $81,598 and PAC donations of $74,775. He began 1992 with no debts and cash reserves of $27,847.

Over the two-year cycle, Barrett spent $97,821 to raise money—a $45,225 increase over 1990. As a percentage of total spending, his fund-raising costs jumped from 9 percent in 1990 to 26 percent in 1992. While direct appeals for votes accounted for 56 percent of his 1990 outlays, such spending accounted for 48 percent of his total spending in 1992.

Similarly, Rep. Chet Edwards (D-Texas) had spent more than $730,000 in 1990 to defeat Republican Hugh D. Shine, who had invested nearly $859,000 in the bitterly contested battle for the open seat created by the retirement of Democratic Rep. Marvin Leath. Challenged in 1992 by a Republican opponent who spent just $17,000, Edwards coasted to victory with 67 percent of the vote, spending "only" $357,418.

Edwards chose to follow the lead of the more experienced incumbents and kept a campaign office open during the off-year. He invested $149,106 in his off-year campaign, spending $61,348 on overhead, $32,685 on staff salaries, $5,876 on telephone service, $4,734 on supplies, $3,213 on rent and utilities, and $3,200 on office equipment. Edwards also invested $57,764 in fund raising in 1991. A birthday celebration in Waco featured Democratic Gov. Ann Richards and attracted approximately 2,500 supporters who paid $10 each to dine on barbecue, Mexican food, and a huge chocolate cake. With costs totaling $22,825, the event barely broke even. Edwards also held one major off-year event aimed at PACs that brought in $168,660 of the $258,792 he raised in 1991.

Even though he had virtually no opposition in 1992, Edwards pumped another $208,312 into his election-year campaign effort. Not surprisingly, only 37 percent of that 1992 spending was put into direct appeals for votes; 42 percent was invested in overhead and fund raising.

Rep. Dick Swett was thought to be a marked man from the moment he upset Republican Rep. Chuck Douglas in 1990, thereby becoming the first Democrat elected to represent New Hampshire's District 2 since 1912. But he soon discovered that incumbency had its distinct advantages. Determined not to be a one-term aberration, Swett spent $319,578 more to defend his seat than he spent to win it. However, much of that 69 percent increase in spending was the result of a dramatic shift in his approach to raising money, not a matter of investing more in direct appeals for votes.

In 1990 fund raising consumed less than 1 percent of Swett's $465,540 treasury, a remarkable feat made possible by his wife's political connections. Katrina Lantos-Swett, the daughter of Rep. Tom Lantos (D-Calif.), had long served as a fund-raiser for her father, and she simply tapped into a network of donors across the country to fill her husband's treasury. The campaign augmented her efforts by holding in-home receptions that cost a total of only $3,463.

For the 1992 campaign, Swett followed his father-in-law's example and turned to Robert H. Bassin Associates of Washington, D.C., for help with PAC fund raising. Over the two-year election cycle, Swett paid Bassin $53,884 for coordinating PAC receptions that helped raise $403,900—more than twice the $186,000 he raised from PACs in 1990.

Fund-raising trips to New York, Atlanta, and Hillsborough, Calif., helped raise $317,968 from individual out-of-state donors who gave at least $200, which accounted for 85 percent of his large donations. To tap small donors, Swett initially turned to Intelligent Software Systems of San Carlos, Calif., a direct-mail consultant used by his father-in-law. As the need for money intensified, Swett also brought in A. B. Data of Milwaukee, Wis. Together, these firms helped push Swett's small contributions to $71,360. Intelligent Software and A. B. Data received $11,571 and $11,629, respectively. In all, Swett spent $155,326 to raise money for the 1992 campaign, an increase of $151,863 over 1990.

Swett's investment in overhead rose 38 percent, from $133,501 in the 1990 cycle to $184,252 in 1992. Having violated the state's voluntary spending limit for the 1990 general election campaign, Swett agreed to pay a $19,209 fine to the state of New Hampshire. He opted not to agree to abide by those voluntary limits in 1992. Payments to his lawyers amounted to $16,705.

In contrast, Swett's spending on direct appeals for votes rose by only 18 percent, from $312,881 in 1990 to $370,316 in 1992. As a percentage of his total spending, Swett's investment in appeals for votes dropped from 67 percent to 47 percent.

Many in the 1990 freshman class quickly realized the importance of constituent stroking. Over the two-year cycle, freshmen who won renomination spent a total of $202,328 on constituent gifts and entertainment.

Rep. Barbara-Rose Collins (D-Mich.) spent $226,735 on her initial reelection effort, but eighteen cents of every dollar went for constituent entertainment and gifts. She invested $25,064 of her campaign funds to celebrate her 1991 inauguration, including $13,364 for a preinaugural prayer breakfast, $3,561 to transport supporters to Washington, and $7,603 for food and room rental at the Hyatt Regency Hotel near Capitol Hill. At the end of the election cycle, the campaign spent $4,500 for tickets to the presidential inaugural ball. Flowers and telegrams to express sympathy over a constituent's death or to celebrate a new constituent's birth cost the campaign $1,222. The campaign spent $5,463 on constituent meals, $2,875 on receptions for senior citizens and other groups, $1,433 on "oval pen stands" and other gifts, and $215 on commemorative plaques. In all, these constituent stroking efforts accounted for $40,772 of Collins's spending.

Trailing far behind Collins in such expenditures was Rep. Neil Abercrombie (D-Hawaii), who invested $14,946 in constituent gifts and entertainment. Abercrombie spent $9,325 on year-end holiday cards, $3,339 on constituent meals and entertainment, $1,234 on various gifts and commemorative awards, and $1,048 on flowers.

Rep. Dick Zimmer (R-N.J.) spent $10,793 on year-end holiday cards and $1,892 to celebrate his inauguration in 1991. Together, these two expenses accounted for 91 percent of the money he invested in constituent stroking.

Zimmer's inaugural party was nothing compared to the celebration hosted by Rep. Rosa DeLauro (D-Conn.). DeLauro paid the New Haven Bus Service $2,950 to ferry supporters to Washington to witness the swearing-in ceremony. A reception for her supporters at America, a restaurant near Capitol Hill, cost the campaign $5,734 and a second reception at a Hyatt hotel near the Capitol added $1,553. The $10,237 tab for her inaugural festivities accounted for 90 percent of her investment in constituent stroking.

Each year, Hobson and fellow Ohio Republican Rep. Paul E. Gillmor invited fifty people from each of their districts to attend what Joyce McGarry, Hobson's press secretary, described as "leadership and government workshops." In 1991 Hobson's campaign spent $595 to sponsor one attendee; $195 for gifts from Rothschild Berry Farm in Urbana, Ohio, to commemorate the event; and $1,222 for a reception. In 1992 conference sponsorship expenses climbed to $1,050, while the cost of the reception rose to $2,534. Hobson also sent out Christmas postcards that cost $3,476 over the two-year cycle. In all, Hobson spent $10,484 on constituent gifts and entertainment—something that had consumed only $64 of his 1990 budget.

Brewster had invested just $89 in constituent entertainment during the 1990 campaign. During the 1992 election cycle, he invested $8,368 in constituent stroking. He spent $1,810 on year-end holiday cards, $1,293 on meals at the House restaurant, $880 on commemorative certificates, $700 on various Christmas gifts, $409 on U.S. flags, $360 on congressional cookbooks, and $202 on calendars purchased from the Oklahoma Democratic party. Tickets to the presidential inaugural festivities cost the campaign $2,370.

Rep. James P. Moran, Jr. (D-Va.) had poured $952,253 into his 1990 battle with Rep. Stan Parris, and only $94 of that massive budget had been put into constituent gifts and entertainment. By 1992, Moran's position had been significantly improved by redistricting, and although Republican Kyle E. McSlarrow put up a strong fight, Moran's new incumbency status prompted him to divert $9,385 of his $902,140 budget to constituent stroking. He invested $3,750 in year-end holiday cards. His inaugural celebration cost $3,530—$1,600 for dinner at the Gas Light restaurant in Alexandria, Va., and $1,930 for a reception at the Radisson Plaza Hotel in Alexandria. He spent $1,402 on constituent events, including a $133 payment for "nursing homes refreshments." Gifts and flowers added $519 and $184, respectively.

While the typical freshman donated $10,336 of his or her own treasury to other candidates, political party organizations, and various causes, some gave away considerably more. The political donations of Rep. John A. Boehner (R-Ohio) amounted to $53,309, or 13 percent of his total spending. Concerned about redistricting, he gave $10,000 to the Ohio Republican Senate Committee; this pushed his donations to party organizations to $13,606. He gave $25,162 to Republican candidates from other states, including $1,000 each to Minority Whip Newt Gingrich (Ga.), Rick Santorum (Pa.), Riggs, Nussle, Charles H. Taylor (N.C.), and John T. Doolittle (Calif.). His donations to such candidates also included campaign packets valued at nearly $17,000. "We did a lot of outreach to Republicans around the country, sending them background information on issues and how to use them in the campaign," noted Barry Jackson, Boehner's chief of staff. Boehner also dipped into his treasury for $9,411 to make donations to other Ohio Republicans vying for various offices. He gave $4,491 to charitable and booster organizations and $640 to ideological groups.

As a challenger in 1990, Dooley had needed every penny he could lay his hands on to defeat Rep. Chip Pashayan. As a result, he donated just $646 to Democratic party organizations, $284 to civic groups, and $75 to other California candidates. However, once elected, Dooley found room in his budget for contributions totaling $46,043, which accounted for 9 percent of his total spending during the 1992 cycle. To protect his own interests and those of fellow California Democrats, Dooley gave $38,188 to IMPAC 2000, the political action committee established to help Democrats with redistricting.

Hobson's donations increased five-fold, from $5,910 in 1990 to $30,368 in 1992. He gave $10,005 to various Republican party organizations, including $8,500 to the Ohio Republican Senate Committee. He gave $7,263 to fellow Ohio Republicans, including $1,000 each to Reps. Bob McEwen and Ralph Regula and $1,100 to his predecessor in District 7, Lt. Gov. Mike DeWine, who decided to challenge Democratic Sen. John Glenn. Hobson donated $6,135 to candidates in other states, including $2,000 to Gingrich and $500 each to Santorum, Riggs, Wayne T. Gilchrest (Md.), Doolittle, Wayne Allard (Colo.), Nussle, and Zeliff. He spent $4,110 on livestock purchased at fairs and 4-H Club events, which accounted for 71 percent of his contributions to charitable and booster organizations. His ideological donations amounted to $1,200.

In 1990 Brewster donated just $890 to charities and Democratic party organizations. Two years later he gave away $22,465. Fellow Democrats Beryl Anthony, Jr. (Ark.), Thomas J. Downey (N.Y.), James A. Barcia (Mich.), Andy Fox (Va.), Laurie Williams (Okla.), and Sam Gejdenson (Conn.) each received checks for $1,000. Eight others received checks for $500.

While $19,858 in donations did not put Rep. William J. Jefferson (D-La.) in the same league with several of his freshman colleagues, those donations amounted to more than twice what he invested in advertising. The chief beneficiary of Jefferson's altruism was the NAACP, which received four contributions totaling $1,250. The Alumni Association of Southern University, Jefferson's alma mater, received a $500 check from his campaign, as did Rev. James

Landrum. Young Democrats of America received two checks totaling $650. Jefferson gave $250 to the Close-Up Foundation, $340 to the Veterans of Foreign Wars, $400 to the Greater St. Matthew Chapel Baptist Church, $202 to the Louisiana Association of the Deaf, and $300 to the Anti-Defamation League of B'nai Brith. He also bought a $218 videocassette recorder for the Flint-Goodrich Hospital in New Orleans. He gave none of his campaign treasury away in 1990.

Following the example of many longtime incumbents, the 1990 freshman class wasted little time in taking advantage of some of the institutionalized perquisites of continuously seeking office. For instance, while Rep. Robert E. "Bud" Cramer (D-Ala.) briefly closed his campaign office, when it reopened in July 1991 his new landlord was the Cramer Corp., a company owned by his uncle. Travel was booked through Cramer Travel, his parent's travel agency. For his 1990 race, Cramer spent just $810 on his campaign car; once elected his campaign began paying $794 a month to lease a new 1991 Ford Explorer. Over the two-year cycle, Cramer spent $20,878 to lease, license, and insure his campaign car; this amounted to 7 percent of his total campaign spending.

During the 1990 campaign, Brewster invested $7,054 in short-term auto leases. Less than six months after taking office, he began making $391 monthly lease payments to Ford Credit. Over the course of the 1992 election cycle, those payments totaled $10,436. The campaign spent $1,375 on automobile repairs, $1,107 to insure and register the car, and $2,654 on gasoline.

Moran paid his daughter Mary Elise $13,500 for running his campaign office. Moran's brother Brian received a $5,000 payment for his campaign efforts, while Moran's son James Edward collected $2,000.

One-third of Collins's $15,790 travel budget was spent in New York during the four-day Democratic National Convention. After investing more than $7,000 of her 1990 campaign funds in clothes and image consulting, she spent more than $1,800 to finish off her wardrobe in early 1991.

Jefferson spent $24,960 on travel; $5,895 of that total was incurred during his stay in New York for the Democratic National Convention, including $2,610 for a party at the New York Hilton.

Rep. Maxine Waters (D-Calif.) tapped her campaign treasury for $5,661 to pay for the annual Congressional Black Caucus weekend in September 1991. Bills at the Hyatt Regency and the Washington

Hilton and Towers were $3,249 and $494, respectively. Limousine service added $528; tickets to the evening gala cost $1,390.

Zeliff tapped his campaign treasury to pay the Washington law firm of Wiley, Rein & Fielding $40,250 for their help in disposing of a nuisance complaint filed with the Federal Election Commission by his 1990 opponent, Democrat Joseph F. Keefe. Keefe charged that a $150,000 loan Zeliff had made to his campaign was improper. Since the loan was made using proceeds from the sale of property Zeliff and his wife jointly owned, Keefe argued that half the loan was really an illegal campaign contribution made by Zeliff's wife. Three accounting firms charged Zeliff's campaign a total of $32,191.

Doolittle, who spent much of the election cycle calling for change and decrying the sorry state of politics as usual, spent $9,206 of his treasury to move his personal belongings from California to Washington.

Although most members of the freshman class of 1992 ran on a platform of change, there was strong evidence even before they were sworn in that the supposedly reform-minded new members had already begun the process of settling in.

State senator Frank Tejeda (D-Texas) was prepared to fight hard to win the state's newly created Hispanic-majority District 28. He opened his campaign office in September 1991 and raised more than $100,000 by the end of the year. However, no other Democrat or Republican bothered to enter the race. His only opposition in November came from libertarian David C. Slatter, who spent just $1,402. Yet, while he was the only freshman elected to a new district who did not face major-party opposition, Tejeda spent $351,961. Only 21 percent of that total was invested in direct appeals for votes.

Tejeda poured 44 percent of his budget into overhead. Monthly rent on his San Antonio office was $850. Salary payments to the eight people who worked on the primary campaign and to the five people who worked on the fall campaign totaled $72,631. Health insurance premiums for campaign manager Frances Ruiz amounted to $1,140. Tejeda spent $10,389 to lease, fuel, and maintain a 1989 Jeep Cherokee.

As a veteran politician, Tejeda knew well the political importance of well-placed charitable contributions. He donated $10,091 to charitable and booster organizations, including $1,664 to sponsor the Southside Junior Cardinals, $1,197 to the St. James Catholic

Church, and $200 to McCollum Band Boosters. Tejeda also realized the importance of constituent stroking, spending $2,461 on Christmas cards, $1,532 on Easter cards, and $933 on flowers, gifts, and entertainment.

Tejeda was by no means alone in embracing the current rules of the electoral game. To celebrate his victory, state senator Robert Menendez (D-N.J.) spent $8,300 of his campaign funds on a luncheon at the J. W. Marriott in Washington, D.C., where approximately 1,000 supporters watched on big-screen televisions as he took the oath of office. While payroll accounted for 15 percent of Human Affairs Commissioner James E. Clyburn's (D-S.C.) $397,090 budget, and his campaign director and press secretary collected "salary" payments for months, he paid no payroll taxes.

Attorney and former state senator Melvin Watt (D-N.C.) paid his son Brian $15,398 for serving as campaign manager. State representative Tim Hutchinson (R-Ark.) paid his wife, Donna, a former executive director of the Arkansas Republican party, $6,642 before taking her off the campaign payroll in August. Hutchinson's press secretary, Samuel A. Sellers, said Donna Hutchinson left the payroll to "avoid any appearance of impropriety."

State representative Cynthia A. McKinney (D-Ga.) paid her mother a $2,500 bonus for serving as the campaign's scheduler. Prior to winning his Democratic primary runoff, Alabama state senator Earl F. Hilliard had needed all his resources for appealing to voters and had paid three brothers a total of only $2,024 for their campaign work. After the runoff, with the nomination in hand and assured of victory in November in his solidly Democratic district, Hilliard found room in the budget for payments to his brothers totaling $8,465. The campaign also paid $2,900 in travel expenses for his wife to attend the Democratic National Convention. His son, Earl F. Hilliard, Jr., collected salary payments totaling $2,000.

Real estate developer Ken Calvert (R-Calif.) tapped his campaign treasury for $2,514 to help pay for moving his belongings to Washington. Compton Mayor Walter R. Tucker III (D-Calif.) spent $1,100 of his treasury to move his car to Washington.

Having raised and spent vast sums to win their seats, virtually all the 1992 freshman class were well acquainted with the Washington PAC community and had no reason to change the status quo on campaign finance. San Matco County Supervisor Anna G. Eshoo (D-

Calif.) had outspent fellow San Mateo supervisor Tom Huening by $282,070 in winning their open seat contest, and her spending advantage had been largely fueled by PACs. During the primary campaign, Eshoo had collected roughly 17 percent of her contributions from PACs, but for the general election campaign against Huening, she upped that to 41 percent. In all, she pulled in $296,322 from PACs.

Governor Michael N. Castle (R-Del.) depended heavily on PACs and out-of-state contributors to fund his successful campaign to replace Democratic Rep. Thomas R. Carper, who retired to run successfully for governor. Castle received $206,868 from PACs, which accounted for 30 percent of his total contributions. Fund-raising events in New York and Philadelphia helped raise $128,750 in large donations from nonconstituents. Together, PACs and out-of-state donors accounted for 49 percent of his total contributions.

By far the clearest indication that reform was not on the minds of every member of the 1992 freshman class was the case of Diamond Bar, Calif., mayor and businessman Jay C. Kim (R-Calif.). In July 1993 the *Los Angeles Times* reported that records provided to the paper showed that Kim had illegally funneled money from his company, JayKim Engineers, to pay many of his 1992 campaign expenses—in violation of federal law. According to the *Times,* Kim used more than $400,000 of corporate money to pay for airline tickets, telephone service, office space, staff, and office supplies. Following these reports, the Federal Bureau of Investigation launched an inquiry into Kim's campaign funding practices.

Table 3-1 What Campaign Money Buys in the 1992 House Races: Average Expenditures by 1990 Freshmen Versus More Entrenched Incumbents

Major Category	Representatives Elected in 1990			Representatives Elected Before 1990			
	Total	Hot Races[a]	Contested Races[b]	Total	Hot Races[a]	Contested Races[b]	Unopposed Seats
Overhead							
Office furniture/supplies	$ 8,501	$ 10,177	$ 7,245	$ 8,741	$ 10,487	$ 7,540	$ 5,364
Rent/utilities	7,533	9,391	6,140	9,357	11,637	7,703	6,715
Salaries	45,000	47,094	43,430	50,650	63,172	42,028	26,567
Taxes	9,999	11,789	8,656	17,395	19,659	15,920	11,294
Bank/investment fees	3,392	4,380	2,651	1,037	1,230	928	151
Lawyers/accountants	9,889	10,055	9,764	10,145	12,301	8,717	4,842
Telephone	9,350	11,086	8,047	8,353	10,887	6,418	7,421
Campaign automobile	1,353	972	1,639	3,449	4,555	2,454	6,128
Computers/office equipment	8,077	8,940	7,430	9,141	10,587	7,942	10,555
Travel	15,497	19,155	12,753	22,016	25,085	19,090	32,856
Food/meetings	1,276	1,568	1,056	3,903	3,417	3,800	13,869
Total Overhead	**119,867**	**134,608**	**108,812**	**144,188**	**173,018**	**122,541**	**125,764**
Fund Raising							
Events	79,766	80,921	78,899	63,394	69,057	59,615	50,024
Direct mail	30,625	45,063	19,797	20,010	26,286	15,861	4,395
Telemarketing	1,370	7	2,393	1,385	2,086	904	0
Total Fund Raising	**111,761**	**125,990**	**101,089**	**84,789**	**97,429**	**76,380**	**54,419**
Polling	**16,567**	**17,869**	**15,590**	**20,241**	**29,177**	**14,121**	**2,400**

Advertising						
Electronic media	156,814	193,364	129,401	138,884	210,152	89,766	2,748
Other media	10,528	9,087	11,609	15,787	16,997	15,478	2,655
Total Advertising	**167,342**	**202,451**	**141,010**	**154,671**	**227,149**	**105,244**	**5,402**
Other Campaign Activity							
Persuasion mail/brochures	56,013	63,592	50,328	71,282	103,048	49,610	6,046
Actual campaigning	35,592	37,200	34,387	42,050	52,981	33,998	31,839
Staff/Volunteers	886	708	1,019	1,525	2,069	1,135	780
Total Other Campaign Activity	**92,491**	**101,500**	**85,734**	**114,857**	**158,098**	**84,744**	**38,666**
Constituent Gifts/Entertainment	**4,817**	**2,311**	**6,697**	**9,135**	**8,680**	**9,220**	**14,727**
Donations to							
Candidates from same state	1,619	1,136	1,981	5,752	2,673	7,435	20,711
Candidates from other states	1,980	456	3,123	4,186	2,301	5,638	4,625
Civic organizations	1,348	649	1,872	3,578	2,831	4,140	4,035
Ideological groups	718	424	939	1,657	1,632	1,734	439
Political parties	4,672	2,469	6,324	13,350	11,289	15,196	8,490
Total Donations	**10,336**	**5,134**	**14,238**	**28,522**	**20,726**	**34,144**	**38,300**
Unitemized Expenses	**11,933**	**10,849**	**12,746**	**16,152**	**17,674**	**14,662**	**22,333**
Total Expenditures	**$535,115**	**$600,712**	**$485,917**	**$572,555**	**$731,951**	**$461,055**	**$302,012**

Note: Totals are for the entire two-year cycle.

[a]Races where incumbent garners 60 percent or less of the vote.
[b]Races where incumbent garners more than 60 percent of the vote.

Table 3-2 What Campaign Money Buys in the 1992 House Races: Expenditures by 1990 Freshmen Versus More Entrenched Incumbents, by Percentage

Major Category	Representatives Elected in 1990			Representatives Elected Before 1990			
	Total	Hot Races[a]	Contested Races[b]	Total	Hot Races[a]	Contested Races[b]	Unopposed Seats
Overhead							
Office furniture/supplies	1.59	1.69	1.49	1.53	1.43	1.64	1.78
Rent/utilities	1.41	1.56	1.26	1.63	1.59	1.67	2.22
Salaries	8.41	7.84	8.94	8.85	8.63	9.12	8.80
Taxes	1.87	1.96	1.78	3.04	2.69	3.45	3.74
Bank/investment fees	.63	.73	.55	.18	.17	.20	.05
Lawyers/accountants	1.85	1.67	2.01	1.77	1.68	1.89	1.60
Telephone	1.75	1.85	1.66	1.46	1.49	1.39	2.46
Campaign automobile	.25	.16	.34	.60	.62	.53	2.03
Computers/office equipment	1.51	1.49	1.53	1.60	1.45	1.72	3.50
Travel	2.90	3.19	2.62	3.85	3.43	4.14	10.88
Food/meetings	.24	.26	.22	.68	.47	.82	4.59
Total Overhead	**22.40**	**22.41**	**22.39**	**25.18**	**23.64**	**26.58**	**41.64**
Fund Raising							
Events	14.91	13.47	16.24	11.07	9.43	12.93	16.56
Direct mail	5.72	7.50	4.07	3.49	3.59	3.44	1.46
Telemarketing	.26	0	.49	.24	.29	.20	0
Total Fund Raising	**20.89**	**20.97**	**20.80**	**14.81**	**13.31**	**16.57**	**18.02**
Polling	**3.10**	**2.97**	**3.21**	**3.54**	**3.99**	**3.06**	**.79**

Advertising					
Electronic media	29.30	26.63	24.26	28.71	19.47	.91
Other media	1.97	2.39	2.76	2.32	3.36	.88
Total Advertising	**31.27**	**29.02**	**27.01**	**31.03**	**22.83**	**1.79**
Other Campaign Activity						
Persuasion mail/brochures	10.47	10.36	12.45	14.08	10.76	2.00
Actual campaigning	6.65	7.08	7.34	7.24	7.37	10.54
Staff/Volunteers	.17	.21	.27	.28	.25	.26
Total Other Campaign Activity	**17.28**	**17.64**	**20.06**	**21.60**	**18.38**	**12.80**
Constituent Gifts/Entertainment	**.90**	**1.38**	**1.60**	**1.19**	**2.00**	**4.88**
Donations to						
Candidates from same state	.30	.41	1.00	.37	1.61	6.86
Candidates from other states	.37	.64	.73	.31	1.22	1.53
Civic organizations	.25	.39	.62	.39	.90	1.34
Ideological groups	.13	.19	.29	.22	.38	.15
Political parties	.87	1.30	2.33	1.54	3.30	2.81
Total Donations	**1.93**	**2.93**	**4.98**	**2.83**	**7.41**	**12.68**
Unitemized Expenses	**2.23**	**2.62**	**2.82**	**2.41**	**3.18**	**7.39**
Total Expenditures	**100.00**	**100.00**	**100.00**	**100.00**	**100.00**	**100.00**

Note: Totals are for the entire two-year cycle.

[a] Races where incumbent garners 60 percent or less of the vote.
[b] Races where incumbent garners more than 60 percent of the vote.

Table 3-3 What Campaign Money Buys 1992 and 1990 House Races: Expenditures by 1990 Freshmen

Major Category	1992 Cycle			1990 Cycle		
	Total	Average	Percent	Total	Average	Percent
Overhead						
Office furniture/supplies	$ 357,062	$ 8,501	1.59	$ 546,380	$ 13,009	2.29
Rent/utilities	316,393	7,533	1.41	331,056	7,882	1.39
Salaries	1,890,018	45,000	8.41	2,956,835	70,401	12.40
Taxes	419,943	9,999	1.87	488,736	11,637	2.05
Bank/investment fees	142,472	3,392	.63	23,292	555	.10
Lawyers/accountants	415,327	9,889	1.85	132,421	3,153	.56
Telephone	392,681	9,350	1.75	688,049	16,382	2.89
Campaign automobile	56,843	1,353	.25	92,631	2,205	.39
Computers/office equipment	339,251	8,077	1.51	318,120	7,574	1.33
Travel	650,856	15,497	2.90	474,128	11,289	1.99
Food/meetings	53,571	1,276	.24	37,910	903	.16
Total Overhead	**5,034,417**	**119,867**	**22.40**	**6,089,559**	**144,990**	**25.55**
Fund Raising						
Events	3,350,158	79,766	14.91	1,477,005	35,167	6.20
Direct mail	1,286,249	30,625	5.72	683,583	16,276	2.87
Telemarketing	57,557	1,370	.26	121,989	2,905	.51
Total Fund Raising	**4,693,964**	**111,761**	**20.89**	**2,282,577**	**54,348**	**9.58**
Polling	**695,813**	**16,567**	**3.10**	**847,039**	**20,168**	**3.55**

Advertising						
Electronic media	6,586,179	156,814	29.30	8,710,734	207,398	36.54
Other media	442,194	10,528	1.97	631,398	15,033	2.65
Total Advertising	**7,028,373**	**167,342**	**31.27**	**9,342,132**	**222,432**	**39.19**
Other Campaign Activity						
Persuasion mail/brochures	2,352,526	56,013	10.47	2,990,681	71,207	12.55
Actual campaigning	1,494,882	35,592	6.65	1,681,440	40,034	7.05
Staff/Volunteers	37,214	886	.17	22,365	532	.09
Total Other Campaign Activity	**3,884,622**	**92,491**	**17.28**	**4,694,486**	**111,773**	**19.69**
Constituent Gifts/ Entertainment	**202,328**	**4,817**	**.90**	**11,449**	**273**	**.05**
Donations to						
Candidates from same state	67,994	1,619	.30	18,961	451	.08
Candidates from other states	83,142	1,980	.37	16,750	399	.07
Civic organizations	56,613	1,348	.25	21,190	505	.09
Ideological groups	30,157	718	.13	5,756	137	.02
Political parties	196,215	4,672	.87	28,029	667	.12
Total Donations	**434,121**	**10,336**	**1.93**	**90,687**	**2,159**	**.38**
Unitemized Expenses	**501,180**	**11,933**	**2.23**	**479,377**	**11,414**	**2.01**
Total Expenditures	**$22,474,819**	**$535,115**	**100.00**	**$23,837,306**	**$567,555**	**100.00**

Note: Totals are for the entire two-year cycle.

Table 3-4 What Campaign Money Buys in the 1992 House Races: Total Expenditures by 1990 Freshmen

Major Category	Boiling Races[a]	Hot Races[b]	Warm Races[c]	Ice Cold Races[d]
Overhead				
Office furniture/supplies	$ 99,991	$ 83,195	$ 126,270	$ 47,607
Rent/utilities	93,520	75,521	105,140	42,211
Salaries	370,146	477,551	710,541	331,779
Taxes	102,076	110,128	133,865	73,874
Bank/investment fees	71,336	7,506	30,658	32,971
Lawyers/accountants	151,849	29,142	157,690	76,646
Telephone	117,637	81,905	144,980	48,160
Campaign automobile	317	17,179	20,878	18,469
Computers/office equipment	74,904	86,023	109,506	68,818
Travel	168,853	175,942	198,369	107,692
Food/meetings	12,859	15,360	16,896	8,456
Total Overhead	**1,263,489**	**1,159,452**	**1,754,793**	**856,683**
Fund Raising				
Events	940,927	515,648	1,337,180	556,403
Direct mail	596,628	214,504	404,307	70,810
Telemarketing	119	0	46,282	11,156
Total Fund Raising	**1,537,674**	**730,152**	**1,787,769**	**638,369**
Polling	**207,874**	**113,771**	**310,209**	**63,959**

	[a]	[b]	[c]	[d]
Advertising				
Electronic media	1,977,238	1,503,319	2,528,538	577,083
Other media	102,075	61,493	173,254	105,373
Total Advertising	**2,079,313**	**1,564,812**	**2,701,792**	**682,456**
Other Campaign Activity				
Persuasion mail/brochures	906,049	238,599	1,010,640	197,237
Actual campaigning	424,638	244,962	594,231	231,051
Staff/Volunteers	2,386	10,361	17,959	6,508
Total Other Campaign Activity	**1,333,073**	**493,923**	**1,622,830**	**434,796**
Constituent Gifts/Entertainment	**15,930**	**25,663**	**109,181**	**51,553**
Donations to				
Candidates from same state	11,745	8,708	16,603	30,938
Candidates from other states	5,700	2,500	22,647	52,296
Civic organizations	3,313	8,376	21,414	23,509
Ideological groups	4,992	2,633	10,232	12,300
Political parties	30,315	14,132	98,890	52,878
Total Donations	**56,065**	**36,349**	**169,786**	**171,921**
Unitemized Expenses	152,341	42,941	143,684	162,214
Total Expenditures	**$6,645,760**	**$4,167,063**	**$8,600,045**	**$3,061,952**

Note: Totals are for the entire two-year cycle.

[a] Those races decided by 10 percentage points or less.
[b] Those races decided by 11-20 percentage points.
[c] Those races decided by 21-40 percentage points.
[d] Those races decided by 41 or more percentage points.

CHAPTER 4

The Angry Electorate?
Incumbents Fight to Survive

All politics is local.

Thomas P. O'Neill,
former House Speaker

On November 21, 1991, Fenn & King Communications of Washington, D.C., which created and placed broadcast advertising for twenty Democratic House incumbents in 1990, sent its clients and prospective clients on Capitol Hill a memorandum warning that "a year ago many incumbent members of Congress, Democrat and Republican, dodged a freight train of anti-incumbent feeling." Among other things, the five-page memo warned that "the anti-status quo, anti-incumbent sentiment in the country is growing, not waning" and cautioned that "relatively obscure challengers can beat incumbents in this climate." While Fenn & King's warning was a bit overstated, Rep. Beverly B. Byron (D-Md.) would have done well to heed their advice.

In seven previous House campaigns, Byron had never received less than 65 percent of the general election vote, and in five of those seven races she had collected 70 percent or more. While furniture salesman Anthony Patrick Puca had taken 36 percent of the Democratic primary votes in 1990, there was little evidence to suggest that Byron was in serious trouble heading into 1992.

Byron's opponent in the March 3 Democratic primary, state representative Thomas H. Hattery, had challenged her in 1980 and come away with only 12 percent of the vote. While most observers expected him to do considerably better this time, few gave him much chance of pulling off an upset.

However, Hattery came out swinging with a heavily negative, anti-incumbent campaign. His persuasion mailers attacked Byron for her 1989 vote in favor of the congressional pay raise; for taking numerous taxpayer-funded junkets, including one to Barbados; and for joining the rest of Congress "in letting the S&L profiteers run wild." Over the final two weeks of the campaign, Hattery aired a companion television commercial that pilloried Byron's junkets in a parody of *Life Styles of the Rich and Famous.* In all, Hattery committed nearly $230,000 to his long-shot primary bid.

For her part, Byron initially seemed unconcerned. She ran no ads directly refuting Hattery's charges. While she spent more than $116,000 during the off-year to maintain her permanent campaign operation, including monthly payments of $2,533 to her one full-time employee, Byron failed to capitalize on the advantage that such an organization is supposed to provide. She spent only $5,000 on polling and may never have seen what was coming. She invested $43,749 in persuasion mail, $4,472 in newspaper ads, $3,700 in phonebanking, $675 in signs, and $440 in bumper stickers. She paid Fenn & King $12,500, and over the final week put $10,235 into airing radio spots that attacked Hattery as "Taxing Tom." As it turned out, her $134,647 preprimary push did not reflect the gravity of her situation.

Hattery carried all six counties in the district and won with 56 percent of the vote. While only one incumbent had failed to win re-nomination in 1990, Hattery's anti-incumbent message carried him to a stunning upset victory in the first congressional primary of 1992, although he would later lose in the general election. It was only the beginning.

Rep. Bill Alexander (D-Ark.) had grown accustomed to stiff primary challenges. In the summer of 1985, Alexander had arranged for a military jet to take a "congressional delegation" on a fact-finding trip to Brazil. When it was revealed that he was the plane's only passenger and that the trip had cost taxpayers $50,000, Alexander found himself faced with the first of what would become strong, biennial anti-incumbent challenges from within his own party.

In 1992 Alexander came up against Blanche Lambert, a thirty-one-year-old former aide to Alexander, who began her bid to unseat him with virtually no money. She could not afford both preprimary polling and broadcast advertising, so she opted to forego the polls. She paid Strother-Duffy-Strother of Washington, D.C., $2,153 to create her preprimary commercials and Media Strategies of Falls Church,

Va., $58,000 to buy air time. Her entire preprimary effort cost approximately $80,000.

Alexander spent $172,007 to keep his permanent campaign running during the off-year, and when Lambert took up the challenge, the fourteen-term incumbent pumped another $170,000 into his primary campaign. However, in a year when "change" was the operative campaign buzzword, Alexander's 487 overdrafts at the House bank proved to be more than voters could forgive.

Ten days before the primary, Lambert unveiled a television commercial that focused on Alexander's initial denial that he had any overdrafts. The spot opened with five seconds of footage showing Alexander's denial; his image was encased in a "Looney Tunes" cartoon box labeled "Bill Toons." Following the denial, a game show buzzer sounded, the Looney Tunes music started, and the words "Alexander had actually bounced 487 checks" appeared on the screen. Alexander received only 39 percent of the primary votes, losing twenty-three of the district's twenty-five counties.

As head of the National Republican Congressional Committee (NRCC), Rep. Guy Vander Jagt (R-Mich.) toured the country throughout the late spring and early summer of 1992 arguing that voters were disgusted with the way Washington worked and about to retire dozens of House members involuntarily. When Peter Hoekstra, a furniture executive with no prior political experience, knocked him out in the August 4 primary, Vander Jagt discovered just how right he had been.

Like many challengers, Hoekstra struggled to raise money. He found forty supporters who were each willing to write letters to one hundred acquaintances asking for donations, but that brought in no more than $15,000. He borrowed $24,300 from a local bank just to keep the campaign sputtering along.

On that budget, Hoekstra could only dream about television advertising. He spent $7,471 to print his campaign literature. Yard signs and posters cost $3,057. He spent $4,371 to send out one mailing to 15,000 past Republican primary voters and several more tightly targeted mailings. Arguing that Vander Jagt was a career politician who was too busy raising money for the national Republican party to stay in touch with his constituents, Hoekstra bicycled thirty miles through the heart of the district, stopping regularly to talk with voters. Whenever he appeared in a parade, his mode of transportation was a 1966

Nash Rambler, made the year Vander Jagt first went to Washington. The sign on the car read, "Isn't it time for a change?"

That message of change echoed throughout each of the three radio spots Hoekstra aired over the primary campaign's final week. One ad hammered Vander Jagt for his reliance on political action committee (PAC) money and pointed out that the fourteen-term incumbent also collected large sums from individual donors who did not live in Michigan. Another spot focused on Vander Jagt's junket to Barbados, which was entirely paid for by lobbyists and unflatteringly profiled on *PrimeTime Live*. "Who does Guy Vander Jagt represent?" the ads asked. Hoekstra's budget for air time was $7,539.

Redistricting had significantly altered Vander Jagt's constituency. The two most populous counties in the new District 2 were entirely new to him, opening the door for Hoekstra's outsider message. Vander Jagt made matters worse for himself. After publicly rejoicing on several occasions about the power of the House banking scandal to bring down long-time House members, he came to the defense of fellow Michigan Republican Robert W. Davis, whose 878 overdrafts at the bank earned him the dubious distinction of being named one of its twenty-two worst abusers. Davis opted to retire rather than try to explain his overdrafts to an angry electorate, but Vander Jagt was stuck with his decision to speak out on Davis's behalf. While that move was undoubtedly the appropriate response for the head of the NRCC, it was not the best message for Vander Jagt the candidate.

Realizing he was in trouble, Vander Jagt spent $60,130 on an eleventh-hour media blitz. Having railed for months against tax-and-spend Democrats, his advertising campaign focused on his ability to deliver pork-barrel projects to the district. It was a hard sell, and he fell 4,369 votes short. In the end, Vander Jagt carried every county that had been part of his old District 9 but lost both of the two newly acquired counties. Discussing his loss the next day, Vander Jagt quietly told reporters, "I don't think it had anything to do with partisanship. There is a much more transcendent feeling out there. And that's just anti-incumbent, throw the bums out, throw the rascals out, all of them, we don't care if they're Republican or Democrat, is the mood at this moment."

Reading Vander Jagt's words or any of the 3,394 stories containing the phrases "anti-incumbent" or "anti-incumbency" that appeared in major daily newspapers and magazines during 1992, one could not have been blamed for assuming that the electorate—every electorate in every jurisdiction—was angry. The question seemed not whether incumbents would lose in droves, but just how bad the carnage would eventually become. As media consultant John Franzen put it, "In one way or another, anti-incumbency was something everyone had to deal with."

Adding to the sense that anti-incumbent sentiment was running rampant were the campaigns of numerous open seat candidates, who repeatedly slammed Congress and politicians in general, since they had no specific incumbent to attack. A mailer touting state senator Karen English's (D-Ariz.) candidacy showed an overweight man sitting in a lawn chair, smoking a cigar. The tagline read: "Washington's been sitting down on the job again."

In Alabama, Republican newspaper executive Terry Everett's campaign slogan was "Send a message, not a politician." Throughout the general election campaign, Everett juxtaposed his political inexperience with the political resume of state treasurer George C. Wallace, Jr., son of the former governor and presidential candidate. "He focused on his status as an outsider, a nonpolitical type, and he frequently attacked Wallace as a person raised by his father to be another politician," recalled Mike Lewis, Everett's press secretary.

To foster his outsider image, businessman and former state representative John Linder (R-Ga.) aired one television commercial showing him helping a group of children clean up a broken piggy bank they had dropped. Proclaiming that the federal government had "broken the bank," the voice-over noted that Linder would "help pick up the pieces."

State senator Bill Baker (R-Calif.) spent $421,707 on campaign literature and advocacy mailers, including one touting his votes against "every legislative pay raise in the state assembly," his record as a champion of "the angry taxpayer," and his displeasure over "the bounced checks, the staggering federal deficit, and the special privileges for members of Congress."

Ironically, the power of the anti-incumbent message was best illustrated by several of the nine incumbent-versus-incumbent match-ups set up by redistricting—match-ups that guaranteed there would be at least nine incumbent losers. The victory of freshman Rep. Jim Nussle (R-Iowa) over three-term Democratic Rep. Dave Nagle showed all too clearly the power of outsider politics. While Nagle campaigned on his ability to deliver federal projects to the district, Nussle positioned himself as a congressional reformer and attacked Nagle as a career politician.

Six weeks before the November general election, Nussle began airing television commercials slamming Nagle for his four overdrafts at the House bank and for initially denying that he had any overdrafts. The most damaging of these spots showed Nagle saying "public opinion be damned" on the House floor, a statement he made in arguing against the release of the House banking records on the grounds that it would violate members' constitutional rights. While Nagle pointed to the projects he had delivered to the district as proof that he was looking out for his constituents' interests, Nussle blasted those same projects as wasteful, pork-barrel spending.

While Nagle paid Fenn & King $288,072 for creating and placing his broadcast advertising, for much of the campaign he ignored the firm's advice to attack Nussle. With early polls showing him ahead by 14 points, Nagle opted to take the high road and stick with his pro-incumbency pitch. One such ad showed Nagle standing near the Mississippi River discussing the need to build and maintain locks and dams. "There are some who say this is pork-barrel spending," Nagle noted. Kneeling next to an oinking pig, he concluded, "This is a river. This is pork. If you're going to represent Iowa in Congress, you'd better know the difference." This humorous message was no match for Nussle's negative bombardment, and while Nagle began counterattacking over the campaign's final two weeks, his efforts proved to be too little, too late.

In Illinois, redistricting pitted two-term Democratic Rep. Glenn Poshard against four-term Democratic Rep. Terry L. Bruce, and Bruce seemed to hold most of the cards. Their redrawn district contained more of Bruce's old constituents. In January 1992 Bruce had campaign cash reserves of $699,486; Poshard began 1992 with just $17,272 in his campaign bank account. Bruce's massive treasury allowed him to commit more than $740,000 to his three-month preprimary effort; Poshard spent only about $150,000 in the first three months of 1992. However, Poshard emerged with 62 percent of the votes, in part because he was successful at turning his financial weakness into a campaign issue. "We were the underdog, fighting the good fight. We were able to set up the contrast between our opponent's reliance on PAC contributions and our refusal to accept them," noted David D. Stricklin, Poshard's press secretary.

Rather than fight the good fight, sixty-five House members opted to retire instead of seeking another term. In addition to Davis, six-term Rep. Vin Weber (R-Minn.) chose not to face voters with his 125 House bank overdrafts. Rep. Chalmers P. Wiley (R-Ohio), with 515 overdrafts, and Carl C. Perkins (D-Ky.), with 514 overdrafts, also decided not to try and explain their problem to voters. Having announced his retirement to seek a Senate seat, Rep. Robert J. Mrazek (D-N.Y.) found his Senate bid derailed by his 920 overdrafts. However, while the press tended to view all retirements as a sign of running from voter anger, members retired for a variety of reasons.

Reps. Robin Tallon (D-S.C.) and Claude Harris (D-Ala.) decided to retire when redistricting reconfigured their districts to create new majority-black constituencies. Republican Rep. George F. Allen, who won a 1991 special election in Virginia's District 7, joined Reps. Frank Annunzio (D-Ill.), Bernard J. Dwyer (D-N.J.), Frank Horton (R-N.Y.), James H. Scheuer (D-N.Y.), and Bill Lowery (R-Calif.), all of whom found retirement preferable to facing fellow incumbents in match-ups created by redistricting. Allen successfully ran for governor in 1993, which may have helped make his decision to retire easier.

Rep. Lawrence J. Smith (D-Fla.) agreed to a $5,000 fine for spending some of his 1990 campaign funds for personal use, including the repayment of a gambling debt. After retiring, Smith spent three months in jail over the incident. In 1990 a former aide to Rep. Gus Yatron (D-Pa.) had accused the twelve-term incumbent of requiring salary kickbacks. Although the aide was ultimately indicted for embezzling campaign money, Yatron decided that his 57 percent victory in 1990 was a precursor of things to come and retired in 1992.

Thanks to a provision in the 1989 ethics and pay law, long-time incumbents who retired before December 31, 1992, were entitled to convert their excess campaign funds to personal use; after that date they lost their right to take the money. Seven members chose to exercise that option, including Reps. Larry J. Hopkins (R-Ky.), Bob Traxler (D-Mich.), and Carl D. Pursell (R-Mich.), who pocketed $665,000, $296,000, and $129,000, respectively. At least eight other House members retired and transferred their excess treasuries into charitable trusts. Reps. Norman F. Lent (R-N.Y.) and Robert A.

Roe (D-N.J.) personally control their trusts, which each contained more than $500,000 in 1992. Roe informed the Federal Election Commission that "in the event that I shall become disabled as determined by a certified physician, the trust property is to be used for my benefit. I have retained the power to amend or revoke the Foundation during my lifetime, or by providing for such amendment or revocation in my Will."

In addition to Mrazek, thirteen House members retired to seek Senate seats or wage gubernatorial campaigns. Although Reps. Barbara Boxer (D-Calif.), Ben Nighthorse Campbell (D-Colo.), and Byron L. Dorgan (D-N.D.) won Senate seats and Democratic Rep. Thomas R. Carper became governor of Delaware, much was made of the fact that the other nine lost along the way.

While virtually all the challengers portrayed themselves as fresh outsiders and their protagonists as elitist, morally bankrupt insiders, that message played very differently from district to district. Although 43 House incumbents fell in either the primary or general elections, 325 incumbents were returned for another term—88 percent of those who sought reelection. Many of those who lost, including the nine incumbents who were defeated by fellow incumbents, owed their defeats to a host of problems that were by no means limited to their incumbency.

Even when it did not create incumbent-versus-incumbent matchups, the redistricting process caused problems for many of those who lost. One obvious example is Rep. Richard Ray (D-Ga.), who lost two-thirds of his former constituents through redistricting.

Despite the ultimate success of Hoekstra's anti-incumbent message, Vander Jagt carried every county that had been part of his old district.

While Charles Hatcher (D-Ga.) was undoubtedly hurt by his 819 House bank overdrafts, his 6-point loss to Sanford D. Bishop, Jr., in the Democratic primary had more to do with the fact that his district changed from one in which 62 percent of electorate was white to one in which only 42 percent was white. Bishop is black; Hatcher is white.

Rep. Ben Erdreich (D-Ala.) lost to former state Republican party chairman Spencer Bachus primarily because redistricting changed Erdreich's constituency from one that had provided George Bush with 57 percent of the vote in 1988 to one that had given Bush 77 percent in 1988.

Rep. Bill Green (R-N.Y.) carried the Manhattan precincts he had represented for fourteen years, but failed to win reelection because he lost by two to one in the Brooklyn and Queens precincts added by redistricting.

Freshman Joan Kelly Horn (D-Mo.), who defeated Rep. Jack Buechner by fifty-four votes in 1990, fell victim to a redistricting deal struck prior to the 1990 election by Buechner and Democrats Richard A. Gephardt and William L. Clay that ceded Democrats from Horn's district to Gephardt and Clay.

Rep. Stephen J. Solarz (D-N.Y.) chose to run in a newly created majority-Hispanic district after his district was obliterated by redistricting. His $3,158,822 million budget brought him within 1,869 votes of victory in the primary.

Rep. Gus Savage (D-Ill.) had defeated fellow Democrat Mel Reynolds twice but could not overcome the effects of redistricting, which replaced many of his southside Chicago constituents with suburban voters less attuned to Savage's vitriolic message and more attuned to Reynold's views.

Redistricting was only one of the problems plaguing incumbents who lost. Some self-destructed; others were overwhelmed.

Rep. Joe Kolter (D-Pa.) fell to third in the Democratic primary following publication of excerpts from an audiotape of one of his campaign strategy sessions. His own worst enemy, Kolter referred to himself during the meeting as a "political whore" and bragged about how he intended to manipulate the electorate.

Albert G. Bustamante (D-Texas) had thirty overdrafts at the House bank, had voted for the congressional pay raise, frequently took congressional junkets, and had just built a new home valued at more than $600,000 in a district where the median value of homes was $75,000. While most incumbents were fighting to keep their old districts intact, Bustamante had voluntarily accepted twenty-one new counties in the redistricting process, giving most of his old constituents to fellow Democratic Rep. Henry B. Gonzalez. However, Bustamante's biggest problem was a federal grand jury investigation that would ultimately lead to his indictment and conviction on federal bribery and racketeering charges. While it would normally be considered an upset when a Democratic incumbent from a heavily Democratic district outspent his Republican challenger by more than $250,000 and still lost, in Bustamante's case, it was no upset.

Freshman Reps. John W. Cox, Jr. (D-Ill.) and Frank Riggs (R-Calif.) were defeated for reelection, but the real surprise was that either one had been elected in the first place. In Cox's case, his brief two-year tenure provided him with the distinction of being the only Democrat to represent his northwestern Illinois district during the twentieth century. Riggs had upset Rep. Douglas H. Bosco in 1990 with a strong outsider campaign, but he owed his victory less to his outsider message than to a third-party candidate who collected 15 percent of the vote. When no third-party candidate surfaced in 1992, Riggs took 45 percent of the vote and still lost.

Rep. Robert J. Lagomarsino's $747,536 budget was no match for the $3.5 million businessman Michael Huffington pumped into his campaign. Although Lagomarsino had collected at least 61 percent of the vote in every election between 1976 and 1986, his electoral position had weakened significantly since that time. In 1988 he had been slightly outspent by Democratic state senator Gary K. Hart and eked out a 3,933-vote victory. In 1990 he had faced Democrat Anita Perez Ferguson, who held him to 55 percent. Put into the same district with fellow Republican Rep. Elton Gallegly following redistricting, Lagomarsino agreed to move further north to meet Huffington, giving Gallegly an easy path to the general election.

In fact, despite all the press reports trumpeting the anti-incumbent mood of the electorate, less than half of the incumbents who lost could be said to have been defeated solely on the strength of an anti-incumbent message. Most incumbents who won did so despite the fact that their challengers sought to tap into the supposed anti-incumbent vein. For a sizable number of incumbents who had overdrafts, had voted for the congressional pay raise, and availed themselves of numerous perquisites of office, the issues never became a problem.

Rep. Henry A. Waxman (D-Calif.) had 434 overdrafts and had voted for the pay raise, but to his liberal westside Los Angeles constituents, neither of those issues mattered. Waxman won the primary with 84 percent of the vote and the general election with 61 percent. While that winning percentage was his lowest ever, the drop did not occur in the face of an all-out effort by Waxman to woo voters. Of the $717,698 he spent on his campaign, $338,803 was simply given away to other candidates, Democratic party organizations, and various causes. Only 23 percent of his gigantic budget was invested in direct appeals for votes.

In Ohio, Democratic Rep. Louis Stokes had 551 overdrafts yet drew no primary opposition and won the general election with 69 percent of the vote. He spent only 20 percent of his $339,188 budget on advertising, persuasion mail, and other grass-roots appeals. Donations and constituent stroking accounted for 23 percent of his budget.

Although Rep. Edolphus Towns (D-N.Y.) had 408 overdrafts and was named one of the House bank's twenty-two worst abusers for the period between September 1988 and October 1991, he cruised to victory with 62 percent of the primary vote and 96 percent of the general election vote. In his overwhelmingly Democratic district, local Republicans did not bother to contest the race. Towns spent $713,723 on his reelection bid, with 36 percent going to direct appeals for votes. He spent $30,738 on constituent stroking, gave away $117,158, invested $174,150 in overhead, and put $113,315 into fund raising.

Rep. Harold E. Ford (D-Tenn.) had 388 overdrafts, had voted for the congressional pay raise, and was facing his second trial on federal charges of conspiring to commit mail, bank, and tax fraud. Nevertheless, he garnered 65 percent of the votes in the four-candidate Democratic primary and won the five-candidate general election with 58 percent. His closest competitor, Republican Charles L. Black, took 28 percent. Overhead consumed 66 percent of Ford's outlays, driven by the $51,413 he paid his legal defense team.

Rep. William L. Clay (D-Mo.) had 328 overdrafts and was named one of the House bank's twenty-two worst abusers. He prevailed in both the primary and general elections with 68 percent of the vote, while devoting 51 percent of his budget to overhead and donations to other candidates, causes, and Democratic party organizations.

With 44 overdrafts, Republican Rep. Dennis Hastert (Ill.) nearly doubled his spending from $312,568 in 1990 to $613,623 in 1992, despite running unopposed in the primary and winning 67 percent of the vote in the general election. However, only 26 percent of his outlays were funneled into direct appeals for votes.

Ultimately, many of those incumbents who felt the need to campaign aggressively to defend themselves against outsider challenges had little difficulty in dispatching their opponents.

Rep. Bill Thomas (R-Calif.) took no chances that his 119 overdrafts at the House bank would prove his undoing. Thomas increased his spending from $496,850 in 1990 to $610,997. He sank $99,439 into advertising, $121,245 into campaign literature and persuasion mail, and $169,632 into other forms of grass-roots voter communication and actual campaigning. He won the Republican primary with 66 percent of the vote and prevailed in the general election with 65 percent, a 5-point increase over his 1990 winning percentage. It did not hurt that his Democratic challenger, Deborah A. Vollmer, had just $23,279 to spend.

Rep. Barbara B. Kennelly (D-Conn.) had spent $404,040 in 1990 to dispatch a Republican challenger who spent only $12,649. With votes in favor of both the congressional pay raise and the 1990 budget agreement that included several tax increases, as well as 60 overdrafts at the House bank, Kennelly bumped her spending up 42 percent to $572,602 in 1992. With no primary opposition and faced in the November general election by Republican Philip L. Steele, who spent just $7,053, Kennelly poured $226,886 into radio and television advertising. She spent $29,152 to put "Kennelly for Congress" signs on one hundred buses and invested $8,420 in newspaper ads, $8,043 in program and journal ads, and $43,970 in campaign literature and persuasion mail. She won with 67 percent of the vote.

Bowing to their fears of an anti-incumbent backlash, some incumbents chose to portray themselves as outsiders. With considerable resources at their disposal, many of those who tried this unlikely ploy were quite successful.

Three-term Rep. Jimmy Hayes (D-La.) spent virtually all of the $83,609 he invested in television, radio, and newspaper advertising during the two weeks leading up to the October 3 open primary. He ran ads promising that he would refuse future congressional pay raises and would not participate in the congressional retirement system.

In the primary, three-term Rep. Wally Herger (R-Calif.) ran television and radio commercials pointing out that he had no overdrafts at the House bank and had, in fact, voted to close the bank; voted against the congressional pay raise; voted against tax increases; and voted for a constitutional amendment requiring a balanced federal budget. Brad Zerbe, Herger's campaign management consultant, said the campaign also sent an "I'm not one of them" mailer to between 80,000 and 90,000 Republican households. His 65 percent vote tally was his largest ever.

Eight-term Rep. Anthony C. Beilenson (D-Calif.) succeeded in turning the tables on Republican state representative Tom

McClintock with a $368,049 persuasion mail campaign that trumpeted Beilenson as "an independent leader for change." One mailing pointed out that McClintock had accepted $928,000 from PACs during his tenure in the state legislature while Beilenson refused PAC money.

New Jersey Democratic Rep. Frank Pallone, Jr., campaigned in a 1974 Ford Maverick to underscore the fact that he had frequently voted against the Democratic House leadership on issues such as the pay raise. He developed a "Declaration of Independence," which cited examples of his breaks from party ranks. His campaign slogan, "Our best hope—their worst nightmare," sought to portray that same outsider image, which he delivered with a $186,528 investment in advertising and a $258,583 investment in persuasion mail and campaign literature.

In the first of his three television spots, five-term Rep. Norman Sisisky (D-Va.) told his viewers that "the greatest satisfaction to me is helping people, whether it's finding a Social Security check that's lost, or getting someone in a veterans hospital, or just breaking down the bureaucratic mess that we have in Washington." To put as much distance as possible between himself and his House colleagues, Sisisky noted, "I didn't come to Congress for free banking or for $10 haircuts or anything else that they got. I came here to do a job for people." In all, Sisisky invested $279,759 in producing and airing his radio and television commercials.

While some of their colleagues were running from incumbency, other successful incumbents chose to embrace its power.

"In the year of the anti-incumbent, we ran against the grain," remarked Robert L. Mitchell, district administrator for six-term Rep. Harold Rogers (R-Ky.). "Rogers likes to work on projects, and he gets things done for the district, so we ran on that." In all, Rogers pumped $383,153 into his pro-incumbency ad campaign.

Similarly, Rep. John M. Spratt, Jr. (D-S.C.), a former bank vice president, paid Geddings Communications of Alexandria, Va., $184,631 to create and place five television and five radio commercials that never mentioned his forty-six House bank overdrafts or his Republican opponent, William T. Horne. Instead, Spratt's ads touted his record of constituent service, his successful efforts to keep Shaw Air Force Base off the base closure list, his work to help protect the state's textile industry, and his efforts on the Armed Services Committee to monitor nuclear waste disposal at the Savannah River nuclear material production plant.

Rep. Tim Johnson (D-S.D.) invested $111,969 in television and radio commercials that trumpeted his work on the Agriculture Committee and his delivery of a federal pipeline project that would bring water to homes and ranches in western South Dakota. Several of his commercials featured constituent testimonials.

After twenty years in the House, Rep. Carlos J. Moorhead (R-Calif.) also felt it would be counterproductive to run against the institution. Instead, he invested $90,333 in ads that recited his accomplishments in office and concluded with Moorhead discussing his plans for the future. He spent $148,623 on brochures and six advocacy mailings that featured testimonials from constituents Moorhead had helped.

Representing a district that is heavily dependent on military spending, Rep. Earl Hutto (D-Fla.) focused many of his ads on his senior position on the Armed Services Committee and on the economic advantages that flowed from that position. Hutto spent $66,376 to air his commercials—about nine times as much as his Republican opponent, Terry Ketchel, spent on broadcast advertising.

In short, while the candidates' messages were undoubtedly important, there was no one message that guaranteed success. Protected by redistricting, unaffected for various reasons by their overdrafts and pay-raise votes, many incumbents had no problems. As former House Speaker Thomas P. O'Neill so eloquently put it, "All politics is local."

For weakened incumbents who survived, as well as successful challengers and open seat candidates, the primary determinant of success was money. Average spending by incumbents in hotly contested races was $716,692—more than twice the $288,654 spent by their challengers. However, excluding Huffington, whose $5,434,569 budget adds more than $150,000 to the average, the typical successful challenger spent $429,075. Average spending by challengers who won their party's nomination but lost the general election was $131,987. This considerable spending advantage allowed successful challengers to spend an average of $111,215 more than unsuccessful challengers on advertising, $47,306 more on persuasion mail, and $31,942 more on phonebanks, yard signs, bumper stickers, and other grass-roots voter contact (see Table 4-1).

Background of Nonincumbent Candidates in the 1992 House Races

	Politicians[a]		Operatives[b]		Novices[c]		
	Number	Percent	Number	Percent	Number	Percent	Total
Challengers	83	23	58	16	217	61	358
Open Seats	94	62	21	14	37	24	152
Total	177	35	79	16	254	50	510

Note: Percentages may not add to 100 percent due to rounding.

[a]Currently in public office or previously held public office.
[b]Served in government, held a senior position in a local or state political party, or unsuccessfully sought public office in the past.
[c]Never held public office or a political party position.

On average, winners in open seat contests spent $498,353, or 60 percent more than the $312,421 spent by the typical loser in such races. With their substantially larger budgets, open seat winners were able to spend 78 percent more than losers on broadcast advertising, 55 percent more on persuasion mail, and 56 percent more on grass-roots appeals for votes.

Successful challengers and open seat candidates had the ability to raise money for one simple reason: connections. In a year symbolized by "change" and marked by a deluge of "outsider" rhetoric, those who succeeded in making it to Washington were anything but outsiders.

Of the 510 candidates who contested the November general elections and challenged House incumbents or sought open seats, 50 percent had never held public office or a political party position; 35 percent were either currently in public office or had previously held public office; and 16 percent were political operatives who had either served in government, held a senior position in a local or state political party, or had unsuccessfully sought public office in the past (see box, above). However, among the 110 challengers and open seat candidates who were successful, only 13 percent were "novices," while 74 percent were "politicians," and 14 percent were "operatives" (see box, page 128). Of the 177 state and local politicians who made bids

Background of Nonincumbent Winners in the 1992 House Races

	Politicians[a]		Operatives[b]		Novices[c]		
	Number	Percent	Number	Percent	Number	Percent	Total
Challengers	16	49	7	21	10	30	33
Open Seats	65	84	8	10	4	5	77
Total	81	74	15	14	14	13	110

Note: Percentages may not add to 100 percent due to rounding.
[a]Currently in public office or previously held public office.
[b]Served in government, held a senior position in a local or state political party, or unsuccessfully sought public office in the past.
[c]Never held public office or a political party position.

for House seats, 81 emerged victorious. Only 14 of the 254 novices were as fortunate.

One reason for the success of state and local politicians was the fact that they were considerably less willing to take on incumbents, even in a year when that was supposedly a much less difficult task. While 217 of the 254 novices, or 85 percent, took on incumbents, only 83 of the 177 politicians, or 47 percent, were so foolhardy. Challenging an incumbent meant almost certain defeat, although politicians were a bit more successful: 207 of the 217 novices who challenged incumbents, or 95 percent, lost; 67 of the 83 politicians who took on incumbents, or 81 percent, met the same fate (see box, page 129). Among the 94 politicians who sought open seats, 65, or 69 percent, won. That success rate would have been higher still had there not be an number of politician-versus-politician match-ups.

Clearly, another major reason for their success was the ability of state and local politicians to channel their already proven fund-raising ability into a new challenge. Those who had the most successful fund-raising organizations also had the greatest success at the ballot box. The 177 state and local politicians who challenged incumbents or sought open House seats reported raising an average of $385,197, including PAC donations of $108,300 (see box, page 130). Among those who were successful, average receipts amounted to $476,220—

Background of Nonincumbent Losers in the 1992 House Races

	Politicians[a]		Operatives[b]		Novices[c]		
	Number	Percent	Number	Percent	Number	Percent	Total
Challengers	67	21	51	16	207	64	325
Open Seats	29	39	13	17	33	44	75
Total	96	24	64	16	240	60	400

Note: Percentages may not add to 100 percent due to rounding.

[a]Currently in public office or previously held public office.

[b]Served in government, held a senior position in a local or state political party, or unsuccessfully sought public office in the past.

[c]Never held public office or a political party position.

$167,824 more than the amount raised by their unsuccessful counterparts. By comparison, the 79 party operatives raised an average of $308,579, of which $62,802 came from PACs; the 15 party operatives who were successful collected an average of $524,744, including PAC donations of $117,413. Excluding Huffington, the successful novices raised $450,877, compared with average receipts of $86,196 for those who lost.

Additional resources translated directly into higher advertising and persuasion mail budgets. The typical successful politician spent $469,033 on his or her campaign, while those who were unsuccessful invested an average of $310,380. Those who prevailed in November invested 57 percent of this $158,653 differential in additional broadcast advertising and advocacy mailers (see Table 4-2).

In the race to succeed retiring Rep. William E. Dannemeyer (R-Calif.), who opted to make an unsuccessful bid for the Senate, Republican state senator Ed Royce got an eight-month jump on his Democratic opponent, Fullerton City Council member Molly McClanahan. Royce announced his decision to run on August 11, 1991; he made his initial payment to fund-raising consultant Ann Hyde Co. of Glendale, Calif., just nine days later. Over the next four months, Royce held three fund-raising events. These three receptions, including one featuring House Minority Whip Newt Gingrich

Average Receipts of Nonincumbents in 1992 House Races

Background	PAC Contributions	Individual Contributions	Total Receipts
Politicians[a]			
Winners	$151,907	$252,041	$476,220
Losers	71,507	184,588	308,396
Total	108,300	215,456	385,197
Operatives[b]			
Winners	117,413	291,680	524,744
Losers	50,003	130,793	257,915
Total	62,802	161,341	308,579
Novices[c]			
Winners	63,255	247,960	450,877
Losers	12,231	42,783	86,196
Total	15,044	54,092	106,297

Note: Total for winning novices does not include receipts of $5,443,247 by Michael Huffington, R-Calif.

[a]Currently in public office or previously held public office.
[b]Served in government, held a senior position in a local or state political party, or unsuccessfully sought public office in the past.
[c]Never held public office or a political party position.

(R-Ga.), raised a total of $164,066 from PACs and individual contributors. By the time McClanahan announced her candidacy on March 25, 1992, Royce had raised more than $180,000 and had cash reserves of more than $100,000. The gap never closed, with Royce ultimately spending $639,833 to McClanahan's $90,114. Royce pulled down 57 percent of the general election votes to McClanahan's 38 percent.

Tillie Fowler (R-Fla.), a Jacksonville City Council member, had decided to challenge Democratic Rep. Charles E. Bennett long before his surprise announcement that he would not seek a twenty-third term. While she had officially announced her candidacy just one week prior to Bennett's abrupt withdrawal, Fowler had been working her local contacts for months to assemble a high-profile finance committee. By the time former Democratic state legislator and judge Mattox Hair decided to run, Fowler had already lined up the support of twenty-two people who had helped Hair raise money for a 1984 state senate campaign. Fowler had eighty people who each agreed to raise between $5,000 and $10,000. Those commitments allowed her to spend $522,363 to Hair's $421,098, a $101,265 differential. Fowler outspent Hair by $74,107 on advertising, and on November 3 she collected 57 percent of the votes.

Republican state senator James C. Greenwood put his fund-raising machinery into overdrive, raising $721,654 for his successful challenge to seven-term Democratic Rep. Peter H. Kostmayer. Starting with an original direct-mail list of roughly 500 donors to his previous state campaigns, Greenwood expanded his base to more than 2,400 contributors by the end of the campaign. That new base yielded direct-mail contributions of more than $120,000, helping to push his small donations to $149,071. Originally hoping to raise $50,000 from PACs, Greenwood's fund-raising advisers targeted 400 PACs as likely contributors; PACs ultimately donated $179,742. Greenwood raised $378,694 from individual contributors who gave at least $200, $33,680 of which came from out-of-state. Although he was outspent by $505,637, Greenwood's substantial budget allowed him to sink $299,486 into advertising and $168,016 into persuasion mail. Greenwood emerged with a 6-point victory.

Republican state senator Michael D. Crapo hired three fund-raising consultants to help him with the difficult task of raising money in Idaho. Rich, Smith & Rich of Boise billed Crapo $43,287 for arranging in-state events and for work on direct-mail fund-raising solicitations. Direct Mail Systems of St. Petersburg, Fla., was paid $24,364 for assisting Rich with production of the direct mail. Ziebart Associates of Washington, D.C., received $26,181 for coordinating PAC receptions. Crapo raised $505,547 from PACs and individuals, which allowed him to outspend Democrat J. D. Williams by more than two to one.

The political operatives who won House seats spent an average of $512,974, while the sixty-four who lost spent an average of $310,380. With their larger budgets, the winners spent an average of $48,095 more on advertising and $45,852 more on persuasion mail (see Table 4-2).

Roosevelt University professor Mel Reynolds had tried in both 1988 and 1990 to oust Democratic Rep. Gus Savage, and his permanent campaign was well established by the time redistricting robbed Savage of part of his base of support. During his two unsuccessful bids, Reynolds had built up an impressive fund-raising base that allowed him to spend $88,548 during the off-year and commit another $389,997 during the first three months of 1992 to his efforts to defeat the six-term incumbent. That investment included $107,623 paid to Fenn & King for developing and placing two preprimary radio commercials.

Few of Savage's Democratic colleagues were sorry to see him lose the primary. Shortly after his upset primary victory, Reynolds flew to Washington, D.C., where House Ways and Means Committee Chairman Dan Rostenkowski (D-Ill.), Speaker Thomas S. Foley (D-Wash.), Majority Leader Gephardt (D-Mo.), Majority Whip David E. Bonior (D-Mich.), Democratic Congressional Campaign Committee Chairman Vic Fazio (D-Calif.), and a host of other Democratic leaders attended a fund-raiser to help retire Reynold's campaign debt.

Attorney Steve Buyer (R-Ind.) had served as Indiana deputy attorney general from 1987 through 1988 and as vice chairman for the White County Republican party from 1988 through 1990. Although he had never held public office, he had the contacts that enabled him to raise $201,400 from individual contributors and $135,834 from PACs. Outspent by $204,359, Buyer funneled 40 percent of his resources into radio and television commercials. With a $34,626 infusion from his own bank account, he managed to spend $15,546 more than Democratic Rep. Jim Jontz on such ads. Buyer emerged with a 2-point victory.

While 254 novices battled for House seats in November, only 14 were elected. Among those who won, there were few Horatio Alger stories.

Huffington spent $5,191,728 of his own money, and his $5,434,569 budget was more than twice as much as any previous House candidate had ever spent.

Everett funded his outsider campaign with $931,291 of his own money, which accounted for 88 percent of his total receipts.

Martin R. Hoke's (R-Ohio) victory over Democratic Rep. Mary Rose Oakar cost $698,460. To help fuel that effort, Hoke tapped his own bank account for $265,000.

A television reporter for fourteen years, Ron Klink (D-Pa.) raised a total of $264,293 to fund his primary victory over Rep. Joe Kolter and his general election win over Republican Gordon R. Johnston. Twenty-one percent of Klink's receipts, $55,006, came from his own bank account.

Businessman Jay Dickey (R-Ark.) personally supplied 32 percent of the $412,465 his campaign took in.

Businessman Dan Miller (R-Fla.) loaned his campaign $122,500, which represented 27 percent of his total receipts.

Whether or not they depended largely on personal wealth to finance their campaigns, the politically successful novices had no trouble raising the necessary money to communicate their messages. Excluding Huffington, the remaining thirteen novices who were elected spent an average of $458,381, including $171,890 on radio and television advertising.

Those novices who lost—a group that included students, teachers, ministers, a typesetter, a homemaker, a geologist, a computer operator, and a hospital technician—spent an average of $85,121. Fifty-six of these less well-heeled challengers spent less than $5,000 on their campaigns.

The power of money was also evident in those races where challengers might have won had they had the money to communicate with voters. For example, Republican Rick Hardy, a political science professor at the University of Missouri, came within 5,883 votes of denying Rep. Harold L.Volkmer (D-Mo.) a ninth term, despite being outspent by more than three to one. While Volkmer's $511,554 treasury allowed him to spend $226,418 on advertising and $50,130 on campaign literature and advocacy mailings, Hardy's more modest $147,139 budget allowed him to spend only $31,984 on advertising and $2,034 on leaflets. "It was a suicide mission," recalled Hardy.

Nevertheless, Hardy nearly pulled off the upset with a strong outsider campaign fueled by more than 500 former students who volunteered to knock on doors. Without the money to advertise, Hardy held press conferences, hoping that the free media would carry his anti-incumbent message. Over the final two weeks of the campaign, when it became clear that the race had tightened, the National Republican Congressional Committee invested $40,000 in additional television and radio air time for Hardy, but it was too little, too late.

Similarly, state senator Edward W. Munster (R-Conn.) garnered 49 percent of the votes in his bid to unseat Democratic Rep. Sam Gejdenson, despite pitting his $142,719 budget against the six-term incumbent's $898,562 treasury. Outspent by a margin of more than ten to one on broadcast advertising, Munster invested much of his $36,423 broadcast advertising budget in cable ads slamming Gejdenson for his fifty-one overdrafts at the House bank and for his vote in favor of the congressional pay raise. At $3 apiece, Munster was able to air his ads thousands of times on CNN and ESPN. "If you don't request a specific time-slot and just saturate the channel, you are virtually guaranteed some prime-time slots," noted Munster. Had he had anything close to Gejdenson's $392,253 broadcast advertising budget, Munster might well have closed the 3,875-vote gap.

Forty-six successful candidates—ten incumbents, eighteen challengers, and eighteen open seat candidates—managed to buck the system, spending less on their campaigns than the people they defeated.

Peter T. King (R-N.Y.) emerged with a 4-point victory, despite being outspent by $897,950 in his open seat contest with Democrat Steve A. Orlins.

Rep. Wayne T. Gilchrest (R-Md.) spent $861,872 less than Democratic Rep. Tom McMillen in an incumbent-versus-incumbent match-up created by redistricting.

Outspent by $808,927, Rick A. Lazio (R-N.Y.) still managed to oust nine-term Rep. Thomas J. Downey, who had 151 overdrafts at the House bank.

In all, thirty-four winners were outspent by at least $100,000, including ten who were outspent by more than $500,000. However, that did not in most cases mean that the victors had limited resources. Only four of the forty-six spent less than $200,000. Thirteen spent more than $500,000, including incumbents Bob Carr (D-Mich.) and Pat Williams (D-Mont.), who spent $1,107,973 and $1,190,716, respectively. While Delaware Gov. Michael N. Castle was outspent by $309,689, his $708,671 budget was more than sufficient to communicate with voters who already knew him well. The same was true for freshman Rep. Thomas H. Andrews (D-Maine), who spent $861,564 to combat Republican Linda Bean's $1,469,959 challenge.

In Senate races, where effective communication with a statewide electorate required a substantial investment in television advertising, money also proved to be a powerful gatekeeper. On average, the twenty-eight incumbents who won renomination spent $4,149,198 on their campaigns. The average challenger spent $1,922,001, less than half the budget of their adversaries. In twelve of these twenty-eight races, the challenger spent less than $500,000 and was little more than a name on the ballot.

Excluding his investment in maintaining his off-year campaign operation, Sen. John B. Breaux (D-La.) outspent Republican Jon Khachaturian $1,193,418 to $94,920.

While Sen. Richard C. Shelby (D-Ala.) was putting $1,212,935 into television and radio advertising, Republican Richard Sellers spent just $146,556 on his entire campaign.

Sen. John McCain (R-Ariz.) spent $875,064 to keep his campaign engine running smoothly during the off-years—nearly three times the $301,362 Democrat Claire Sargent spent trying to unseat him in his first reelection bid.

Over the six-year election cycle, Sen. Tom Daschle (D-S.D.) spent $1,010,233 on campaign salaries and taxes, $397,387 of which was spent during 1992. Following his narrow victory in 1986, Daschle expected another serious challenge in 1992. Daschle's Republican opponent, former schoolteacher Charlene Haar, never posed a serious threat, as she managed to scrape together $406,547 for her token effort.

These four races and eight similar financial mismatches helped ensure that there would not be massive turnover in the Senate as a result of anti-incumbent sentiment.

Even in those cases where challengers were well funded, their treasuries were generally dwarfed by the resources available to the incumbent in the race.

In Missouri, Democratic challenger Geri Rothman-Serot spent $1,114,580 in her unsuccessful bid to unseat Republican Sen. Christopher S. Bond. After spending $1,111,859 to maintain his permanent campaign during the off-years, Bond was able to respond to Rothman-Serot's challenge with a $3,770,172 burst in 1992 to secure a second term.

Indiana Democrat Joseph H. Hogsett spent $1,544,475 on his challenge to Sen. Daniel R. Coats. Coats invested $816,501 in his campaign during 1991 and pumped $2,967,657 into his reelection effort in 1992.

Rep. Les AuCoin (D-Ore.) spent $2,641,756 trying to unseat Republican Sen. Bob Packwood. However, that was $548,278 less than Packwood spent during the off-years. In 1992 Packwood poured another $4,768,629 into the defense of his seat.

In New York, State Attorney General Robert Abrams spent a total of $6,374,304 to secure the Democratic nomination and challenge Republican Sen. Alphonse M. D'Amato. D'Amato's fund-raising ability allowed him to invest $3,753,302 in maintaining his permanent campaign and still spend $8,065,930 on his election-year push.

The successful challengers had campaign treasuries that looked more like a typical incumbent's. Former San Francisco mayor Dianne Feinstein spent $8,041,099 to defeat Republican Sen. John Seymour. While many challengers struggled to raise $500,000, Feinstein poured $3,277,559 into producing and airing her broadcast ads, and that sizable investment was augmented by a $1,235,000 infusion from the Democratic Senatorial Campaign Committee.

Cook County Recorder of Deeds Carol Moseley-Braun had only about $580,000 to invest in her long-shot bid to oust Sen. Alan J. Dixon in the Illinois Democratic primary, but she had plenty of help. Over the final six weeks of the primary campaign fellow Democratic challenger Albert F. Hofeld spent between $200,000 and $300,000 a week on television commercials blasting Dixon's record. Dixon, in turn, pounded Hofeld with a barrage of television commercials that virtually ignored Moseley-Braun, who slipped through to a 3-point win over Dixon. Once the nomination was hers, Moseley-Braun raised more than $6 million for her general election contest with Chicago attorney Richard Williamson, who spent $2,468,282.

In North Carolina, Lauch Faircloth and Sen. Terry Sanford were old political allies. However, when Faircloth opted in 1991 to become a Republican and challenge Sanford for his seat, Faircloth quickly gained a new friend and powerful ally: Sen. Jesse Helms (R-N.C.).

Carter Wren, a longtime aide to Helms, devised Faircloth's media strategy. Hanover Communications of Raleigh, N.C.—a key player in Helms's past campaigns under its old name, Campaign Management—produced and placed Faircloth's commercials. So great was the overlap between Helms's and Faircloth's campaign organizations that it even confused those responsible for filling out the campaign financial statements filed with the Federal Election Commission. One page of a Faircloth expense statement filed in July 1992 read: Helms for Senate Committee. Faircloth hired Helms's direct-mail fundraiser and during 1992 raised enough to outspend Sanford $2,904,061 to $2,295,449.

In all, the thirteen challengers and open seat candidates elected to the Senate in 1992 reported spending $47,449,564, an average of $3,649,966. The thirty-three losing challengers and open seat candidates spent a total of $55,445,809, an average of $1,680,176 (see Table 4-3).

More than anything else, this explains why twenty-four of the twenty-eight incumbents who won renomination were reelected on November 3. While the negative images associated with incumbency were of concern to virtually every senator, in the vast majority of cases those images melted under the heat generated by an average spending advantage of $1,969,790.

Table 4-1 What Campaign Money Buys in the 1992 House Races: Average Expenditures by Nonincumbents

	Challengers		Open Seats	
Major Category	*Winner*	*Loser*	*Winner*	*Loser*
Overhead				
Office furniture/supplies	$ 6,724	$ 2,582	$ 7,649	$ 5,110
Rent/utilities	7,469	2,453	7,520	5,199
Salaries	41,918	14,798	52,352	35,491
Taxes	6,033	2,119	7,415	5,853
Bank/investment fees	611	165	589	434
Lawyers/accountants	3,443	659	3,215	1,613
Telephone	9,893	3,517	9,359	6,511
Campaign automobile	1,046	162	653	547
Computers/office equipment	4,964	2,220	4,539	3,983
Travel	8,429	3,270	10,193	6,569
Food/meetings	446	189	633	320
Total Overhead	**90,975**	**32,133**	**104,117**	**71,630**
Fund Raising				
Events	32,648	6,771	30,509	17,028
Direct mail	10,322	4,685	10,810	6,982
Telemarketing	1,618	419	169	1,033
Total Fund Raising	**44,588**	**11,874**	**41,487**	**25,044**
Polling	**14,364**	**4,362**	**16,747**	**10,288**

Advertising				
Electronic media	146,894	41,560	153,186	86,054
Other media	10,537	4,656	12,394	8,447
Total Advertising	**157,431**	**46,216**	**165,580**	**94,502**
Other Campaign Activity				
Persuasion mail/brochures	67,859	20,553	108,541	69,962
Actual campaigning	44,737	12,795	50,005	32,068
Staff/Volunteers	516	107	785	371
Total Other Campaign Activity	**113,112**	**33,456**	**159,331**	**102,401**
Constituent Gifts/Entertainment	**820**	**25**	**909**	**17**
Donations to				
Candidates from same state	103	43	325	49
Candidates from other states	31	4	69	7
Civic organizations	328	104	615	183
Ideological groups	71	26	190	38
Political parties	398	139	489	317
Total Donations	**932**	**315**	**1,689**	**594**
Unitemized Expenses	**6,853**	**3,607**	**8,493**	**7,946**
Total Expenditures	**$429,075**	**$131,987**	**$498,353**	**$312,421**

Note: Total for winning challengers does not include expenditures of $5,434,569 by Michael Huffington, R-Calif.

Table 4-2 What Campaign Money Buys in the 1992 House Races: Average Expenditures by Politicians, Operatives, and Novices

Major Category	Politicians[a]			Operatives[b]			Novices[c]		
	Total	Winner	Loser	Total	Winner	Loser	Total	Winner	Loser
Overhead									
Office furniture/supplies	$ 6,087	$ 7,122	$ 5,214	$ 5,582	$ 7,722	$ 5,080	$ 2,000	$ 7,960	$ 1,652
Rent/utilities	5,935	7,018	5,022	5,629	10,546	4,477	2,008	6,528	1,744
Salaries	41,340	47,840	35,855	29,379	51,843	24,114	12,620	51,413	10,357
Taxes	6,432	6,909	6,029	3,533	3,913	3,444	1,867	10,407	1,369
Bank/investment fees	373	499	267	413	566	377	207	1,139	152
Lawyers/accountants	2,603	3,612	1,751	1,306	2,391	1,052	508	2,092	416
Telephone	8,401	9,433	7,531	6,765	9,537	6,115	2,547	9,295	2,154
Campaign automobile	685	843	552	557	995	454	47	34	48
Computers/office equipment	4,424	4,343	4,492	3,678	5,403	3,274	1,792	5,398	1,581
Travel	8,056	9,999	6,416	6,915	7,977	6,666	2,511	8,929	2,137
Food/meetings	535	589	489	280	486	232	125	568	99
Total Overhead	**84,870**	**98,208**	**73,617**	**64,037**	**101,379**	**55,285**	**26,231**	**103,762**	**21,709**
Fund Raising									
Events	25,308	33,117	18,720	13,557	24,721	10,940	5,201	24,331	4,085
Direct mail	11,018	10,114	11,781	7,246	9,056	6,822	2,701	14,824	1,994
Telemarketing	800	242	1,271	543	1,019	432	369	2,133	266
Total Fund Raising	**37,127**	**43,474**	**31,771**	**21,346**	**34,796**	**18,193**	**8,271**	**41,288**	**6,345**
Polling	**13,437**	**16,078**	**11,209**	**10,119**	**18,425**	**8,172**	**2,995**	**12,178**	**2,459**

Advertising									
Electronic media	117,079	141,505	96,470	97,751	175,169	79,606	31,541	171,890	23,354
Other media	8,630	10,289	7,229	10,144	15,388	8,916	4,369	16,235	3,676
Total Advertising	**125,709**	**151,794**	**103,699**	**107,896**	**190,557**	**88,522**	**35,910**	**188,125**	**27,031**
Other Campaign Activity									
Persuasion mail/brochures	76,303	101,172	55,320	62,123	114,095	49,942	15,916	44,484	14,250
Actual campaigning	36,156	46,951	27,048	29,311	47,570	25,032	12,324	54,670	9,854
Staff/Volunteers	455	720	230	422	827	328	102	443	82
Total Other Campaign Activity	**112,914**	**148,843**	**82,599**	**91,857**	**162,493**	**75,301**	**28,342**	**99,596**	**24,185**
Constituent Gifts/Entertainment	**479**	**1,009**	**32**	**98**	**387**	**30**	**51**	**623**	**18**
Donations to									
Candidates from same state	210	337	102	46	35	48	20	37	19
Candidates from other states	42	78	11	8	0	9	1	0	1
Civic organizations	420	635	239	177	206	170	67	239	57
Ideological groups	106	176	48	57	103	46	19	79	16
Political parties	411	491	343	196	143	208	123	609	94
Total Donations	**1,189**	**1,717**	**743**	**483**	**488**	**482**	**230**	**964**	**187**
Unitemized Expenses	7,259	7,910	6,710	5,389	4,450	5,609	3,665	11,845	3,187
Total Expenditures	**$382,984**	**469,033**	**$310,380**	**$301,224**	**$512,974**	**$251,595**	**$105,694**	**$458,381**	**$85,121**

Note: Total for winning novices does not include expenditures of $5,434,569 by Michael Huffington, R-Calif.

[a]Currently in public office or previously held public office.
[b]Served in government, held a senior position in a local or state political party, or unsuccessfully sought public office in the past.
[c]Never held public office or a political party position.

Table 4-3 What Campaign Money Buys in the 1992 Senate Races: Expenditures by Nonincumbents

Major Category	Winners			Losers		
	Total	Average	Percent	Total	Average	Percent
Overhead						
Office furniture/supplies	$ 727,785	$ 55,983	1.53	$ 922,010	$ 27,940	1.66
Rent/utilities	504,687	38,822	1.06	632,641	19,171	1.14
Salaries	5,269,885	405,376	11.11	6,036,935	182,937	10.89
Taxes	954,435	73,418	2.01	1,620,194	49,097	2.92
Bank/investment fees	79,430	6,110	.17	26,348	798	.05
Lawyers/accountants	366,776	28,214	.77	272,487	8,257	.49
Telephone	1,068,357	82,181	2.25	1,319,947	39,998	2.38
Campaign automobile	55,191	4,245	.12	53,355	1,617	.10
Computers/office equipment	623,018	47,924	1.31	644,804	19,540	1.16
Travel	1,419,502	109,192	2.99	1,624,610	49,231	2.93
Food/meetings	39,185	3,014	.08	40,110	1,215	.07
Total Overhead	**11,108,250**	**854,481**	**23.41**	**13,193,442**	**399,801**	**23.80**
Fund Raising						
Events	3,461,174	266,244	7.29	3,098,358	93,890	5.59
Direct mail	6,095,890	468,915	12.85	6,047,722	183,264	10.91
Telemarketing	698,378	53,721	1.47	491,917	14,907	.89
Total Fund Raising	**10,255,442**	**788,880**	**21.61**	**9,637,997**	**292,061**	**17.38**
Polling	**1,176,772**	**90,521**	**2.48**	**1,363,965**	**41,332**	**2.46**

Advertising						
Electronic media	20,408,864	1,569,913	43.01	25,239,788	764,842	45.52
Other media	270,347	20,796	.57	387,185	11,733	.70
Total Advertising	**20,679,211**	**1,590,709**	**43.58**	**25,626,973**	**776,575**	**46.22**
Other Campaign Activity						
Persuasion mail/brochures	1,040,340	80,026	2.19	1,849,613	56,049	3.34
Actual campaigning	2,711,355	208,566	5.71	3,156,181	95,642	5.69
Staff/Volunteers	30,458	2,343	.06	15,904	482	.03
Total Other Campaign Activity	**3,782,153**	**290,935**	**7.97**	**5,021,698**	**152,173**	**9.06**
Constituent Gifts/ Entertainment	**40,158**	**3,089**	**.08**	**12,023**	**364**	**.02**
Donations to						
Candidates from same state	1,266	97	0	7,708	234	.01
Candidates from other states	3,000	231	.01	26	1	0
Civic organizations	8,519	655	.02	7,054	214	.01
Ideological groups	2,500	192	.01	6,061	184	.01
Political parties	14,404	1,108	.03	15,704	476	.03
Total Donations	**29,689**	**2,284**	**.06**	**36,553**	**1,108**	**.07**
Unitemized Expenses	377,889	29,068	.80	553,158	16,762	1.00
Total Expenditures	**$47,449,564**	**$3,649,966**	**100.00**	**$55,445,809**	**$1,680,176**	**100.00**

CHAPTER 5

The "Year of the Woman"
Sweeping Phenomenon or Political Cliché?

> Our spending decisions, particularly on TV, were directly influenced by the fact that our opponent was a woman.
>
> *Wes Gullett, campaign manager for*
> *Sen. John McCain (R-Ariz.)*

On the eve of the 1960 elections, sixteen women held seats in the House of Representatives; in 1980 that number still stood at sixteen. In 1990, fueled by the rise in the number of women elected to state and local offices, sixty-eight women had sought House seats. Only twenty-eight of those 1990 hopefuls had come away victorious, including twenty-four incumbents (but excluding Eleanor Holmes Norton, Washington, D.C.'s nonvoting delegate). While nine women contested Senate seats in 1990, only incumbent Nancy Landon Kassebaum (R-Kans.) was successful. In thirty years, despite all the societal changes that had increased opportunities for women in other fields, women's representation in the House had grown from 4 percent to 6 percent. Over that same time span, the number of women in the Senate rose from one to two.

Then, virtually overnight, the logjam seemed to break. On November 3, 1992, voters in 101 congressional districts across the country were given the opportunity to cast their ballots for a woman who had won either the Republican or Democratic nomination. In five of those districts, both major party candidates were women. In addition, women finished second in Louisiana's open primaries against Republican Rep. Robert L. Livingston in District 1 and Democratic Rep. William J. Jefferson in District 2, but since both Livingston and Jefferson emerged with more than 50 percent of the vote, they were exempted under state election law from having to run in the November general election. In Massachusetts, Republicans chose not to challenge Rep. Joseph P. Kennedy II, and his only opposition came from independent Alice Harriett Nakash. Charles E. Schumer (D-N.Y.) escaped a Republican challenge, but drew limited opposition from Conservative party nominee Alice E. Gaffney. Women contested eleven of the thirty-six Senate seats up for grabs in November.

Given these numbers, it was little wonder that the primary contests that yielded this record field of female candidates also spawned in major newspapers and magazines more than 3,000 stories that contained the phrase "Year of the Woman." However, like "change" and "anti-incumbency," the phrase took on a life of its own. News reports placed emphasis on the body count, implying a cohesion among these women that simply did not exist.

Emblematic of this analysis was an Associated Press story on the fund-raising success enjoyed by Cook County Recorder of Deeds Carol Moseley-Braun (D-Ill.) and several other women seeking Senate seats. Assessing the Year of the Woman, the article noted that "the reason for the number of female candidates is the same rationale given for fund-raising success: the Senate Judiciary Committee's treatment of Anita Hill and her charges of sexual harassment against Supreme Court Justice Clarence Thomas."

Hill provided the cause celebre if not the impetus for several high-profile campaigns. Moseley-Braun noted in one of her fund-raising letters that "the hearings on the Clarence Thomas nomination gave us all a rude awakening. Of the 100 members of the United States Senate, the most important legislative body in the country, 98 are men. . . . A few days after the vote, I announced my candidacy for the United States Senate." A fifteen-minute video shown at in-home fund-raisers hit the issue several times.

Lynn Yeakel (D-Pa.), the founder and president of a Philadelphia-based organization that raises money for various women's groups, came within 3 points of upsetting Republican incumbent Arlen Specter in their Senate race. In one of her two television commercials shown before the Democratic primary, she took aim at Specter, who had taken the lead in attacking Hill's credibility. Opening with a brief segment of Specter's questioning of Hill, the ad quickly cut to a still photograph of Specter, as Yeakel asked, "Did this make you as angry as it made me? I'm Lynn Yeakel and it's time we do something about the mess in Washington."

DIVERSITY, NOT UNIFORMITY

While most of the press coverage focused on high-profile Senate races such as Moseley-Braun's and Yeakel's, female candidates, like their male counterparts, were scattered from one end of the liberal-conservative spectrum to the other. Their reasons for running, as well as the messages they delivered, went well beyond the controversy surrounding Hill's treatment by the Senate.

Lynn Woolsey (D-Calif.), who won the House seat vacated by Democratic Rep. Barbara Boxer, promised in an introductory mailer that she would "fight to protect a woman's right for reproductive choice, for passage of the ERA, for gay and lesbian rights." The cover of one of her brochures featured two pictures—one showing six members of the Senate Judiciary Committee, the other showing Hill being sworn in as a witness at that committee's hearings into her allegations against Thomas. Black lettering on a red background proclaimed: "Anita Hill made a lot of people realize we need more women like Lynn Woolsey in Congress." Another brochure focused on education, issues affecting the elderly, job creation, and, to pay for it all, her promise to fight for at least a 50 percent reduction in the defense budget.

Fellow California Democrat Patricia Garamendi, who lost an open seat contest to Republican Richard W. Pombo, found common ground with Woolsey on a host of issues, including abortion rights and health care, but her position on defense cuts was considerably more cautious. In one mailer she promised to support "sensible cuts in the defense budget while implementing conversion and adjustment programs to prevent economic disaster in communities impacted by those cuts." That same mailer touted Garamendi's commitment to "strong crime-fighting programs," an issue never discussed in Woolsey's mailings. None of Garamendi's advocacy mailers mentioned Hill.

Narrowly reelected in 1992, Rep. Barbara F. Vucanovich (R-Nev.) opposed abortion. An article in *McCall* magazine had dubbed her one of the top ten congressional enemies of women's issues. Asked by a reporter why she had chosen not to join the Congressional Caucus on Women's Issues, Vucanovich replied, "I can't see spending money on a caucus to have Pat Schroeder out there representing me."

Douglas T. Gray, administrative assistant to Democratic state senator Pat Danner, who defeated Republican Rep. Tom Coleman in

Missouri, noted that Danner had not used gender as an issue in her campaign."She even wanted to be called 'Congressman' at first," Gray added. "She did not want to be a woman in the Congress; she just wanted to be a member."

Republican Donna Peterson, who unsuccessfully challenged Rep. Charles Wilson (D-Texas), certainly was among the most conservative of the 121 women who sought House or Senate seats. Noting that she was "a conservative Texan with a strong background of service to America," one of Peterson's brochures pointed out that she was "the first woman from Southeast Texas to graduate from the United States Military Academy at West Point." Among the positions outlined in the brochure was her dedication "to traditional moral values," stating that she opposed "minority status for homosexuals and federal funding for abortions" and favored "school prayer and Pledge of Allegiance."

In addition to largely ignoring the diversity of opinion among those women running, press reports also ignored that fact that the Year of the Woman was not happening everywhere. While it was presented as a national phenomenon, half of the women contesting House seats on November 3 came from just six states—California, Florida, New York, Ohio, Texas, and Wisconsin. In sixteen states, including Pennsylvania, only one woman was successful in winning either the Republican or Democratic nomination for a House seat. In five of those sixteen states, the lone woman was an incumbent. In fifteen states, including Massachusetts, no women captured a major party's nomination for a House seat.

Even when they successfully navigated their party's primary, women frequently had a more difficult time doing so than their male counterparts. Twenty-five of the eighty-four women who challenged House incumbents or sought open seats, or 30 percent, fought their way through crowded fields in which they received less than 50 percent of the votes. The comparable percentage for nonincumbent men was 23 percent.

Judy Jarvis (R-Calif.) captured 21 percent of the primary votes against nine men. Woolsey won the nomination with just 26 percent of the vote in a nine-candidate field. Ellen E. Wedum (D-Ind.) prevailed with 27 percent in a four-candidate contest. Nydia M. Velazquez (D-N.Y.) collected 33 percent of the primary votes against Rep. Stephen J. Solarz and four others. In six other races with similar results, the women who captured the most votes were still required by state election laws to win primary runoffs after failing to garner at least 50 percent of the primary votes.

In the Senate, four of the ten women who sought to challenge incumbents or contest open seats failed to receive the support of 50 percent of their party's primary voters. In Missouri, Geri Rothman-Serot grabbed 36 percent in the fourteen-candidate Democratic primary free-for-all to pick a challenger to Republican Sen. Christopher S. Bond. Moseley-Braun took 38 percent of the Democratic primary vote in upsetting Sen. Alan J. Dixon. Yeakel and Boxer each collected 44 percent.

The so-called Year of the Woman was also much more of a Democratic party phenomenon than a broad-based political phenomenon. Of the eighty-four women who provided the major opposition for House incumbents or sought open House seats, fifty-four were Democrats, twenty-eight were Republicans, and two were independents. Former South Dakota Republican party leader Charlene Haar was the only Republican among the ten women who sought open Senate seats or challenged incumbents, prompting Susan Brankin Hirschmann, executive director of the conservative Eagle Forum political action committee (PAC), to remark to one reporter, "What the media really means by 'The Year of the Woman' is 'The Year of the Radical Democratic Pro-Abortion Woman.' "

Dolly Madison McKenna (R-Texas), who unsuccessfully challenged Democratic Rep. Michael A. Andrews, said the Year of the Woman helped her campaign by instantly giving her more credibility and by providing her with national publicity that she would not have received otherwise. Peterson had precisely the opposite reaction. "I was constantly having to defend myself in this conservative district that I am not some radical, liberal feminist," she recalled.

On election day, forty-seven women were elected to the House, including twenty-three incumbents (but excluding Norton), raising women's representation in the House to an all-time high of 11 percent. The net gain by women of nineteen seats was the direct result of the decisions by sixty-five incumbents to retire from politics or seek other offices. Only one of the open House seats was previously occupied by a woman. Mirroring the pattern for nonincumbent victors in general, those women who joined the 1992 freshman class tended to be open seat contestants. While forty-nine women challenged incumbents, only four emerged victorious. Among the thirty-five women who contested open seats, twenty won. This 57 percent batting average was 8 points higher than the success rate for men in open seat contests.

In the Year of the Woman, the four victories by women challengers represented an 8 percent success rate, which was essentially the same as the 9 percent success rate recorded by men who challenged incumbents—29 of 309. Further belying the gender hype, none of the women who successfully challenged House incumbents won primarily because of anger over Hill's treatment or their opponent's position on abortion and other issues on which women might be expected to have the edge.

Blanche Lambert (D-Ark.) upset her former boss, Rep. Bill Alexander, in the Democratic primary largely as a result of his 487 overdrafts at the House bank. Danner's campaign was built on an anti-incumbent message that included attacks on Coleman's vote in favor of the congressional pay raise, his penchant for taxpayer-funded travel, and his heavy use of the congressional franking privilege. Velazquez narrowly ousted Solarz in the New York Democratic primary because redistricting had dismantled his predominantly Jewish district in Brooklyn, and he had chosen to seek refuge in a district gerrymandered to elect a Hispanic. While her campaign slogan was "there are too many millionaires and not enough women" in Congress, former city council member Carolyn B. Maloney (D-N.Y.) owed her victory over liberal, pro-choice Republican Bill Green to redistricting, which added heavily Democratic precincts in Brooklyn and Queens to Green's wealthy Manhattan constituency. Green carried the Manhattan precincts he had represented for fourteen years, but lost by a two-to-one margin in the newly acquired precincts.

As these four victorious women were ending the House careers of men, four men were replacing female members for many of the same reasons. In Maryland, Democratic state representative Thomas H. Hattery rode a negative, anti-incumbent campaign to a Democratic primary victory over Rep. Beverly B. Byron. Hattery then lost the general election to Republican Roscoe G. Bartlett, who tarred Hattery with the negatives of incumbency. Rep. Joan Kelly Horn (D-Mo.) had won her seat by just 54 votes in 1990, and when redistricting added Republicans to her constituency, she fell to Republican James M. Talent by 8,865 votes. Attorney and businessman Martin R. Hoke

(R-Ohio) ended the sixteen-year House career of Rep. Mary Rose Oakar largely because of her status as one of the House bank's twenty-two worst abusers and the political fallout over erroneous reports in the *Cleveland Plain Dealer* that she had placed ghost employees on the House post office staff. Three-term Rep. Liz J. Patterson (D-S.C.) was ousted by the anti-incumbent onslaught of attorney Bob Inglis. "Our strategy was to run against Congress, not Patterson," recalled Jeff Parker, Inglis's campaign manager. "We said, 'Here are some things you don't like about Congress, but guess what, Patterson shares some of those same characteristics.'"

In the Senate, the number of women jumped from two to six (a seventh, Kay Bailey Hutchison, R-Texas, won a June 1993 special election to fill the seat vacated by Democratic Sen. Lloyd Bentson). Two of the four newly elected members—Moseley-Braun and former San Francisco mayor Dianne Feinstein (D-Calif.)—upset incumbents, although Feinstein's opponent, Sen. John Seymour, had been appointed to the seat in 1991 by Gov. Pete Wilson, who had resigned the seat in order to make his successful gubernatorial bid. State senator Patty Murray (D-Wash.) and Boxer took open seats.

Once again, the single biggest key to success for those who sought to become House or Senate incumbents was incumbency in some other office. Thirty-eight of the eighty-four women who sought open House seats or challenged House incumbents had held neither public office nor a political party post; thirty currently held or had recently held public office; and sixteen had some prior political experience (see box, page 152). However, of the twenty-four women who won House seats for the first time in 1992, nineteen were "politicians," including five state senators, a former state senator, five state representatives, and three city council members. Three of the successful women were "operatives," and only two were "novices" (see box, page 153). None of the twenty-eight novices who challenged incumbents won (see box, page 154).

Six of the ten women who sought open Senate seats or challenged incumbents were politicians—Boxer, Feinstein, Moseley-Braun, Murray, state senator Jean Lloyd-Jones (D-Iowa), and city council member Rothman-Serot. All four of the newly elected senators came from this group. Although voters were supposedly anxious to throw incumbents out of office, in reality most voters simply traded one set of career politicians for another.

Background of Nonincumbent Female Candidates in the 1992 House Races

	Politicians[a]		Operatives[b]		Novices[c]		
	Number	Percent	Number	Percent	Number	Percent	Total
Challengers	11	37	10	63	28	74	49
Open Seats	19	63	6	38	10	26	35
Total	30	36	16	19	38	45	84

Note: Percentages may not add to 100 percent due to rounding.
[a]Currently in public office or previously held public office.
[b]Served in government, held a senior position in a local or state political party, or unsuccessfully sought public office in the past.
[c]Never held public office or a political party position.

As was the case with nonincumbents in general, women with political experience proved to be more successful on election day in large part because they were more successful fund-raisers. In the House, the thirty-five women who contested open seats spent a total of $17,426,029, an average of $497,887. The twenty winners—sixteen of whom were politicians—spent $12,729,474, or $636,474 on average. These twenty women spent $186,584 more on average than the men who won open seats.

In contrast, the fifteen losers in these open seat contests—only three of whom were politicians—spent a total of $4,696,555, an average of $313,104. If the $1,701,907 spent by the three politicians who lost is removed from the equation, the typical loser's outlays amounted to $249,554 (see Table 5-1).

Having headed the Washington state Republican party for eleven years, Jennifer Dunn was adept at raising money. When Republican Rep. Rod Chandler decided to leave Congress to wage an unsuccessful Senate campaign, Dunn decided it was time to turn that fund-raising prowess to her own advantage. "We raised most of our money by Jennifer Dunn personally asking for it," recalled campaign manager John Myers. With the help of friends and volunteers, Dunn worked her way through the 5,000 names in her personal files, raising $492,444 from individual donors and $168,373 from PACs. Helped

Background of Nonincumbent Female Winners in the 1992 House Races

	Politicians[a]		Operatives[b]		Novices[c]		
	Number	Percent	Number	Percent	Number	Percent	Total
Challengers	3	16	1	33	0	0	4
Open Seats	16	84	2	67	2	100	20
Total	19	79	3	13	2	8	24

Note: Percentages may not add to 100 percent due to rounding.

[a]Currently in public office or previously held public office.
[b]Served in government, held a senior position in a local or state political party, or unsuccessfully sought public office in the past.
[c]Never held public office or a political party position.

by a $25,000 infusion from her own bank account, Dunn was able to outspend businessman George O. Tamblyn by $287,578.

State senator Eddie Bernice Johnson (D-Texas) had one substantial advantage in the contest for the state's newly created District 30: she chaired the state senate's congressional redistricting committee and had a major role in drawing the district's boundaries to her liking. Once that battle was won, Johnson had no trouble collecting $114,176 from PACs and $149,761 from individual contributors. Her Republican opponent spent only $4,707, and Johnson coasted to victory.

San Diego Port Commissioner Lynn Schenk (D-Calif.) had extensive experience in state Democratic politics and fund raising—experience that undoubtedly spelled the difference in her match-up with Republican Judy Jarvis, a registered nurse who, like Schenk, took a pro-choice stance on abortion. Schenk raised $653,104 from individual contributors and $300,129 from PACs; comparable figures for Jarvis were $87,799 and $149,993, respectively. Schenk's fund-raising prowess allowed her to spend $1,122,504, including $470,292 on broadcast advertising and $243,352 on campaign literature and persuasion mailers. Jarvis spent just $40,973 on her broadcast advertising campaign and $160,345 on advocacy mailings and handouts.

San Mateo County Supervisor Anna G. Eshoo (D-Calif.) had spent $1.1 million on an unsuccessful challenge to Republican Rep. Tom

Background of Nonincumbent Female Losers in the 1992 House Races

	Politicians[a]		Operatives[b]		Novices[c]		
	Number	Percent	Number	Percent	Number	Percent	Total
Challengers	8	73	9	69	28	78	45
Open Seats	3	27	4	31	8	22	15
Total	11	18	13	22	36	60	60

Note: Percentages may not add to 100 percent due to rounding.
[a]Currently in public office or previously held public office.
[b]Served in government, held a senior position in a local or state political party, or unsuccessfully sought public office in the past.
[c]Never held public office or a political party position.

Campbell in 1988, and when Campbell announced his decision to seek the open Senate seat created by the retirement of Democratic Sen. Alan Cranston, Eshoo simply turned on the fund-raising spigot. Among those Eshoo turned to for help was Gloria Steinem, who was the featured guest at an afternoon fund-raiser in April 1992. Billed in the invitation as a "Tea for Two Terrific Women" and sponsored by Palo Alto City Council member Liz Kniss, the event drew 200 supporters who each paid $100 to witness an informal conversation between Eshoo and Steinem. All of the attendees left with a signed copy of Steinem's book, *Revolution from Within.* The campaign asked Steinem back in June for a sit-down luncheon attended by more than a dozen supporters who each paid $500. Dozens of events such as these helped Eshoo raise $610,938 from individual contributors and $296,322 from PACs. She ultimately spent $957,101 on her campaign, outspending her Republican opponent, fellow San Mateo County Supervisor Tom Huening, by $282,070. She invested $196,994 of that spending advantage in persuasion mail and coasted to an 18-point win.

Having served on the staff of former California Sen. John V. Tunney and as a White House aide in the Carter administration, attorney and businesswoman Jane Harman (D-Calif.) had the political connections to raise $598,176 from individual contributors and $199,208 from PACs. Married to the founder of Harman International Industries, a manufacturer of high fidelity audio equipment with assets of more than $350 million, Harman also had the personal wealth to augment her fund-raising efforts whenever necessary. In winning the seven-candidate Democratic primary and her general election contest with Los Angeles City Council member Joan Milke Flores, Harman tapped her personal bank account for a total of $823,000. Harman was able to invest $630,998 in television and radio advertising. While Flores spent $905,455 and matched Harman dollar-for-dollar on persuasion mail and grass-roots appeals for votes, she had nothing left for broadcast advertising in the pricey Los Angeles market. Harman emerged with a 6-point win.

While only four women succeeded in defeating incumbents in the 1992 House races, those who did spent an average of $406,006—almost twice as much as the average expenditure of $208,508 by the forty-five challengers who lost (Table 5-2). While these winners did not outspend their male counterparts, once Michael Huffington's (R-Calif.) $5,434,569 outlays are removed from the equation, spending by successful female challengers was only 6 percent less than the average spending reported by successful male challengers.

Lambert, the only political operative to vanquish an incumbent, immediately began to reap the benefits of her primary victory over Alexander. Facing a Republican opponent with only $28,372 to spend in an overwhelmingly Democratic district, Lambert was virtually assured of victory in the November general election. Able to spend only about $80,000 in the months leading up to the May 26 primary, she discovered there were suddenly many people anxious to help her after her primary win. Over the final six months of 1992, she raised $310,404, including $159,950 from PACs. Flush with cash, she spent about $246,000 while collecting 70 percent of the vote against her underfunded Republican opponent.

Although Coleman outspent Danner $548,902 to $413,246, $60,017 of his spending advantage was invested in maintaining his off-year campaign operation. By pouring 61 percent of her treasury into broadcast advertising and 18 percent of her funds into other direct appeals for votes, Danner was able to come within $19,475 of Coleman's outlays for communicating with voters. Her ability to tap PACs for $183,992 and individual contributors for $149,538 flowed directly from her service in the state senate and the fact that her chief fund-raiser—her son Steve—was also a state senator.

Unsuccessful challengers were not nearly so well-heeled. While the forty-five losers spent an average of $208,508, eighteen of these women spent less than $25,000, including six challengers who spent less than $5,000. Deborah A. Vollmer (D-Calif.) scraped together $23,279 for her challenge to Republican Rep. Bill Thomas. Thomas countered by spending $610,997, a 23 percent increase over his 1990 outlays, and cruised to victory with 65 percent of the vote. Republican businesswoman Martha A. "Mickey" Strickland spent $20,119 on her challenge to Democratic Rep. Tom Bevill, who invested $514,418 in his reelection bid and emerged with 69 percent of the vote. The $15,152 budget of homemaker Lisa A. Donaldson (D-Mich.) was no match for Republican Rep. Dave Camp's $401,290 response.

In the Senate, the limited number of races and the even smaller number of female candidates make detailed comparisons between winners and losers and between women and men problematic, at best. The dramatic differences in the resources required to run a statewide race in Kansas and California further complicate the comparisons. Nevertheless, led by Boxer's $10,445,695 open seat effort, the four successful women who challenged incumbents or contested open seats spent an average of $6,696,062 (see Table 5-3). Feinstein spent $8,041,099 to defeat Seymour. Moseley-Braun's campaign cost $6,957,821. All three raised millions of dollars more than their male opponents. Of the four winners, only Murray was outspent by her male opponent, but her $1,339,632 budget was still sufficient to get her message out.

Among the six women who lost Senate bids, the average outlay was $1,296,156. However, when you exclude Yeakel's $5,213,198 challenge to Specter, the women whose Senate bids fell short spent an average of only $512,747. While Claire Sargent (D-Ariz.) had a positive message that echoed Moseley-Braun's, Boxer's, Feinstein's, and Murray's on issues such as abortion and health care, she had only $301,362 with which to deliver it. Her opponent, Republican Sen. John McCain, spent $3,740,479.

Lloyd-Jones refused PAC money, which cut her off from labor support, and she raised only $191,758 from individual contributors. With a $175,057 infusion from her own bank account, she managed to spend $409,737 on her challenge to Sen. Charles E. Grassley (R-Iowa). Grassley took $1,077,564 from PACs and raised $1,378,527 from individual contributors, which allowed him to run a $2,429,899 campaign that included $641,465 in broadcast advertising.

Their substantial cash advantage over unsuccessful female challengers did not mean that all male incumbents could afford to entirely ignore the gender issue, although some clearly did. While Sargent had few resources, her campaign was built around the hope that she could pry Republican women away from McCain. McCain invested much of his money to make certain that did not happen.

McCain invested $92,065 in polls which showed him that, among other things, his support among pro-choice Republican women was soft. To shore up that support, McCain's media advisers, Smith & Harroff of Alexandria, Va., developed a series of commercials highlighting McCain's positions on issues relating to the environment, health care, and senior citizens. "The message we tried to get out was that even though McCain is pro-life, he's a good guy, and that there are other issues besides abortion to consider," recalled Wes Gullett, McCain's campaign manager.

Given the nature of Yeakel's early attacks over his treatment of Hill, Specter could not afford to hope the gender issue would fizzle. Instead, he developed a host of appeals targeted at mending his severely damaged image with women voters. In July he began airing commercials that touted his record of support for increased funding of breast cancer research. Later, he rolled out a sixty-second commercial featuring Teresa Heinz, the widow of the late Republican senator John Heinz, asking voters not to judge Specter by his tough questioning of Hill. Hundreds of copies of a video touting Specter's record on abortion rights and other issues deemed important to women were passed out to women who had been organized under the name "Women for Specter," who in turn showed the video to other women at coffees and various in-home gatherings. To drive up Yeakel's negatives, one of Specter's ads slammed her for failing to pay $17,000 in back taxes until the day before she announced her candidacy.

Remarkably, after seizing on Specter's treatment of Hill as the rallying cry for her primary campaign, Yeakel all but abandoned the issue once she had the nomination. Of the nearly two dozen commercials that aired heavily from late September until election day, only one even mentioned Hill, and it ran only over the final week of the campaign.

While Rep. David Price (D-N.C.) was not overly concerned by Republican Lavinia "Vicky" Goudie's $13,188 challenge, he was still careful to run television commercials touting his pro-choice stance on abortion to guard against any drop in his support among women. Price won with 65 percent of the vote.

A number of men who prevailed in open seat contests had to deal with the gender issue at some point in the process, and in several cases it did not require a well-funded female opponent to sensitize them to the problem. In California, Democrat Bob Filner was concerned as much with Libertarian Barbara Hutchinson as he was with Republican Tony Valencia. Afraid that Hutchinson might run just well enough to give Valencia the victory in the solidly Democratic District 50, Filner devoted one of his two television commercials to attacking what he described as her "strange" beliefs.

Sanford D. Bishop, Jr. (D-Ga.), who ousted Rep. Charles Hatcher in the Democratic primary and faced Republican Jim Dudley in the general election, spent $1,000 for advice on women's issues. "In the 'Year of the Woman,' I wanted to make sure I had all my bases covered," Bishop explained.

Arguing that she was the true agent of change in the Year of the Woman, Binghamton Mayor Juanita M. Crabb (D-N.Y.) was considered the early favorite to win the Democratic nomination in the race to succeed retiring Rep. Matthew F. McHugh. However, state representative Maurice D. Hinchey successfully blunted that argument with television ads listing endorsements from female legislators and a radio spot featuring actress Mary Tyler Moore. Hinchey took 54 percent of the primary votes.

Fund Raising: Women Helping Women

One area in which the Senate Judiciary Committee's treatment of Anita Hill had a powerful impact was fund raising. Throughout 1992, but particularly in the primary campaigns, female candidates depended heavily on the financial support of other women, many of whom had been energized to contribute by what they saw during Thomas's confirmation hearings. EMILY's List, a PAC dedicated to raising money for pro-choice Democratic women, directly donated $365,318 to House and Senate candidates in 1992. More importantly, through its fund-raising direct-mail program, the organization collected approximately $6 million in earmarked contributions from its members, bundled them, and passed them on to fifty-five female candidates. WISH List, a PAC dedicated to assisting pro-choice Republican women, directly contributed $73,109 to 19 candidates, including 6 incumbents. The Women's Campaign Fund donated a total of $390,399 to 71 Democratic candidates, a total of $112,668 to 24 Republicans, and $10,000 to Lynn H. Taborsak in Connecticut, who waged an independent campaign to oust Republican Rep. Gary A. Franks following her Democratic primary loss to James J. Lawlor. The National Organization for Women's PAC donated $322,385 to 102 candidates, virtually all of them women. The National Women's Political Caucus Victory Fund and the National Women's Political Caucus Campaign Support Committee, two connected PACs, donated $136,220 and $69,800, respectively, to a total of 75 women.

Contributions from women's groups and individual donations from women were particularly crucial to Boxer's success in her primary battle with Rep. Mel Levine and Lt. Gov. Leo T. McCarthy. Prior to the primary, Boxer received $197,369 in individual contributions from 1,676 members of EMILY's List. Through the Hollywood Women's Political Committee she attracted donations from actresses Joanne Woodward, Marlo Thomas, Marsha Mason, and Katherine Hepburn, among others. Singer Bonnie Raitt performed at a Beverly Hills event that raised $70,000 for the campaign.

Having never raised more than $500,000 for her House races and beginning with a donor list of roughly 7,000, Boxer poured nearly $1.2 million into a preprimary direct-mail fund-raising effort that churned out more than 1.5 million letters. Capitalizing on the fall-out from Hill's testimony, most of the mail contained a pro-feminist pitch. By the end of the primary, Boxer's direct-mail program had helped her raise well over $4 million, roughly two-thirds of which came from women. Her donor list had grown to more than 54,000.

Yeakel also looked to other women to supply the early seed money for her Senate contest. "When we were first hired by the campaign, I told them they couldn't raise money through direct mail," recalled David H. Gold, president of Gold Communications in Austin, Texas. "Yeakel was at 1 percent in the polls, and I even made a bet that the direct mail wouldn't work. It was a bet I didn't mind losing."

One of the preprimary appeals Gold put together for Yeakel was a four-page mailing that featured a picture of Specter on the envelope. Inside, the message dovetailed with the campaign's television commercial, asking recipients if Specter's treatment of Hill had made them angry and inviting them to send money if the answer was yes. Like Boxer, approximately two-thirds of Yeakel's preprimary money came from women.

In the House, women's groups directly donated a total of $49,006 to Elaine Baxter (D-Iowa), $49,005 to Elizabeth Furse (D-Ore.), $47,151 to Eshoo, $46,155 to Karen Shepherd (D-Utah), $43,073 to Garamendi, $40,132 to Harman, $40,112 to Anita Perez Ferguson (D-Calif.), and $30,000 or more to seven other candidates.

However, while women's groups extended a helping hand to numerous candidates, they could not be expected to support all the women running. There simply was not enough money to allow for that kind of generosity. Thirty-three of the eight-four female challengers and open seat candidates in House races received no direct contributions from any of the women's PACs. While they comprised 20 percent of the female challengers and open seat candidates, Californians received 34 percent of the money donated by women's PACs.

Most of the money went to the experienced politicians, rather than political operatives or novices. Collectively, Boxer, Feinstein, Moseley-Braun, Murray, and Rothman-Serot received $293,672 in direct contributions from PACs representing women's organizations. Yeakel and Sargent, the two novices who received direct contributions from these PACs, collected $52,068 and $12,720, respectively. The only other Senate candidate to receive direct financial assistance, Democratic activist Gloria O'Dell, collected just $6,000 for her token challenge to Sen. Bob Dole (R-Kan.). Lloyd-Jones and Haar received no assistance from women's PACs in their uphill battles against male incumbents.

In the House, twenty-six of the thirty female challengers and open seat candidates who had held elective office received direct contributions totaling $642,585 from PACs representing women's groups. Nine of the sixteen operatives received such help, collecting a total of $208,331. The only Democrat not to receive any assistance was Ada E. Deer (Wis.), who refused all PAC funds. Seventeen of the thirty-eight novices received some money from women's organizations, but these contributions totaled just $176,942.

Much of this financial help was provided prior to the primary. Once candidates had secured their party's nomination, the traditional money sources kicked in immediately for those considered likely to succeed. Following her primary victory, Boxer's contributor profile shifted so dramatically that by election day men accounted for 60 percent of her donations of $200 or more. While Yeakel's experience was not as dramatic, she also saw a substantial shift. "We started out targeting women, but we quickly discovered that many men on our lists were just as enthusiastic as women about supporting a female candidate," noted Yeakel's direct-mail fund-raiser.

WOMEN INCUMBENTS

Among the 110 women seeking House seats in the general election were 26 incumbents. While they were routinely added to the body count to enhance the Year of the Woman hype, female incumbents faced a very different political reality than the women seeking to join them in the House. With the possible exception of the four members of the 1990 freshman class, these women had all of the problems and benefits of incumbency. As a result, their campaigns looked remarkably like those of their male counterparts, both in terms of how much they spent and how they spent it (see Table 5-4).

On average, female incumbents reported spending $564,024 on their campaigns, only 1 percent less than their male counterparts. In hotly contested races, female incumbents reported spending an average of $688,631, or only 4 percent less than the average spending reported by the 139 men facing similarly difficult reelection bids. Average spending by incumbents in less competitive races showed women outspending men by $5,029, a 1 percent advantage.

Overall, the 26 women who sought reelection reported committing 29 percent of their budgets to advertising; the comparable figure for male incumbents was 27 percent. On average, both male and female incumbents invested 20 percent of their budgets in advocacy mailings, leaflets, yard signs, buttons, bumper stickers, phonebanks, rallies, and other grass-roots campaign expenses. Spending on overhead and fund raising was virtually identical, as well. While women tended to invest slightly more than men in constituent stroking, the difference was essentially meaningless (see Table 5-5).

At the operational level, women and men faced the same redistricting problems and the same anti-incumbent sentiments. The solutions were gender neutral, as well.

Vucanovich and Rep. James Bilbray (D-Nev.) had worked out a mutually beneficial redistricting deal that ceded Republicans in

Bilbray's district to Vucanovich and moved more Democratic areas from Vucanovich's old district into Bilbray's District 1. Yet despite that deal, Vucanovich drew just 48 percent of the general election votes, escaping with a 5-point victory in a five-candidate field.

Reno Mayor Pete Sferrazza pumped 92 percent of his $198,391 budget into advertising and advocacy mailings that hammered Vucanovich for her acceptance of PAC money, her vote in favor of the congressional pay raise, and her anti-abortion stance. Vucanovich responded by spending $315,455 more on her 1992 campaign than she had in 1990. She increased her outlays for broadcast advertising from $48,052 in 1990 to $216,415 in 1992. Her investment in persuasion mail jumped from $4,389 to $38,368.

Given that her opponent was also a politician with a record, Vucanovich worked hard to tar him with the anti-incumbent stain. When Sferrazza attacked her for supporting the congressional pay raise, Vucanovich struck back with an ad attacking him for supporting a pay raise for Reno government employees during his tenure as mayor. Portraying him as a career politician, Vucanovich slammed Sferrazza for missing numerous mayoral commission meetings and for presiding over a 60 percent increase in city government spending. Leaping on the "change" bandwagon, the five-term incumbent also touted her support for congressional reforms.

Pounded by Monroe County legislator William P. Polito for accepting $1.5 million from PACs during her six years in Congress and accused of being just another tax-and-spend liberal, Rep. Louise M. Slaughter took the opposite approach from Vucanovich. To defend her seat, Slaughter depended on the free media to critique the accuracy of Polito's charges. She invested most of her $305,376 broadcast advertising budget in pro-incumbency television spots, including one testimonial that described how Slaughter had helped restore electricity to a constituent's home following an ice storm.

Had it not been for her $387,004 spending advantage, nine-term Rep. Marilyn Lloyd (D-Tenn.) would probably not have pulled out her 2,930-vote victory over Republican Zach Wamp. Wamp put $78,370 into advertising and $45,138 into advocacy mailings that included calls for voters to "Wamp Congress" and attacks on Lloyd's 1989 vote in favor of the congressional pay raise.

Lloyd opened her reelection bid with positive television commercials showing her visiting with school children and senior citizens, but as the race grew tighter, her advertising campaign grew progressively nastier. One of her commercials dredged up Wamp's "criminal" past, which included writing two bad checks for a total of $20 when he was in college. While her mailers initially pointed to federal projects she had helped bring to the district, they mirrored the negative television spots by campaign's end. In all, she spent $266,123 on broadcast advertising and $50,261 on leaflets and persuasion mailers.

While the task for most female challengers and open seat candidates was to demonstrate leadership and decisiveness, Rep. Jolene Unsoeld had somewhat the opposite problem. Having established a reputation for toughness, the anti-incumbent mood of the electorate prompted her to project a softer image in some of her advertising. One spot developed by Fenn & King Communications of Washington, D.C., consisted largely of home movies of a younger Unsoeld hiking in the mountains and playing with her small children. "We decided we needed to soften her image a bit," explained Peter Fenn.

Freshman Rep. Maxine Waters (D-Calif.) had no difficulties with her initial reelection campaign. In an overwhelmingly Democratic district, facing a Republican opponent who had just $6,919 to spend on his challenge, Waters invested only 26 percent of her $207,957 budget in direct appeals for votes. Virtually all of the $35,682 she spent on advocacy mailings was spent prior to the Democratic primary.

Instead of worrying about her campaign, Waters was free to allocate her funds to other activities. In January 1991 she invited between 100 and 200 supporters to Washington to witness and celebrate her swearing in. While guests paid for their own transportation and lodging, Waters tapped her campaign treasury to pay for the party. A reception at the Washington Court Hotel cost the campaign $3,820, and other miscellaneous expenses added $550. Waters also tapped her campaign funds to cover $5,661 in expenses incurred during the annual Black Caucus Weekend in September 1991. The campaign picked up the tab for $4,346 in transportation and lodging expenses connected with her stay in New York during the 1992 Democratic National Convention.

While Donald McDonough, general strategist for state representative Maria Cantwell (D-Wash.), was absolutely correct when he noted that "women candidates symbolized change" in 1992, the politics of victory looked the same, regardless of gender.

Table 5-1 What Campaign Money Buys in the 1992 House Races: Average Expenditures by Open Seat Candidates

Major Category	Female Candidates			Male Candidates		
	Total	Winner	Loser	Total	Winner	Loser
Overhead						
Office furniture/supplies	$ 7,824	$ 10,334	$ 4,477	$ 5,969	$ 6,707	$ 5,268
Rent/utilities	7,127	10,318	2,874	6,149	6,538	5,780
Salaries	60,772	78,465	37,181	39,025	43,189	35,069
Taxes	6,838	9,856	2,813	6,587	6,559	6,614
Bank/investment fees	410	377	455	543	663	428
Lawyers/accountants	3,375	3,020	3,849	2,141	3,284	1,054
Telephone	8,946	11,595	5,414	7,657	8,575	6,785
Campaign automobile	239	418	0	709	735	684
Computers/office equipment	5,357	6,300	4,101	3,938	3,922	3,953
Travel	8,841	13,138	3,112	8,274	9,160	7,433
Food/meetings	499	735	185	472	597	354
Total Overhead	**110,229**	**144,555**	**64,461**	**81,464**	**89,928**	**73,423**
Fund Raising						
Events	28,139	37,453	15,721	22,576	28,072	17,355
Direct mail	12,251	17,894	4,727	7,925	8,324	7,546
Telemarketing	276	472	14	691	62	1,288
Total Fund Raising	**40,666**	**55,819**	**20,462**	**31,192**	**36,459**	**26,189**
Polling	**17,946**	**23,975**	**9,906**	**12,248**	**14,210**	**10,383**

Advertising						
Electronic media	153,753	206,129	83,919	109,983	134,609	86,588
Other media	7,107	7,240	6,929	11,446	14,203	8,827
Total Advertising	**160,860**	**213,369**	**90,848**	**121,429**	**148,812**	**95,415**
Other Campaign Activity						
Persuasion mail/brochures	106,191	121,525	85,745	84,514	103,985	66,016
Actual campaigning	48,561	60,177	33,072	38,939	46,436	31,817
Staff/Volunteers	460	633	228	617	838	406
Total	**155,211**	**182,336**	**119,045**	**124,070**	**151,259**	**98,240**
Constituent Gifts/Entertainment	276	481	2	527	1,059	21
Donations to						
Candidates from same state	340	592	3	144	231	61
Candidates from other states	14	25	0	46	85	8
Civic organizations	299	486	49	433	661	217
Ideological groups	134	226	11	109	177	45
Political parties	473	794	45	384	382	385
Total Donations	**1,260**	**2,123**	**109**	**1,116**	**1,536**	**716**
Unitemized Expenses	**11,439**	**13,815**	**8,272**	**7,261**	**6,626**	**7,865**
Total Expenditures	**$497,887**	**$636,474**	**$313,104**	**$379,306**	**$449,890**	**$312,251**

Table 5-2 What Campaign Money Buys in the 1992 House Races: Average Expenditures by Challengers

Major Category	Female Candidates			Male Candidates		
	Total	*Winner*	*Loser*	*Total*	*Winner*	*Loser*
Overhead						
Office furniture/supplies	$ 3,928	$ 3,176	$ 3,994	$ 2,798	$ 7,231	$ 2,354
Rent/utilities	2,515	3,892	2,393	2,964	7,980	2,463
Salaries	21,589	38,599	20,077	16,535	42,392	13,949
Taxes	2,415	0	2,630	2,478	6,895	2,037
Bank/investment fees	135	433	108	217	637	175
Lawyers/accountants	2,632	9,605	2,013	634	2,563	441
Telephone	4,842	9,167	4,457	3,968	9,996	3,365
Campaign automobile	254	0	277	239	1,195	143
Computers/office equipment	2,379	1,644	2,444	2,480	5,438	2,184
Travel	5,090	8,582	4,780	3,516	8,407	3,027
Food/meetings	111	179	105	228	484	203
Total Overhead	**45,891**	**75,277**	**43,279**	**36,058**	**93,217**	**30,342**
Fund Raising						
Events	12,741	25,068	11,645	8,510	33,731	5,987
Direct mail	7,627	505	8,260	4,802	11,724	4,110
Telemarketing	408	429	406	545	1,788	420
Total Fund Raising	**20,775**	**26,002**	**20,311**	**13,857**	**47,244**	**10,518**
Polling	**8,909**	**16,636**	**8,222**	**4,678**	**14,039**	**3,742**

Advertising						
Electronic media	84,702	124,113	81,198	45,640	150,149	35,189
Other media	5,116	6,704	4,975	5,194	11,084	4,605
Total Advertising	**89,817**	**130,816**	**86,173**	**50,834**	**161,233**	**39,794**
Other Campaign Activity						
Persuasion mail/brochures	32,647	91,736	27,394	23,544	64,448	19,454
Actual campaigning	21,851	60,097	18,452	14,673	42,542	11,886
Staff/Volunteers	232	774	183	130	479	95
Total Other Campaign Activity	**54,729**	**152,607**	**46,029**	**38,347**	**107,470**	**31,435**
Constituent Gifts/Entertainment	**112**	**807**	**50**	**93**	**822**	**20**
Donations to						
Candidates from same state	70	525	29	45	43	45
Candidates from other states	5	0	5	7	36	4
Civic organizations	93	145	89	129	354	106
Ideological groups	51	0	56	26	81	21
Political parties	176	319	163	160	409	135
Total Donations	**394**	**989**	**341**	**367**	**924**	**311**
Unitemized Expenses	**4,002**	**2,873**	**4,103**	**3,881**	**7,421**	**3,527**
Total Expenditures	**$224,630**	**$406,006**	**$208,508**	**$148,115**	**$432,371**	**$119,690**

Note: Total for winning male candidates does not include expenditures of $5,434,569 by Michael Huffington, R-Calif.

Table 5-3 What Campaign Money Buys in the 1992 Senate Races: Average Expenditures by Nonincumbents

Major Category	Female Candidates			Male Candidates		
	Total	*Winner*	*Loser*	*Total*	*Winner*	*Loser*
Overhead						
Office furniture/supplies	57,892	111,527	22,135	29,747	31,298	29,230
Rent/utilities	40,059	80,390	13,172	20,465	20,348	20,504
Salaries	395,924	759,877	153,289	204,099	247,820	189,526
Taxes	80,108	133,243	44,684	49,265	46,829	50,077
Bank/investment fees	5,600	13,519	320	1,383	2,817	905
Lawyers/accountants	24,318	58,465	1,554	11,002	14,768	9,747
Telephone	92,382	170,331	40,415	40,680	43,004	39,906
Campaign automobile	5,255	9,848	2,194	1,555	1,756	1,489
Computers/office equipment	55,086	103,710	22,670	19,916	23,131	18,844
Travel	109,086	212,256	40,306	54,257	63,387	51,214
Food/meetings	1,586	3,692	183	1,762	2,713	1,445
Total Overhead	**867,295**	**1,656,856**	**340,921**	**434,132**	**497,869**	**412,886**
Fund Raising						
Events	274,004	631,497	35,676	106,097	103,909	106,826
Direct mail	561,780	1,245,984	105,645	181,272	123,550	200,513
Telemarketing	70,849	170,508	4,409	13,384	1,816	17,239
Total Fund Raising	**906,633**	**2,047,989**	**145,730**	**300,753**	**229,276**	**324,579**
Polling	**54,588**	**108,686**	**18,523**	**55,413**	**82,448**	**46,401**

Advertising						
Electronic media	1,383,283	2,404,458	702,499	883,773	1,199,003	778,696
Other media	13,003	18,837	9,113	14,653	21,666	12,315
Total Advertising	**1,396,286**	**2,423,296**	**711,613**	**898,426**	**1,220,670**	**791,011**
Other Campaign Activity						
Persuasion mail/brochures	66,990	112,439	36,691	61,668	65,621	60,351
Actual campaigning	134,205	288,447	31,377	125,708	173,063	109,923
Staff/Volunteers	2,235	5,135	301	667	1,102	522
Total Other Campaign Activity	**203,429**	**406,020**	**68,369**	**188,043**	**239,786**	**170,796**
Constituent Gifts/Entertainment	**2,749**	**6,872**	**0**	**686**	**1,408**	**445**
Donations to						
Candidates from same state	82	37	112	226	124	261
Candidates from other states	0	0	0	84	333	1
Civic organizations	337	381	307	339	777	193
Ideological groups	236	381	139	172	108	194
Political parties	275	196	327	760	1,513	509
Total Donations	**930**	**996**	**885**	**1,582**	**2,856**	**1,157**
Unitemized Expenses	**24,208**	**45,347**	**10,115**	**19,138**	**21,834**	**18,240**
Total Expenditures	**3,456,118**	**6,696,062**	**1,296,156**	**1,898,172**	**2,296,146**	**1,765,514**

Table 5-4 What Campaign Money Buys in the 1992 House Races: Average Expenditures by Incumbents

Major Category	Female Candidates			Male Candidates		
	Total	Winner	Loser	Total	Winner	Loser
Overhead						
Office furniture/supplies	$ 8,540	$ 8,455	$ 9,197	$ 8,798	$ 8,642	$ 11,038
Rent/utilities	10,890	10,739	12,046	9,062	8,787	13,009
Salaries	54,089	54,059	54,314	50,087	48,005	80,026
Taxes	20,045	20,783	14,387	16,115	15,929	18,784
Bank/investment fees	511	381	1,511	1,373	1,413	804
Lawyers/accountants	9,404	9,341	9,887	10,205	9,691	17,597
Telephone	8,010	7,991	8,159	8,605	8,239	13,865
Campaign automobile	575	650	0	3,369	3,083	7,474
Computers/office equipment	8,881	8,333	13,086	9,014	8,875	11,017
Travel	14,694	15,202	10,806	21,851	21,196	31,272
Food/meetings	2,906	3,126	1,215	3,637	3,692	2,835
Total Overhead	**138,545**	**139,059**	**134,608**	**142,114**	**137,552**	**207,721**
Fund Raising						
Events	59,773	59,988	58,120	66,141	64,718	86,607
Direct mail	19,646	21,131	8,261	21,421	21,261	23,722
Telemarketing	99	112	0	1,496	1,573	389
Total Fund Raising	**79,518**	**81,231**	**66,382**	**89,059**	**87,553**	**110,718**
Polling	**20,632**	**19,505**	**29,273**	**19,993**	**18,687**	**38,771**

Advertising					
Electronic media	147,825	127,130	306,481	141,305	130,631	294,810
Other media	18,467	18,753	16,279	14,725	14,691	15,213
Total Advertising	**166,292**	**145,883**	**322,760**	**156,030**	**145,322**	**310,023**
Other Campaign Activity						
Persuasion mail/brochures	76,809	70,687	123,748	69,666	66,131	120,502
Actual campaigning	37,360	35,373	52,591	42,585	41,352	60,325
Staff/Volunteers	670	553	1,567	1,578	1,601	1,255
Total Other Campaign Activity	**114,839**	**106,612**	**177,906**	**113,830**	**109,084**	**182,082**
Constituent Gifts/Entertainment	**10,278**	**10,313**	**10,010**	**8,441**	**8,487**	**7,786**
Donations to						
Candidates from same state	3,372	3,714	750	5,354	5,620	1,522
Candidates from other states	3,314	3,660	667	3,933	4,111	1,364
Civic organizations	3,513	3,730	1,848	3,266	3,236	3,693
Ideological groups	1,613	1,707	895	1,526	1,572	863
Political parties	9,716	10,548	3,342	12,322	12,800	5,459
Total Donations	**21,529**	**23,359**	**7,502**	**26,401**	**27,339**	**12,902**
Unitemized Expenses	**12,392**	**8,587**	**41,564**	**15,790**	**15,571**	**18,947**
Total Expenditures	**$564,024**	**$534,549**	**$790,005**	**$571,658**	**$549,595**	**$888,950**

Note: Totals are for the entire two-year cycle.

Table 5-5 What Campaign Money Buys in the 1992 House Races: Expenditures by Incumbents, by Percentage

Major Category	Female Candidates			Male Candidates		
	Total	Winner	Loser	Total	Winner	Loser
Overhead						
Office furniture/supplies	1.51	1.58	1.16	1.54	1.57	1.24
Rent/utilities	1.93	2.01	1.52	1.59	1.60	1.46
Salaries	9.59	10.11	6.88	8.76	8.73	9.00
Taxes	3.55	3.89	1.82	2.82	2.90	2.11
Bank/investment fees	.09	.07	.19	.24	.26	.09
Lawyers/accountants	1.67	1.75	1.25	1.79	1.76	1.98
Telephone	1.42	1.49	1.03	1.51	1.50	1.56
Campaign automobile	.10	.12	0	.59	.56	.84
Computers/office equipment	1.57	1.56	1.66	1.58	1.61	1.24
Travel	2.61	2.84	1.37	3.82	3.86	3.52
Food/meetings	.52	.58	.15	.64	.67	.32
Total Overhead	**24.56**	**26.01**	**17.04**	**24.86**	**25.03**	**23.37**
Fund Raising						
Events	10.60	11.22	7.36	11.57	11.78	9.74
Direct mail	3.48	3.95	1.05	3.75	3.87	2.67
Telemarketing	.02	.02	0	.26	.29	.04
Total Fund Raising	**14.10**	**15.20**	**8.40**	**15.58**	**15.93**	**12.45**
Polling	**3.66**	**3.65**	**3.71**	**3.50**	**3.40**	**4.36**

Advertising					
Electronic media	26.21	23.78	38.79	24.72	23.77	33.16
Other media	3.27	3.51	2.06	2.58	2.67	1.71
Total Advertising	**29.48**	**27.29**	**40.86**	**27.29**	**26.44**	**34.88**
Other Campaign Activity						
Persuasion mail/brochures	13.62	13.22	15.66	12.19	12.03	13.56
Actual campaigning	6.62	6.62	6.66	7.45	7.52	6.79
Staff/Volunteers	.12	.10	.20	.28	.29	.14
Total Other Campaign Activity	**20.36**	**19.94**	**22.52**	**19.91**	**19.85**	**20.48**
Constituent Gifts/Entertainment	**1.82**	**1.93**	**1.27**	**1.48**	**1.54**	**.88**
Donations to						
Candidates from same state	.60	.69	.09	.94	1.02	.17
Candidates from other states	.59	.68	.08	.69	.75	.15
Civic organizations	.62	.70	.23	.57	.59	.42
Ideological groups	.29	.32	.11	.27	.29	.10
Political parties	1.72	1.97	.42	2.16	2.33	.61
Total Donations	**3.82**	**4.37**	**.95**	**4.62**	**4.97**	**1.45**
Unitemized Expenses	**2.20**	**1.61**	**5.26**	**2.76**	**2.83**	**2.13**
Total Expenditures	**100.00**	**100.00**	**100.00**	**100.00**	**100.00**	**100.00**

Note: Totals are for the entire two-year cycle.

CHAPTER 6

Independent and Coordinated Expenditures
A World of Unlimited Possibilities

*This is not a contest between two men. This is a battle between
me and the special interests I have been opposing.*

Rep. Mike Synar (D-Okla.),
commenting on his 1992 campaign

During his fourteen-year House career, Rep. Mike Synar
(D-Okla.) had succeeded in alienating a number of moneyed
interests. As one of the leading advocates of raising fees paid
by ranchers who graze their cattle on public lands, Synar had angered
ranchers throughout the West. Tobacco companies had taken um-
brage at his strong support for a total ban on all advertising and
promotion of tobacco products. Health insurance companies had been
alienated by his position on mandatory universal coverage. An advo-
cate of a strong national energy policy, Synar had frequently irritated
the oil lobby. His support of a seven-day waiting period on handgun
purchases and a ban on the sale of combat assault weapons had en-
raged the National Rifle Association (NRA). In 1992 it was payback
time, and in the solidly Democratic District 2, the battleground was
the Democratic primary.

Synar's primary opponent was Muskogee District Attorney Drew
Edmondson, son of the late Rep. Ed Edmondson, who had represented
District 2 from 1953 to 1973, and the nephew of a former governor and
senator. Sensing a golden opportunity to rid themselves of a longtime foe,
political action committees (PACs) representing tobacco, health insurance, petroleum, and ranching interests pumped more than $150,000
into Edmondson's campaign coffers. The NRA's PAC kicked in $9,900.
Edmondson received individual contributions from ranchers totaling
more than $100,000. Together these interests donated more than 30
percent of the $836,742 Edmondson spent on his challenge.

175

However, that sizable boost proved to be just the first installment of anti-Synar money that came pouring into the district. Taking full advantage of a 1976 Supreme Court ruling that affirmed the right of individuals and organizations to spend unlimited sums in support of or in opposition to candidates—as long as there is no communication between the organization and the candidates it supports or opposes—the NRA invested $226,088 in an independent campaign—$141,275 in opposition to Synar and $84,813 in support of Edmondson.

The NRA spent $127,561 on anti-Synar radio and television commercials, attacking him in one television spot for voting "with liberals like Ted Kennedy and Barney Frank over 90 percent of the time." One radio ad, a parody of the game show *Jeopardy,* began with a mock contestant saying, "I'll take 'No Home on the Range' for $400." The game show host then read, "He owns a beautiful home in Washington, D.C., but doesn't even have a trailer in Oklahoma," and asked the contestant for the question that the statement answered. "Who is Mike Synar?" came the instant response.

Full-page newspaper ads costing the NRA a total of $43,479 criticized Synar as "the only congressman from Oklahoma who voted to take away your guns," attacked his votes against constitutional amendments to balance the federal budget and ban flag-burning, and cautioned voters that "if Synar wins, hunters lose." The NRA opened an office in the district and spent $14,007 on travel for the staff who orchestrated the anti-Synar campaign. A series of letters sent to NRA members attacking Synar and endorsing Edmondson cost $13,887. Additional funds were invested in bumper stickers and a phonebanking operation that placed calls to the roughly 10,000 NRA members in the district.

Synar also had supporters willing to invest in independent campaigns on his behalf, although they were token efforts compared with the massive display put on by the NRA. The Small Business Coalition spent $10,364 on Synar's behalf, while independent campaigns launched by Teamsters Local 523, the AFL-CIO, and the National Committee to Preserve Social Security and Medicare cost $5,000, $4,679, and $2,187, respectively.

Coupled with his own spending, the NRA's sizable investment in the race helped carry Edmondson to a second-place finish in the four-candidate primary on August 25 and to within 6,578 votes of unseating Synar in the September 15 runoff. In effect, the NRA's cash infusion increased Edmondson's budget by 27 percent, allowing him to outspend Synar and his supporters by nearly $220,000 during the first nine months of 1992.

Similarly, in the race for the Senate seat vacated by Pete Wilson (R-Calif.), who successfully ran for governor, records filed with the Federal Election Commission (FEC) show that former San Francisco mayor Dianne Feinstein (D-Calif.) outspent Republican Senate appointee John Seymour by $1,166,863—$8,041,099 to $6,874,236. Feinstein's campaign reported spending $3,277,559 on television and radio advertising, or $1,371,408 more than Seymour spent on his commercials. Those numbers do not begin to tell the story of their confrontation.

The National Republican Senatorial Committee (NRSC) paid $2,449,955 to Target Enterprises of Hollywood, Calif., the firm responsible for placing Seymour's commercials, to buy additional air time. The California Association of Realtors and the National Association of Realtors (NAR) spent a total of $267,050 on Seymour's behalf, primarily for advocacy mailings, newspaper advertising inserts, and phonebanks. The conservative English Language PAC invested $49,718, and ten other organizations spent a total of $12,362 on independent campaigns, either in support of Seymour or in opposition to Feinstein. Together, the party coordinated expenditures and the independent campaigns that benefited Seymour amounted to $2,779,085, effectively increasing his budget by 40 percent.

Feinstein had her share of outside support, as well. The Democratic Senatorial Campaign Committee (DSCC) dedicated $1,313,826 of its coordinated campaign to Feinstein, including eight payments totaling $1,235,000 to her media adviser, Morris & Carrick of New York. The DSCC's coordinated expenditures also included $30,000 for postage, $29,000 for a pro-choice voter guide, and $12,500 for demographic research. The balance of its outlays went for opposition research, travel, fund raising, and subscriptions to political journals. The Democratic State Central Committee of California spent $175,976 in support of Feinstein's candidacy, including three payments totaling $50,000 to Morris & Carrick; three payments totaling $74,501 to Gold Communications Co. of Austin, Texas, for persuasion mailers; and two payments amounting to $30,453 for postage. The Democratic National Committee (DNC) picked up $15,920 of her polling costs with Greenberg-Lake of Washington, D.C. Feinstein also had the benefit of $44,767 in independent support from a dozen organizations, including the AFL-CIO and the National Abortion Rights Action League (NARAL). In all, the party coordinated expenditures and the independent campaigns on Feinstein's behalf totaled $1,550,489, essentially increasing her budget by 19 percent.

When all the party money and independent expenditures were added to their own campaign expenditures, Seymour and his supporters had narrowly outspent Feinstein and her supporters $9,653,321 to $9,591,588. What looked like a contest in which the two protagonists spent a total of $14,915,335 was actually a $19,244,909 battle. Feinstein won that fight 54 percent to 38 percent on election day.

In the race to succeed retiring Sen. Tim Wirth (D-Colo.), records filed with the FEC show former Republican state senator Terry Considine outspending Democratic Rep. Ben Nighthorse Campbell by nearly $500,000. To make matters worse, while Considine skated through the Republican primary without opposition, Campbell was forced to spend more than $400,000 to prevail in a three-candidate Democratic primary that included former governor Richard D. Lamm and the party's 1990 Senate nominee, Josie Heath. In the general election, Considine outspent Campbell by $274,836 on broadcast advertising and by $129,657 on persuasion mail.

As in virtually every closely contested Senate race, the party coordinated expenditures for Campbell and Considine were nearly identical. Together, the DSCC and the DNC paid out $245,156 in support of Campbell, including $82,400 to Joe Slade White & Co. of New York for creating broadcast ads; $89,990 to Shafto & Barton of Houston, Texas, for placing the ads; and $59,314 to Mellman & Lazarus of Washington, D.C., for polling. The NRSC countered with $275,427 in expenditures for Considine, $275,082 of which went to his media adviser, Barnhart Advertising of Denver.

However, Considine's vocal opposition to abortion rights drew the attention of NARAL, which targeted him for defeat. In the final month of the campaign, NARAL invested $149,986 to elect Campbell, including payments totaling $65,420 to Greer, Margolis, Mitchell & Associates of Washington, D.C., for television buys during the final week and a $40,825 payment to Great Lakes Communication of Milwaukee, Wis., for phonebanking. Campbell emerged with a 9-point victory in the general election.

Although most of the 435 House races and 37 Senate races did not involve the level of outside financial assistance channeled into the Synar-Edmondson, Feinstein-Seymour, and Campbell-Considine races, dozens of contests were similarly targeted. Coordinated campaign expenditures by national Democratic and Republican committees totaled $39,092,810—$16,484,017 by the NRSC; $11,283,934 by the DSCC; $5,181,932 by the National Republican Congressional Committee (NRCC); $4,179,032 by the Democratic Congressional Campaign Committee (DCCC); $1,139,809 by the DNC; and $824,086 by the Republican National Committee (RNC). Independent campaigns added another $10,000,025.

PARTY COORDINATED EXPENDITURES

The level of national party coordinated expenditures is established by federal election law, and in 1992 such expenditures were limited to $27,620 for each House race, except in the six states with only one congressional district, where the limit was doubled to $55,240. The national party committee limits for Senate races are based on state voting age population and ranged in 1992 from a low of $55,240 to a maximum of $1,227,322. State parties were allowed to contribute an equal amount or transfer their spending quotas to the national party committees, effectively doubling the national committee's spending limits.

Sixty-eight Senate candidates received some support from their national party committee. In thirty-nine cases, the state parties transferred their entire spending limit to the national parties, which in turn provided essentially the maximum possible support to the candidate. Among the candidates in this group were former television commentator Bruce Herschensohn (R-Calif.), $2,454,644; Seymour, $2,449,955; Sen. Alfonse M. D'Amato (R-N.Y.), $1,512,543; Robert Abrams (D-N.Y.), $1,508,835; and Sen. Arlen Specter (R-Pa.), $1,008,903.

In eleven additional cases, the national party committees spent their maximum allotment and picked up at least a portion of the state parties' spending limit, as well. National Democratic party committees spent their allotted $1,227,322 on behalf of Rep. Barbara Boxer (D-Calif.), who successfully battled Herschensohn for the vacant seat created by the retirement of Democratic Sen. Alan Cranston, and picked up $403,680 of the California Democratic party's limit. The state party spent only $132,914 of its remaining $823,642 allotment. The DSCC and the DNC combined to spend $1,329,746 on behalf of Feinstein, including $102,424 of the state party's allotment. As with Boxer, the California Democrats did not come close to spending the balance of its $1.2 million spending limit for Feinstein. Other Senate candidates receiving more than the national party maximum but less than the combined national and state allotment were Lynn Yeakel (D-Pa.), $842,275; Sen. John Glenn (D-Ohio), $622,896; Cook County Recorder of Deeds Carol Moseley-Braun (D-Ill.), $478,329; Sen. Christopher S. Bond (R-Mo.), $379,904; and state senator Patty Murray (D-Wash.), $379,614.

None of the five women who were elected to Senate seats received the maximum combined national and state party limit. FEC records show that Yeakel received $164,780 less than the maximum, despite being involved in one of the more high-profile Senate races in the country.

In two cases—Sens. Kent Conrad (D-N.D.) and Tom Daschle (D-S.D.)—the national party committees spent their limit but picked up none of the state party's allotment. In fifteen cases the national party committees did not bother to spend the maximum, since it was clear that the races were essentially uncontested. For example, the DSCC spent only $42,643 of the $100,647 it was allowed to spend in support of Gloria O'Dell (Kan.), who challenged Sen. Bob Dole. The DSCC invested only $35,756 of the $114,292 it was allowed to spend in support of Claire Sargent's challenge to Sen. John McCain (R-Ariz.). Democratic Sens. Bob Graham (Fla.) and Dale Bumpers (Ark.) did not need the DSCC's money, taking only $656 and $156, respectively.

One Senate race where party money clearly made a difference was in Georgia. Democratic Sen. Wyche Fowler, Jr., received a 49 percent plurality of the 2,251,576 votes cast in the November 3 general election. However, Georgia's state election law requires a candidate to garner a 50 percent or greater majority in the election or face a runoff. Having fallen just short, Fowler was forced into a runoff with Republican Paul Coverdell, who had collected 48 percent.

Immediately following the general election, the NRSC requested that the FEC issue an advisory opinion on whether the runoff should constitute a new election, thus providing the state and national parties with an opportunity to spend another $535,607 on each candidate's behalf. On its face, the request was clearly contrary to a 1983 FEC ruling that declared that a runoff was a continuation of the general election, not a new election. The decision was of particular interest to the Republicans, since they had exhausted their limit in the general election. The Democrats had stopped $200,000 short of the limit, anticipating that a runoff would occur.

When the FEC failed to rule on its request, the NRSC decided to spend nearly $450,000 during the three weeks leading up to the runoff. The Democrats spent only the remaining $200,000 of their general election limit, assuming that they could not spend more. In an election that drew only 1,253,991 voters to the polls—997,585 fewer than had voted in the general election—Coverdell won by 16,237 votes. The DSCC filed a complaint with the FEC asking that the NRSC be fined for its actions, since the FEC has no power to overturn election results.

In March 1993, after Coverdell had been sworn in, the FEC ruled in a similar case that a runoff to fill the Senate seat vacated by Lloyd Bentsen (D-Texas) constituted a continuation of the special election. In this case, the NRSC supported applying a single spending limit to the party committees. Nevertheless, one month later the FEC split 3-3 along party lines, and the DSCC's complaint against the NRSC for overspending on behalf of Coverdell was dropped.

In the House, 589 of the 859 candidates who contested the November general elections benefited from at least some coordinated expenditures by their party's national committees. At the low end, the NRCC spent $32 in support of John M. Shimkus, who challenged Democratic Rep. Richard J. Durbin in Illinois' District 20. At the high end, 159 House candidates received the maximum $27,620 in national party coordinated assistance. While the state party committees shifted their full coordinated limit to the federal party committees in only 17 cases, thereby providing those candidates with the $55,240 combined maximum, the national parties spent at least $40,000 on behalf of 102 candidates.

National party committees were not nearly as careful to balance spending in contested House races, since even the maximum allotment placed severe limits on their ability to have an impact on races where the average incumbent spent $571,089 and the average open seat candidate invested $406,611. For example, open seat candidate Judy Jarvis (R-Calif.) received the full $55,240 national-state allotment from the NRCC; her Democratic counterpart, Lynn Schenk, received only $7,265 in coordinated support from the DCCC. However, since Schenk's campaign was able to outspend Jarvis by $745,514, the difference in the level of coordinated party support provided Jarvis with only a marginal boost, at best. Schenk received 51 percent of the vote to Jarvis's 43 percent in the marginally Republican District 49.

In Georgia's District 1, the DCCC spent $54,239 in support of school principal Barbara Christmas, including $40,925 for "media services," $7,500 for polling, and $5,000 for opposition research. The NRCC spent $25,000 to augment state representative Jack Kingston's advertising buys. With Kingston spending $273,922 on advertising and Christmas investing only $164,014 in her ads, the $15,925 net gain in advertising supplied by the DCCC was undoubtedly small consolation to Christmas. Including the party money, Kingston still outspent Christmas on advertising by $93,983. He collected 58 percent of the votes.

The coordinated expenditures did yield more advertising. The NRSC invested 91 percent of its $16,484,017 in broadcast advertising; the DSCC spent 85 percent of its $11,283,934 on such ads (see Tables 6-1 and 6-2). Given the nature of House races, less of the DCCC's and NRCC's coordinated assistance was invested in broadcast ads—77 percent and 32 percent, respectively—and more was spent on persuasion mail, particularly on the Republican side (see Tables 6-3 and 6-4).

In several instances, Republican candidates relied on the NRCC to provide their entire advocacy mailing effort. In Maine, Rep. Olympia J. Snowe did not invest any of her campaign's resources in mailers; instead, the NRCC's in-house team designed her mail and spent $44,360 on printing and postage.

In other cases, the party's assistance amounted to matching funds. Republican Douglas Carl (Mich.), who unsuccessfully challenged Rep. David E. Bonior, spent $36,119 on his own persuasion mail effort; the NRCC kicked in $45,667 for printing, postage, and mailing lists. However, the boost Carl received from the NRCC was no match for Bonior's $556,380 spending advantage on television and radio advertising.

While the DCCC's and NRCC's coordinated spending frequently failed to have much impact on the final outcome of the campaign, in some cases the assistance clearly helped tighten the race. Bill Townsend (R-Pa.), who challenged Democratic Rep. Austin J. Murphy, was outspent by more than six to one. Townsend spent just $4,692 of his $50,280 budget on persuasion mail. Townsend came within 3,307 votes of pulling off the upset, in large part because the NRCC spent $39,391 on his mailers.

In the case of the DNC, its coordinated assistance in House races appeared to be little more than poorly disguised expenditures on behalf of presidential nominee Bill Clinton. FEC records show that the DNC invested $908,866 in House campaigns across the country, all of which was spent on polls (see Table 6-3). In contrast, the DCCC spent $404,596 on polls, roughly 10 percent of its budget. The RNC spent just $11,940, or 1 percent of its $824,086 investment in House campaigns, on polls. While polling is an important part of any campaign, many of the DNC's polls were conducted in districts where the outcome of the House race was never in doubt but where the attitudes of voters concerning the presidential race was of great interest.

In California, a state considered a must win if Democratic presidential nominee Bill Clinton was to be elected, the DNC paid Greenberg-Lake of Washington, D.C., $73,878 to conduct polls in fourteen House districts represented by Democrats: fifteen-term Rep. Don Edwards; eleven-term Rep. Ronald V. Dellums; ten-term Rep. Pete Stark; nine-term Rep. George Miller; nine-term Rep. Henry A. Waxman; eight-term Rep. Leon E. Panetta; seven-term Rep. Julian C. Dixon; seven-term Rep. Robert T. Matsui; six-term Rep. Tom Lantos; five-term Rep. Howard L. Berman; five-term Rep. Esteban E. Torres; two-term Rep. Nancy Pelosi; Rep. Gary A. Condit, a 1989 special election winner; and freshman Rep. Maxine Waters. None of these incumbents was facing a difficult race. All eventually won with 60 percent of the vote or more. Four won with 83 percent of the vote or better, and three others received between 70 and 80 percent. Only three of the candidates spent any of their own resources on polls of their constituents, and the $5,277 the DNC spent in each district could not have produced results that would have been of more than marginal interest to any of the incumbents. However, collectively these results would have been of considerable interest to the Clinton camp. Perhaps not coincidentally, Greenberg-Lake was also Clinton's pollster.

In Ohio, another key battleground in the presidential contest, the DNC paid $12,026 each for polls in districts represented by Democrats Marcy Kaptur, Louis Stokes, James A. Traficant, Jr., and Douglas Applegate. None of the four candidates was ever in danger: Kaptur garnered 74 percent of the general election vote, Stokes grabbed 69 percent, Traficant collected a whopping 84 percent, and Applegate received 68 percent. Greenberg-Lake split the polling duties with Mellman & Lazarus of Washington, D.C., in each of the four districts. Clinton's advisers thought the state sufficiently crucial to the election that the Clintons and Gores visited the state forty-five times during the fall campaign.

The DNC spent $16,039 on polls in each of four Michigan districts, only one of which produced a race in which the Democratic incumbent failed to get at least 65 percent of the vote. In Pennsylvania, yet another key state in the Clinton strategy to reach 270 electoral votes, Greenberg-Lake conducted polls in six districts for $7,393 each. Among the five incumbents who "benefited" from this effort, none received less than 65 percent of the vote. The DNC thought challenger Bill Sturges's $59,027 challenge to Republican Rep. George Gekas warranted sending in Greenberg-Lake, despite the fact that Gekas ultimately collected 70 percent of the vote.

In all, Greenberg-Lake received $410,872 from the DNC for its work on House campaigns. That represented 45 percent of the DNC's investment in polling for House races.

Without question, the best example of how much more the DNC's polls meant to the presidential campaign than to the House members who received them was the case of Rep. William H. Natcher (D-Ky.). Elected in a 1953 special election, Natcher had run unopposed in seven of his twenty House campaigns. In those twenty campaigns, he had received less than 60 percent of the vote only three times. Throughout his entire House career, he had never accepted a campaign contribution. He funded his campaigns, which rarely exceeded $7,000, from his own pocket. His 1992 opponent was a college student, who Natcher completely ignored. Nevertheless, the DNC paid Lauer, Lalley & Associates of Washington, D.C., $17,633 for a poll of Natcher's constituents, who again showed their strong support by giving him 61 percent of the vote.

In contrast, when the DCCC felt polling assistance was called for, it generally paid the candidate's own pollster rather than sending in one of its own. Challenger Paul McHale (D-Pa.), who knocked off Republican Rep. Don Ritter, received $8,750 in coordinated polling assistance from the DCCC. The payment went to McHale's pollster, Cooper & Secrest Associates of Alexandria, Va.

INDEPENDENT EXPENDITURES

While the money involved was substantially less than the aggregate invested by the various national Republican and Democratic party committees, independent expenditures topped $10 million in the 1992 election cycle. This money was concentrated in a relatively small number of races where those interested in influencing the outcome felt they had the best chance of success. The NRA invested $3,021,715 in independent campaigns (see box, page 186), but spent $1,272,884 of that total in just ten races. The National Association of Realtors, which ranked a distant second among organizations putting money into independent campaigns, dedicated $852,926 of its $1,536,067 investment to five races. While the American Medical Association (AMA) spent $1,024,210 on its independent efforts, $868,042 of that total, or 85 percent, was spent in support of five candidates.

In addition to its efforts to defeat Synar, the NRA pumped $172,011 into an independent campaign in support of Specter (see box, page 187), most of which was invested in mailings. Prior to the Republican primary, the NRA spent $81,219 to send letters to its members urging them to vote for Specter. In the fall campaign against Yeakel, the NRA spent another $84,558 on mailings to its members.

In a newly drawn District 29, which was designed to maximize the chances of electing a new Hispanic member from Texas, Gene Green, who is white, emerged with the Democratic nomination after three rounds of bitter campaigning against Houston City Council member Ben Reyes. Green succeeded by sinking $124,441 into commercials and $298,572 into preprimary mailings that reminded voters that Reyes had declared personal bankruptcy, had been delinquent in paying his property taxes, had been arrested for driving under the influ-

The Top Fifteen Organizations
Waging Independent Campaigns

Rank	Organization	For	Against	Total
1	National Rifle Association	$2,529,241	$492,474	$3,021,715
2	National Association of Realtors	1,536,067	0	1,536,067
3	American Medical Association	1,024,210	0	1,024,210
4	National Right to Life Committee	797,896	10,415	808,311
5	AFL-CIO	741,579	1,636	743,215
6	National Abortion Rights Action League	477,055	242,506	719,561
7	Clean Up Congress	155,807	13,626	169,433
8	California Teachers Association	153,114	0	153,114
9	Public Citizen	0	150,193	150,193
10	California Association of Realtors	143,992	0	143,992
11	Auto Dealers & Drivers for Free Trade	125,539	0	125,539
12	Handgun Control	123,373	700	124,073
13	Pennsylvania AFL-CIO	123,259	0	123,259
14	Minnesota Concerned Citizens for Life	92,129	15,135	107,264
15	National Council of Senior Citizens	83,869	11,408	95,277

Note: Figures include "independent expenditures" and "communication costs," as reported by the organizations to the Federal Election Commission.

ence of alcohol, and had been placed on probation after pleading no contest to misdemeanor charges of theft and violating campaign finance laws.

The NRA spent $157,926 on an independent campaign on Green's behalf, including $41,411 for radio commercials and $11,647 for a phonebanking operation. While there was supposedly no coordination between Green's campaign and the NRA effort, letters mailed to voters by the NRA echoed Green's messages. One letter called atten-

The Top Ten Independent Campaigns Waged by the National Rifle Association

Race	Expenditures	For or Against	Total
1 Oklahoma District 2			$226,088
Mike Synar (D)	$141,275	against	
Drew Edmondson (D)	84,813	for	
2 Pennsylvania Senate			172,011
Arlen Specter (R)	172,011	for	
3 Texas District 29			157,926
Gene Green (D)	156,698	for	
Ben Reyes (D)	1,228	against	
4 California Senate			130,316
Bruce Herschensohn (R)	130,316	for	
5 Arkansas District 4			128,239
Beryl Anthony, Jr. (D)	86,412	against	
W. J. "Bill" McCuen (D)	41,827	for	
6 Pennsylvania Senate			101,938
Harris Wofford (D)	71,115	against	
Dick Thornburgh (R)	30,823	for	
7 Wisconsin Senate			99,942
Bob Kasten (R)	99,942	for	
8 Missouri District 6			94,502
Tom Coleman (R)	61,209	against	
Patsy Danner (D)	33,293	for	
9 Georgia Senate			87,081
Paul Coverdell (R)	87,081	for	
10 North Carolina Senate			74,241
Lauch Faircloth (R)	74,241	for	

Note: Figures include "independent expenditures" and "communication costs" as reported by the National Rifle Association to the Federal Election Commission.

tion to a district attorney's investigation into alleged ties between Reyes and a local drug ring. After dispatching Reyes, Green easily won the November election.

Herschensohn benefited from a $130,316 NRA campaign, all of which was spent on mailings to its California members.

Arkansas Secretary of State W. J. "Bill" McCuen ousted Rep. Beryl Anthony, Jr., in a June 9 primary runoff that McCuen's media adviser, Jim Duffy of Washington, D.C.-based Strother-Duffy-Strother, described as a "media war." Yet, while Duffy produced four television spots, including ads attacking Anthony's vote for a congressional pay raise and his 109 overdrafts at the House bank, this effort to defeat Anthony was significantly enhanced when the NRA dedicated $128,239 of its resources to oust the seven-term incumbent. Radio and newspaper ads condemning Anthony for supporting the Brady Bill cost the NRA $116,549.

The NRA sponsored a radio spot similar to the *Jeopardy* game show parody used to attack Synar, in which the mock contestant began, "I'll take 'Two-Faced Politicians' for $1,000." Following the *Jeopardy* format, the game show host then provided the answer to a question: "He tells folks in Arkansas that he's a hunter, but voted for a nationwide ban on dozens of commonly used hunting rifles." "Uh, who is Beryl Anthony?" shot back the contestant.

The single most expensive independent campaign of the 1992 elections was the $329,289 effort mounted by the NAR in support of Rep. Les AuCoin (D-Ore.), who fell short in his challenge to Republican Sen. Bob Packwood (see box, page 189). Terris & Jaye of San Francisco, Calif., received $200,000 for producing advocacy mailers. Fenn & King Communications of Washington, D.C., collected $87,745 for creating and placing broadcast ads. Target Inc. of Washington, D.C., received $38,584 for polling. National Telecommunications Services of Washington, D.C., collected $2,960 for phonebanking.

In another losing battle, the NAR spent $169,950 in support of Republican Rep. Rod Chandler, who lost an open Senate seat contest to state senator Patty Murray in Washington. John Maddox & Associates of Alexandria, Va., collected $150,000 for creating and placing television commercials. American Viewpoint, also of Alexandria, received the remaining $19,950 for polling.

The only winner among the top five candidates targeted by the NAR was Rep. E. Clay Shaw, Jr. (R-Fla.), who won a seventh term

The Top Five Independent Campaigns Waged by Various Organizations

Organization	Race	Expen-ditures	For or Against
National Association of Realtors			
Les AuCoin (D-Ore.)	Senate	$329,289	for
Rod Chandler (R-Wash.)	Senate	169,950	for
E. Clay Shaw, Jr. (R-Fla.)	House	130,629	for
John Seymour (R-Calif.)	Senate	123,058	for
Beryl Anthony, Jr. (D-Ark.)	House	100,000	for
American Medical Association			
Vic Fazio (D-Calif.)	House	255,085	for
Bob Packwood (R-Ore.)	Senate	227,809	for
Scott McInnis (R-Colo.)	House	184,910	for
Michael A. Andrews (D-Texas)	House	118,985	for
Gary A. Franks (R-Conn.)	House	81,256	for
National Right to Life Committee			
Mike DeWine (R-Ohio)	Senate	27,644	for
Don Davis (R-N.C.)	House	27,419	for
Morrison J. Hosley, Jr. (R-N.Y.)	House	24,564	for
Richard Ray (D-Ga.)	House	23,141	for
Bruce Herschensohn	Senate	19,982	for
AFL-CIO			
Harris Wofford (D-Pa.)	Senate	155,583	for
Wyche Fowler, Jr. (D-Ga.)	Senate	40,801	for
Les AuCoin (D-Ore.)	Senate	21,260	for
Ben Nighthorse Campbell (D-Colo.)	Senate	17,614	for
John S. Devens (D-Alaska)	House	14,967	for
National Abortion Rights Action League			
Russell D. Feingold (D-Wis.)	Senate	148,426	for
Steven D. Pierce (R-Mass.)	House	144,091	against
Ben Nighthorse Campbell (D-Colo.)	Senate	137,487	for
Pat Williams (D-Mont.)	House	77,885	for
Judith M. Ryan (R-Calif.)	House	59,827	for

Note: Figures include "independent expenditures" and "communication costs," as reported by the organizations to the Federal Election Commission.

by defeating Democratic state senator Gwen Margolis in what proved to be Shaw's costliest race ever. Shaw spent $1,136,419 to Margolis's $932,420. The NAR weighed in with a $125,208 effort on behalf of Shaw, including a $97,508 payment to Public Opinion Strategies of Alexandria, Va., for advocacy mailers, $17,700 to the same firm for polling, and $10,000 to John Maddox for additional polls.

In preparation for what it assumed would be a contentious fight over health care reform, the AMA weighed in heavily in an attempt to affect the outcome of several races. The organization spent $255,085 in support of Rep. Vic Fazio (D-Calif.): $195,885 for television commercials produced and placed by Fenn & King; $43,000 for radio spots, also produced and placed by Fenn & King; and $16,200 for polling with Mellman & Lazarus.

The AMA spent $227,809 in support of Packwood, including $121,404 paid to National Media of Alexandria, Va., for producing and placing broadcast ads. James R. Foster & Associates of Carrollton, Texas, received $92,405 from the AMA to produce pro-Packwood mailings. To refine the messages delivered by those ads and mailings, the AMA paid Tarrance & Associates of Alexandria, Va., $14,000 for polling.

The AMA spent $184,910 to help put state representative Scott McInnis (R-Colo.) over the top in his open seat contest with Lt. Gov. Mike Callihan, $102,800 of which was poured into a television campaign designed by Sandler-Innocenzi of Washington, D.C. The AMA also paid John Maddox $43,690 for persuasion mail and $22,920 for phonebanking, while Public Opinion Strategies collected $15,500 for polling. The AMA's sizable investment equaled 43 percent of what McInnis spent on his own campaign.

Rep. Michael A. Andrews (D-Texas) also received a considerable push from the AMA, which spent $15,600 on polls conducted by Mellman & Lazarus and paid Fenn & King $103,385 to produce and place radio commercials on his behalf. The ads never mentioned health care, but instead trumpeted Andrews's support for a middle-class income tax cut, his support for troop reductions in Europe, and his record as a crime fighter.

Rounding out their top five targeted races, the AMA backed freshman Rep. Gary A. Franks (R-Conn.) in his contest with Democrat James J. Lawlor and state representative Lynn H. Taborsak, who ran as an independent following her loss in the Democratic primary. The AMA spent $81,256 on Franks's behalf, including payments of $10,500 to American Viewpoint for polling, $39,009 for radio spots, and $31,747 for targeted mailings.

The National Right to Life Committee focused considerable effort on the presidential campaign, spending $801,573 on an independent campaign in support of George Bush. While it spent some money in 208 House and Senate races, the organization spent no more than $27,644 in support of any one candidate.

The AFL-CIO was the fifth most active organization among those waging independent campaigns, although for the most part its efforts were on par with those of the National Right to Life Committee. Primarily, these campaigns consisted of phonebanking and mailings directed to its members. The one notable exception was the special election contest between appointed Sen. Harris Wofford (D-Pa.) and former U.S. attorney general and Pennsylvania governor Dick Thornburgh. The union spent $155,583 in support of Wofford, most of which went for advocacy mailings to its members.

Seventy-nine percent of the money invested by NARAL in its independent campaigns was funneled into five races, including $148,426 to support Democratic state senator Russell D. Feingold in his successful bid to topple Wisconsin Sen. Bob Kasten. NARAL spent $85,000 on radio and television commercials and $43,000 on phonebanking to back Feingold.

As these examples suggest, many races that fostered one major independent campaign also drew other organizations into the fray. The NAR's $329,289 campaign on behalf of AuCoin was largely offset by the $227,809 effort by the AMA on behalf of Packwood. The American Auto Dealers and Drivers and the NRA also threw their support behind Packwood, with independent campaigns totaling $65,539 and $43,106, respectively. The Feingold-Kasten race spawned fifteen independent campaigns.

Although federal law requires those waging independent efforts to report their spending to the FEC, the law would appear to have several gaping loopholes.

Rep. Dan Glickman (D-Kan.) had to fight off four independent efforts against him, including a $68,983 campaign by the NRA. However, the cost of the biggest independent campaign against him will never be known. Following his vote in favor of imposing federal regulations on the cable television industry, Multimedia Cablevision of Wichita began airing editorials denouncing Glickman and urging viewers to vote for his Republican opponent, state senator Eric R. Yost. The editorials aired more than 100 times a day on as many as ten cable stations, including CNN. Because Multimedia Cablevision called the spots editorials, the firm did not have to report the cost of this campaign to the FEC. Glickman paid $10,790 in legal fees to Perkins Coie of Washington, D.C., for their work in reaching an agreement with Multimedia Cablevision, which ultimately allowed him to run 600 free spots over the campaign's final week.

Similarly, televangelist Pat Robertson's Christian Coalition distributed more than 40 million "nonpartisan" voter guides. The leaflets, distributed in all fifty states, told voters which candidates opposed abortion, homosexual rights, higher taxes, gun control, and congressional term limits. Because its voter guides are supposedly nonpartisan, the Christian Coalition was not required to report any of the costs associated with the 40 million fliers.

If efforts to place voluntary spending limits on candidates are eventually pushed through Congress, it will almost certainly produce an explosion of independent campaigns. Having already declared such spending a protected form of free speech, it is unlikely that the Supreme Court would uphold any congressional action designed to stop them.

Table 6-1 What Campaign Money Buys in the 1992 Senate Races: Coordinated Expenditures by National Parties

Major Category	From the Democratic Party			From the Republican Party		
	Total	DSCC	DNC	Total	NRSC	RNC
Overhead						
Office furniture/supplies	$ 15,000	$ 15,000	$ 0	$ 679	$ 679	$ 0
Rent/utilities	11,475	11,475	0	0	0	0
Salaries	35,538	35,538	0	0	0	0
Lawyers/accountants	21,247	21,247	0	0	0	0
Campaign automobile	0	0	0	25,963	25,963	0
Computers/office equipment	5,350	5,350	0	0	0	0
Travel	25,008	25,008	0	23,910	23,910	0
Total Overhead	**113,618**	**113,618**	**0**	**50,552**	**50,552**	**0**
Fund Raising						
Events	45,547	45,547	0	393	393	0
Direct mail	45,136	45,136	0	0	0	0
Total Fund Raising	**90,682**	**90,682**	**0**	**393**	**393**	**0**
Polling	730,426	611,075	119,351	54,225	54,225	0
Advertising						
Electronic media	9,684,431	9,608,431	76,000	14,960,225	14,960,225	0
Other media	2,249	2,249	0	28,722	28,722	0
Total Advertising	**9,686,680**	**9,610,680**	**76,000**	**14,988,947**	**14,988,947**	**0**
Other Campaign Activity						
Persuasion mail/brochures	389,690	389,690	0	1,109,714	1,109,714	0
Actual campaigning	503,781	468,190	35,592	280,187	280,187	0
Total Other Campaign Activity	**893,471**	**857,879**	**35,592**	**1,389,900**	**1,389,900**	**0**
Total Expenditures	**$11,514,876**	**$11,283,934**	**$230,943**	**$16,484,017**	**$16,484,017**	**$ 0**

Table 6-2 What Campaign Money Buys in the 1992 Senate Races: Coordinated Expenditures of National Parties, by Percentage

Major Category	From the Democratic Party			From the Republican Party		
	Total	DSCC	DNC	Total	NRSC	RNC
Overhead						
Office furniture/supplies	.13	.13	0	0	0	0
Rent/utilities	.10	.10	0	0	0	0
Salaries	.31	.31	0	0	0	0
Lawyers/accountants	.18	.19	0	0	0	0
Campaign automobile	0	0	0	.16	.16	0
Computers/office equipment	.05	.05	0	0	0	0
Travel	.22	.22	0	.15	.15	0
Total Overhead	**.99**	**1.01**	0	**.31**	**.31**	0
Fund Raising						
Events	.40	.40	0	0	0	0
Direct mail	.39	.40	0	0	0	0
Total Fund Raising	**.79**	**.80**	0	0	0	0
Polling	**6.34**	**5.42**	**51.68**	**.33**	**.33**	0
Advertising						
Electronic media	84.10	85.15	32.91	90.76	90.76	0
Other media	.02	.02	0	.17	.17	0
Total Advertising	**84.12**	**85.17**	**32.91**	**90.93**	**90.93**	0
Other Campaign Activity						
Persuasion mail/brochures	3.38	3.45	0	6.73	6.73	0
Actual campaigning	4.38	4.15	15.41	1.70	1.70	0
Total Other Campaign Activity	**7.76**	**7.60**	**15.41**	**8.43**	**8.43**	0
Total Expenditures	**100.00**	**100.00**	**100.00**	**100.00**	**100.00**	0

Table 6-3 What Campaign Money Buys in the 1992 House Races: Coordinated Expenditures by Party National Parties

Major Category	From the Democratic Party			From the Republican Party		
	Total	DSCC	DNC	Total	NRSC	RNC
Overhead						
Office furniture/supplies	$ 500	$ 500	$ 0	$ 0	$ 0	$ 0
Salaries	106,356	106,356	0	0	0	0
Lawyers/accountants	5,506	5,506	0	0	0	0
Travel	27,566	27,566	0	0	0	0
Food/meetings	0	0	0	5,540	5,540	0
Total Overhead	**139,928**	**139,928**	**0**	**5,540**	**5,540**	**0**
Fund Raising						
Events	3,472	3,472	0	2,700	2,700	0
Telemarketing	1,326	1,326	0	0	0	0
Total Fund Raising	**4,799**	**4,799**	**0**	**2,700**	**2,700**	**0**
Polling	1,313,462	404,596	908,866	376,606	364,666	11,940
Advertising						
Electronic media	3,201,151	3,201,151	0	2,281,348	1,667,912	613,436
Other media	0	0	0	16,797	16,797	0
Total Advertising	**3,201,151**	**3,201,151**	**0**	**2,298,145**	**1,684,709**	**613,436**
Other Campaign Activity						
Persuasion mail/brochures	275,069	275,069	0	3,202,417	3,066,764	135,654
Actual campaigning	153,489	153,489	0	120,610	57,554	63,056
Total Other Campaign Activity	**428,559**	**428,559**	**0**	**3,323,027**	**3,124,318**	**198,709**
Total Expenditures	**$5,087,898**	**$4,179,032**	**$908,866**	**$6,006,018**	**$5,181,932**	**$824,086**

Table 6-4 What Campaign Money Buys in the 1992 House Races: Coordinated Expenditures of National Parties, by Percentage

Major Category	From the Democratic Party			From the Republican Party		
	Total	DSCC	DNC	Total	NRSC	RNC
Overhead						
Office furniture/supplies	.01	.01	0	0	0	0
Salaries	2.09	2.54	0	0	0	0
Lawyers/accountants	.11	.13	0	0	0	0
Travel	.54	.66	0	0	0	0
Food/meetings	0	0	0	.09	.11	0
Total Overhead	**2.75**	**3.35**	0	**.09**	**.11**	0
Fund Raising						
Events	.07	.08	0	.04	.05	0
Telemarketing	.03	.03	0	0	0	0
Total Fund Raising	**.09**	**.11**	0	**.04**	**.05**	0
Polling	25.82	9.68	100.00	6.27	7.04	1.45
Advertising						
Electronic media	62.92	76.60	0	37.98	32.19	74.44
Other media	0	0	0	.28	.32	0
Total Advertising	**62.92**	**76.60**	0	**38.26**	**32.51**	**74.44**
Other Campaign Activity						
Persuasion mail/brochures	5.41	6.58	0	53.32	59.18	16.46
Actual campaigning	3.02	3.67	0	2.01	1.11	7.65
Total Other Campaign Activity	**8.42**	**10.25**	0	**55.33**	**60.29**	**24.11**
Total Expenditures	**100.00**	**100.00**	**100.00**	**100.00**	**100.00**	**100.00**

CHAPTER 7

Political Consultants
The Real Winners

Mike was a first-time candidate, and most of the people around him hadn't been involved in congressional campaigns before. We made sure we had the help we needed when we needed it.

John Hoehne, chief of staff
for Rep. Michael D. Crapo (R-Idaho)

B y mid-October 1992, former Mendocino County supervisor Dan Hamburg (D-Calif.) knew his bid to oust freshman Rep. Frank Riggs was in trouble. Hamburg also knew that with just three weeks left in the campaign, he was rapidly running out of time. Convinced that the race could be won but that his current strategy would fail, he dropped his chief consultants, Directions By King & Associates and Hopcraft Communications, both of Sacramento, Calif. "We needed more punch," recalled Meg O'Donnell, Hamburg's campaign finance director.

With the blessing of the Democratic Congressional Campaign Committee (DCCC), which dispatched a staffer to serve as his campaign manager during the final push, Hamburg brought in the Campaign Group of Philadelphia, Pa., to refocus his radio and television commercials and Campaign Performance Group of San Francisco, Calif., to develop advocacy mailers. In turn, Campaign Performance brought in Terris & Jaye, also of San Francisco, to help with both the conceptualization and production of the mailings.

"Hamburg had run the typical California campaign, making mail the main focus," recalled Richard M. Schlackman, president of Campaign Performance. "I spent the whole weekend in a hotel room going over poll results, and they had the right message. It just wasn't being communicated effectively. We did mail in the southern part of the district where TV was too expensive, but in the northern areas we bought television. Cable buys were $12 a point in Humbolt [County],

197

so we bought lots of CNN. We'd have been crazy not to buy that time."

On election day, Hamburg carried Humbolt and Mendocino counties in the north and District 1's portion of Solano County in the south by sufficiently wide margins to offset losses in the district's other four counties. His margin of victory: 6,410 votes.

Although the circumstances are rarely this dramatic, Hamburg's experience reflects the professionalization of modern politics, a process in which candidates turn themselves over to a cadre of highly skilled advisers who develop campaign strategy, mold and project the candidate's image, make certain people show up to vote on election day, and find the money to pay for it all.

Well before any ballots were cast on November 3, congressional candidates across the country had seen to it that political consultants would emerge from the 1992 campaigns as huge financial winners. When all the bills were finally totaled, $248,515,641—or 46 percent of the $542,248,774 spent by the 933 House and Senate candidates who contested the general election—had been funneled through media consultants, fund-raisers, persuasion mail specialists, pollsters, general and campaign management consultants, and get-out-the-vote specialists.

While the percentage of total spending accounted for by payments to consultants was virtually identical to the 45 percent recorded in 1990, the amount of money involved was substantially greater. Fueled by incumbents' concerns over the mood of the electorate, the greater number of challengers with sufficient resources to make races competitive, and the record number of open seat contests, consultant billings in congressional campaigns jumped more than $60 million between 1990 and 1992, a 32 percent rise.

In addition to the nearly $249 million shelled out by House and Senate candidates, party coordinated campaigns generated another $32,268,249 in consultant fees. We did not have the resources required to collect and code the additional millions paid to consultants by state party organizations or those waging independent campaigns on behalf of congressional candidates.

MEDIA CONSULTANTS

The biggest winners in this bonanza were the media consultants, who fashioned and projected the images that spelled the difference between winning and losing in many competitive races. During the 1992 election cycle, these "kingmakers" billed congressional campaign committees a total of $165,589,508—a 42 percent increase over 1990. The national party committees kicked in another $27,212,742.

As in 1990, Squier/Eskew/Knapp/Ochs Communications of Washington, D.C., led the way, billing fourteen campaigns a total of $11,273,185 (see Table 7-1). The firm billed Sen. Christopher J. Dodd (D-Conn.), $1,831,630; Sen. Bob Graham (D-Fla.), $1,743,642; Sen. Richard C. Shelby (D-Ala.), $1,211,492; Sen. Terry Sanford (D-N.C.), $1,037,228; and Sen. Dale Bumpers (D-Ark.), $931,181. In addition, Squier/Eskew handled the media chores for two unsuccessful Senate candidates seeking open seats and one unsuccessful challenger, billing Rep. Les AuCoin (D-Ore.), $1,131,196; Rep. Richard Stallings (D-Idaho), $375,952; and challenger Joseph H. Hogsett (D-Ind.), $1,229,031. The firm's leading clients in the House were Rep. Vic Fazio (D-Calif.), $669,827; and 1991 special election victor John W. Olver (D-Mass.), $573,556.

When the additional $1,195,674 in coordinated expenditures coming in from national Democratic party committees are all factored in, Squier/Eskew's 1992 billings amounted to $12,468,859, a 52 percent increase over 1990. Including party coordinated expenditures, the firm's eight Senate clients accounted for 85 percent of those revenues.

Greer, Margolis, Mitchell & Associates of Washington, D.C., landed six Senate and two House campaigns in 1992, and its billings jumped from $2,388,526 in 1990 to $11,096,778. Ranked twelfth in terms of total billings in 1990, this 365 percent increase moved Greer, Margolis into second place in 1992. Their work on the Senate campaign of Rep. Barbara Boxer (D-Calif.) accounted for nearly half of the firm's receipts, with Boxer paying $4,299,960 and the Democratic Senatorial Campaign Committee (DSCC) adding $1,217,000. Sen. Wyche Fowler, Jr. (D-Ga.) paid Greer, Margolis $2,579,820 in his loosing bid for a second term, and the DSCC added $510,000. Sens. Wendell H. Ford (D-Ky.), Kent Conrad (D-N.D.), and Patrick J. Leahy (D-Vt.) paid Greer, Margolis $947,393, $337,842, and $210,035, respectively. The firm's most lucrative House account belonged to Rosa DeLauro (D-Conn.), who contributed $394,496 to Greer, Margolis's receipts.

National Media of Alexandria, Va., collected more than twice as much from its House and Senate clients in 1992 as they had in 1990, but that growth did no more than maintain its third-place ranking. National Media worked on eighteen campaigns, including six Senate races. Lt. Gov. Mike DeWine (R-Ohio) paid them $1,595,353 during his unsuccessful bid to oust Sen. John Glenn. Sen. Don Nickles (R-Okla.) paid the firm $1,216,607. Former attorney general and Pennsylvania governor Dick Thornburgh pumped $1,976,126 through the firm during his unsuccessful 1991 special election contest with Sen. Harris Wofford, who had been appointed to the seat following the death of Sen. John Heinz. Although Sen. Bob Dole (R-Kan.) did not have much of a race, his advertising campaign generated $481,168 worth of business for the firm. Unsuccessful challengers Brook Johnson (R-Conn.) and Steve Sydness (R-N.D.) paid the firm $1,207,012 and $110,970, respectively. National Media's two most profitable House races involved Reps. E. Clay Shaw, Jr. (R-Fla.) and Jim Bunning (R-Ky.), who paid $543,424 and $438,137, respectively. The firm collected another $1,418,228 in national party coordinated expenses, including $892,000 for DeWine's campaign and $279,182 for Johnson's.

Multi Media Services Corp. of Alexandria, Va., owed its fourth-place ranking largely to Sen. Alfonse M. D'Amato (R-N.Y.), who paid the time-buyer $4,982,589. With the National Republican Senatorial Committee (NRSC) spending $1,507,718 on D'Amato's behalf, that one campaign accounted for 70 percent of Multi Media's $9,270,463 total billings. The unsuccessful campaign of Richard Williamson (R-Ill.) against Carol Moseley-Braun generated revenues of $1,673,251, including $944,052 in party coordinated expenditures.

Another media buyer, Target Enterprises of Hollywood, Calif., earned most of its money from two Senate campaigns. Target collected $2,665,048 from Bruce Herschensohn (R-Calif.) and $2,454,644 from the NRSC. Payments of $1,338,360 by Sen. John Seymour (R-Calif.) were augmented by a $2,449,955 infusion from the NRSC.

FUND-RAISERS

Whether they relied primarily on political action committees (PACs) or on individual donors to fund their campaigns, whether they raised their money primarily through events or by mail, most candidates hired at least one fund-raising consultant to help fill their 1992 campaign coffers. Of the $84,954,183 congressional candidates spent on fund-raising events, direct-mail solicitations, and telemarketing, $29,336,066 was paid to professional fund-raisers. This represented a drop of about $8.7 million between 1990 and 1992, a 23 percent decrease explained largely by a reduction in spending on direct-mail consultants. In 1992 only three direct-mail fund-raisers had billings of at least $1 million; in 1990 eight firms had topped the $1 million mark and two had exceeded $2 million.

This marked dropoff in direct-mail expenses was largely due to the absence of Sen. Jesse Helms (R-N.C.) from the 1992 candidate roster. In 1990 Helms paid five direct-mail consultants a total of $4.6 million, including $1,334,275 to Bruce W. Eberle & Associates of Vienna, Va.; $1,246,726 to Computer Operations of Raliegh, N.C.; and $1,039,027 to Jefferson Marketing, also of Raleigh.

Without the campaigns of Democratic Sens. Tom Harkin (Iowa), Paul Simon (Ill.), and John Kerry (Mass.), who together spent $2,979,082, Coyle, McConnell & O'Brien of Washington, D.C., dropped from first to ninth on the list.

While Response Dynamics of Vienna, Va., saw its billings drop from $1,872,116 in 1990 to $1,763,935 in 1992, the company emerged as the top direct-mail fund-raiser, having leap-frogged from third place (see Table 7-2). The firm charged Rep. Robert K. Dornan (R-Calif.) $967,651 for list rental, production, postage, and processing returns. Dornan's payments accounted for 55 percent of the money paid to Response Dynamics by House and Senate candidates in 1992. Among the company's other major clients were Sens. Seymour and John McCain (R-Ariz.), who were billed $310,340 and $295,837, respectively.

Karl Rove & Co. of Austin, Texas, jumped from fourth in 1990 to second in 1992, despite the fact that its earnings dropped by $555,635. Rove's major clients included Thornburgh, $336,725; Sen. Bob Kasten (R-Wis.), $330,388; and Sen. Christopher S. Bond (R-Mo.), $279,479. Terry Considine (R-Colo.), who lost an open Senate seat contest to Rep. Ben Nighthorse Campbell, paid Rove $160,515.

On the strength of the $562,599 paid by former San Francisco mayor Dianne Feinstein's (D-Calif.) Senate campaign and the $400,586 paid by Lynn Yeakel's (D-Pa.) Senate campaign, Gold Communications Co. of Austin, Texas, saw its total revenues rise from $327,830 in 1990 to $1,146,223 in 1992, a 250 percent increase. Feinstein and Yeakel accounted for 84 percent of Gold's earnings.

Robbed of the large direct-mail operations run by 1990 candidates Sens. Simon (D-Ill.), J. Bennett Johnston (D-La.), and Carl Levin (D-Mich.), A. B. Data of Milwaukee, Wis., took in $1,416,097 less in 1992 than it had two years earlier. A. B. Data's best client in 1992, Senate hopeful Robert Abrams (D-N.Y.), paid the company $359,814. Sen. Glenn and Rep. Les Aspin (D-Wis.) spent $303,813 and $101,493, respectively.

Pamela D. Needham of Washington, D.C., topped the list of 359 fund-raising event planners who worked for congressional candidates (see Table 7-3), collecting 91 percent of the $495,337 she earned in the 1992 cycle from one campaign. Sen. Barbara A. Mikulski (D-Md.) paid Needham $452,167 over the six-year cycle to coordinate her fund-raising receptions.

Scott Gale, president of Fundraising Management Group in Washington, D.C., took the opposite approach, collecting a total of $432,577 from eleven campaigns. Gale billed Abrams $95,536; Shelby, $75,203; Senate challenger Tony Smith (D-Alaska), $68,954; and Wofford, $36,247. Democratic Reps. Greg Laughlin, Martin Frost, and Pete Geren, all Texans, paid Fundraising Management $46,345, $42,913, and $15,973, respectively.

Robert H. Bassin Associates of Washington, D.C., raised money for four Democratic Senate candidates, collecting $70,191 from Glenn, $33,147 from Hogsett, $32,952 from Campbell, and just $4,785 from Conrad. Among his fifteen clients seeking House seats, Olver rung up bills totaling $55,544. Rep. Dick Swett (D-N.H.) was not far behind, paying $53,884. Robert E. Andrews (D-N.J.) spent $37,839. Swett's father-in-law, Tom Lantos (D-Calif.), paid Bassin $30,573.

Fraioli/Jost of Washington, D.C., pulled in $402,316 by working on twenty-six House and Senate campaigns, earning as little as $1,160 from Rep. Gary L. Ackerman (D-N.Y.) to as much as $73,290 from Rep. Richard H. Lehman (D-Calif.). In addition to Lehman, the firm's most lucrative contracts were Stallings, $67,271; Rep. Pat Williams (D-Mont.), $36,282; and Rep. Richard J. Durbin (D-Ill.), $29,521.

While John L. Plaxco & Associates of Los Angeles, Calif., worked for three candidates, Feinstein accounted for 92 percent of the company's billings—$365,220. Plaxco also received $15,603 from House Majority Leader Richard A. Gephardt (D-Mo.) and $14,316 from Lehman.

None of the top five fund-raising event planners in 1992 had been among the top five in 1990.

Outlays for telemarketing dropped from $5,115,550 in 1990 to $2,644,737 in 1992, a 48 percent decline that was largely explained by the absence of Senate candidates who relied heavily on this tool during the 1990 election cycle. In the 1990 cycle, Simon alone had spent $706,298 with his telemarketers.

Although forty-three firms provided telemarketing services to congressional candidates during the 1992 cycle, five firms received 66 percent of the $2,416,207 paid to professional telemarketers.

Most campaigns avoided telemarketing because of its high costs and increasing public dissatisfaction with telephone sales pitches. Gordon & Schwenkmeyer of El Segundo, Calif., topped the list of telemarketers, billing its clients a total of $596,164. However, 92 percent of those earnings came from two campaigns: Feinstein paid $317,292 and Moseley-Braun paid $233,966. The firm's next biggest client was Rep. Bill Richardson (D-N.M.), who paid them $33,796 for telemarketing and another $31,098 for their help on his fund-raising direct-mail program.

Meyer Associates of St. Cloud, Minn., received a total of $424,247 from ten campaigns, $229,963 of which was paid by Sen. Tom Daschle (D-S.D.). AuCoin, who lost his bid to unseat Sen. Bob Packwood, spent $56,507. Reps. Pete Stark (D-Calif.), Lane Evans (D-Ill.), and Tim Johnson (D-S.D.) paid Meyer $43,858, $24,504, and $18,462, respectively.

Rounding out the top five telemarketing consultants were Optima Direct of Washington, D.C., which billed its clients a total of $280,571; Product Development of Costa Mesa, Calif., which collected 99 percent of its $143,028 from Herschensohn; and Synhorst & Schraad of Russell, Kan., which collected a total of $139,651 for its work on twelve campaigns, including $50,743 for its efforts on behalf of Sen. Charles E. Grassley (R-Iowa).

PERSUASION MAIL SPECIALISTS

Persuasion mail remained an integral part of virtually every 1992 campaign, particularly in House races, where television frequently proved not to be an economical means of communicating with voters. In Los Angeles, New York, Chicago, and other major media markets, most candidates relied almost exclusively on advocacy mailers to communicate their messages. The consultants who designed those mailings received $17,457,860 from candidates and another $1,740,549 from the national party committees. In all, eleven persuasion mail consultants collected more than $500,000.

As in 1990, Campaign Performance was the biggest player by far (see Table 7-4). While the firm had only one Senate candidate among its clients, it worked to one degree or another for forty Democratic House candidates. Some simply paid Campaign Performance a retainer to guarantee access to its expertise in the event a race developed, but most put Schlackman and his colleagues to work. For its efforts, Campaign Performance collected $2,693,376 from its clients and $40,847 from national Democratic party committees—more than doubling its 1990 receipts. The company billed three clients more than $200,000: California Reps. Fazio and George E. Brown, Jr., and unsuccessful open seat candidate Steve A. Orlins (D-N.Y.). Democratic Reps. Robert Andrews, Norman Y. Mineta (Calif.), and Tom McMillen (Md.) each paid the firm more than $100,000, as did Thomas H. Hattery (D-Md.), who defeated Rep. Beverly B. Byron in the primary before losing in the general election to Roscoe G. Bartlett. Another eleven campaigns paid Campaign Performance between $50,000 and $100,000.

Although its billings were nearly $1.9 million less than Campaign Performance's, Karl Rove collected $691,547 more from its clients in 1992 than it had in 1990. Payments from national Republican party committees jumped from $52,534 in 1990 to $479,833 in 1992. While Bond paid them $79,934, the NRSC picked up the tab for mailers costing $226,888. Although Sens. Nickles and Kasten paid the firm nothing for work on advocacy mailings, the party paid Rove $141,276 to produce mailings for Nickles and $111,670 to create mailers for Kasten. In the House, Reps. Joe L. Barton, Lamar Smith, and Jack Fields, all Texas Republicans, paid Rove $127,088, 58,219, and $56,955, respectively.

McNally, Temple & Associates in Sacramento, Calif., placed third in the persuasion mail rankings. The firm worked on five House campaigns, the most lucrative of which was the $291,019 effort of Michael Huffington (R-Calif.). It collected $277,629 from Bill Baker

(R-Calif.), who won an open seat contest with Democrat Wendell H. Williams.

The November Group of Washington, D.C., worked on thirteen House campaigns and one Senate campaign. Sen. Ernest F. Hollings (D-S.C.) paid the firm $31,550 and the DSCC spent another $40,800 on his behalf. Democratic Reps. Thomas J. Downey (N.Y.) and Gerry E. Studds (Mass.) paid the company $181,570 and $138,608, respectively. The party picked up another $10,000 in expenses for Studds. Gwen Margolis (D-Fla.), who lost to Republican Clay Shaw, paid $50,746.

Direct Mail Systems of St. Petersburg, Fla., created voter persuasion mail for nine House campaigns. Shaw paid them $157,508, and Rep. Michael Bilirakis (R-Fla.) anted up $114,519. Dan Miller (R-Fla.) and John L. Mica (R-Fla.), who both won open seats, spent $109,337 and $73,405, respectively.

POLLSTERS

In a year marked by tighter races, it should come as no surprise that candidates paid their polling consultants a total of $16,627,764—32 percent more than pollsters collected from House and Senate campaigns during the 1990 election cycle. These payments were augmented by checks totaling $2,474,719 from the national party committees.

Greenberg-Lake of Washington, D.C., collected a total of $1,770,613 from congressional candidates, the DSCC, the DCCC, and the Democratic National Committee (DNC), a 23 percent increase over 1990. Even without the huge sums the firm collected for working on Bill Clinton's presidential campaign, these payments were enough to vault the firm to the top of the polling list (see Table 7-5). While twenty-five candidates paid Greenberg-Lake directly, the party committees together paid the firm for its involvement in sixty-one campaigns, including forty-nine in which the candidates did not tap their own treasuries to pay for the polls. The firm's two biggest Senate clients, Dodd and Boxer, paid $176,173 and $151,774, respectively. The DSCC kicked in an additional $24,860 for Dodd, and the DNC picked up $16,735 of Boxer's polling costs. Among House candidates, the company's top clients were Democratic Reps. David E. Bonior (Mich.), Downey, and Bob Carr (Mich.), who paid $135,691, $109,873, and $104,907, respectively. Of the three, only Carr had an additional $3,775 picked up by the party.

Cooper & Secrest Associates of Alexandria, Va., the leading pollster of the 1990 cycle, worked on thirty-seven House campaigns and two Senate campaigns. While the firm's billings increased by a modest 2 percent over 1990, that was not enough to hold on to its top ranking. On the Senate side, Cooper & Secrest collected $295,288 from Fowler and $51,507 from Stallings. McMillen and Studds were the firm's best House clients, paying $98,101 and $64,234, respectively. Another twelve candidates, only two of whom were nonincumbents, paid Cooper & Secrest between $30,000 and $50,000.

As in 1990, Garin-Hart ranked third on the revenue list, collecting $1,061,152 from twenty-six campaigns and another $340,368 in Democratic party coordinated expenditures. Sens. Conrad, Hollings, Graham, and Leahy paid Garin-Hart $114,250, $74,717, and $51,500, respectively. The firm received $90,500 from AuCoin and $37,377 from Feinstein. Topping the list of clients involved in House open seat contests were Jane Harman (D-Calif.) at $76,445 and Orlins at $52,035. Due to tight races or redistricting, Democratic Reps. Michael A. Andrews (Texas), Peter Hoagland (Neb.), Fazio, and Richard J. Durbin (Ill.) each paid between $43,000 and $53,000 for Garin-Hart's services. Rep. John D. Dingell (D-Mich.), who was neither affected by redistricting nor seriously challenged, paid the firm $45,000.

Mellman & Lazarus of Washington, D.C., provided polling services to twenty-one campaigns. Boxer topped the company's client list with direct payments of $107,860 and coordinated payments by the DSCC of $163,207. Glenn paid the firm $221,993 and received a DNC stipend of $5,740. Six other Senate campaigns tapped the firm's expertise. Among House candidates using Mellman & Lazarus, Gephardt's $78,821 outlay led the pack. Rep. Gerry Sikorski (D-Minn.), who had 697 overdrafts, was not far behind with direct payments of $73,802 and a $5,000 infusion from the DCCC.

The top pollster used by Republican candidates, Arthur J. Finkelstein & Associates of New York, collected $1,109,708. Although Finkelstein provided polling for fifteen campaigns, four Senate campaigns accounted for 77 percent of his firm's billings. Finkelstein served as both D'Amato's pollster and general campaign strategist, collecting $356,194 for his polling services alone. Lauch Faircloth (R-N.C.), who defeated Democratic Sen. Terry Sanford, paid Finkelstein $280,226. Polls conducted for Williamson and Nickles brought the firm $128,437 and $86,450, respectively. Former Rep. Joseph J. DioGuardi (R-N.Y.), who lost a rematch with Democratic Rep. Nita Lowey, paid Finkelstein $57,229. Five other House candidates each paid Finkelstein more than $20,000 for polling.

GENERAL AND CAMPAIGN MANAGEMENT CONSULTANTS

With the increased specialization in the political consulting industry, some candidates have begun hiring consultants to coordinate the activities of their various consultants.

Geto & De Milly of New York was paid $444,082 to handle the day-to-day operations of the Abrams Senate campaign (see Table 7-6). While other firms created the campaign's ads, produced the commercials, and bought much of the air time, Geto & De Milly also collected $2,262,199 for consulting on the media campaign and purchasing time. Abrams paid an additional $11,250 to rent space in the firm's Manhattan office.

Kam Kuwata's firm, Kuwata Communications of Santa Monica, Calif., received $261,419 for managing Feinstein's successful special election campaign against Seymour to fill the remaining two years of former Sen. Pete Wilson's term. After the election, Feinstein named Kuwata director of her Los Angeles congressional office. In early 1994 he changed hats again, leaving the congressional staff to begin managing Feinstein's 1994 campaign for a full six-year term.

Seymour also had a campaign management consultant, Richard H. McBride of RHM in Round Rock, Texas. RHM collected $200,538 for coordinating the day-to-day campaign activities, including those undertaken by the other thirty-one consultants Seymour employed.

Rep. Robert H. Michel (R-Ill.) ran his 1992 campaign as he had every campaign since 1986, when his campaign manager, MaryAlice Erickson, created her own management firm. That firm, Campaigns & Elections of Peoria, Ill., collected $188,433 for running Michel's permanent campaign throughout the 1992 cycle. Erickson managed a small direct-mail fund-raising operation, arranged fund-raising events, published and mailed out a newsletter, sent out Michel's year-end holiday cards, sent congratulations to recent high school graduates, and coordinated the activities of his fund-raising, polling, and public relations consultants.

Some candidates opted not to turn their entire operations over to a single firm, but leaned heavily on general consultants for strategic advice. In some cases, those planning the general campaign strategy and orchestrating the activities of other consultants were also acting in some other campaign capacity.

In addition to his polling fees, Finkelstein was also paid to mold the strategy on four campaigns. D'Amato paid $265,295 for this service (see Table 7-7). In the House, Sam Johnson (R-Texas) paid $38,486 for Finkelstein's input to his 1991 special election. Stephen A. Sohn (R-Mass.) paid Finkelstein $34,500 for general advice on his losing effort against Rep. Edward J. Markey. Rep. Duncan Hunter (R-Calif.) paid Finkelstein a $2,000 retainer.

Campaign Design Group of Washington, D.C., collected $105,103 from Boxer and $39,686 from the DSCC for work on Boxer's behalf. State senator Patty Murray (D-Wash.) paid the firm $75,536. Lynn Woolsey (D-Calif.) paid Campaign Design $2,076 for their input on her open seat campaign.

Spencer-Roberts & Associates of Irvine, Calif., received $193,740 for providing general strategic advice to Seymour and $18,757 for its work on the successful House campaign of real estate executive Ken Calvert (R-Calif.). Eddie Mahe, Jr. & Associates of Washington, D.C., provided general consulting services to three House and two Senate campaigns. His two biggest clients, DeWine and Sen. Frank H. Murkowski (R-Alaska), paid $109,475 and $60,802, respectively.

While Maxwell & Associates of Alexandria, Va., usually handled fund raising for campaigns, the firm consulted with three campaigns on their overall strategies. Grassley paid $129,004 for that service. The firm received $21,577 from Jim Ross Lightfoot (R-Iowa) and $14,498 from John J. Rhodes III (R-Ariz.).

GET-OUT-THE-VOTE SPECIALISTS

In the largely bygone days of machine politics, candidates depended on block and precinct captains in their party organizations to make certain that supporters made their way to the polls on election day. In the age of entrepreneurial politics, most candidates have taken on that task for themselves. While most run in-house phonebanking operations, many candidates have begun to contract out that labor-intensive process to consultants. In all, candidates contesting the 1992 elections paid such consultants $5,351,046. Coordinated payments by the national party committees added $400,497.

The Tyson Organization of Fort Worth, Texas, received $567,098 for its phonebanking efforts on behalf of seven candidates (see Table 7-8). Senators Shelby and Fowler paid Tyson $191,996 and $31,114, respectively. The company billed Democratic Reps. Frost, $101,045; Geren, $84,565; Mike Synar (Okla.), $81,340; Bart Gordon (Tenn.), $58,757; and Bob Clement (Tenn.), $18,280.

Campaign Telecommunications of New York received $441,077 from ten campaigns for phonebanking, including $225,047 paid by Brook Johnson. Other Republicans who made use of the firm's services included Rep. Newt Gingrich (Ga.), $45,096; Nickles, $43,847; Rep. Richard H. Baker (La.), $34,533; Dornan, $21,790; Hunter, $20,000; and Rep. Randy "Duke" Cunningham (Calif.), $14,880. Although Bond did not hire them directly, the NRSC paid for $81,307 worth of telephone calls made on his behalf.

Telemark in Wilsonville, Ore., had a client list with a distinctly bipartisan flavor, an unusual phenomenon in the consulting business. Packwood's phonebanking payments totaled $223,000 and accounted for 45 percent of the firm's receipts. Another Republican client was Thornburgh, who paid the firm $76,545. Among the firm's nine House clients were Democrats Olver and Bob Filner (D-Calif.), who paid $43,977 and $32,229, respectively.

Payco American Corp. of Brookfield, Wis., collected $340,689 for its phonebanking efforts on behalf of a dozen Republican candidates, including $117,609 from Robert F. Bennett (Utah), who won an open Senate seat.

Shelby was Timbes & Yeager's sole phonebanking client, but the Mobile, Ala., firm collected $293,693 for helping to place 250,000 calls on his behalf prior to the primary.

HOUSE CANDIDATES AND CONSULTANTS:
A HOST OF APPROACHES

During the 1992 cycle, Huffington led all House candidates in spending on consultants, pumping $3,054,032 of his record-breaking $5,434,569 campaign through his advisers (see Table 7-9). He paid Ringe Media of Purcellville, Va., $546,197 for creating his broadcast advertising. Crest Films of New York collected $280,501 for production work. Specialized Media Services of Charlotte, N.C., billed Huffington $1,089,540 to cover the cost of air time and the firm's advertising placement fees. Target Enterprises collected $151,648 for purchasing additional air time.

To drive his advertising campaign and monitor the mood of the electorate, Huffington employed a bevy of research firms. Hill Research Consultants of Woodlands, Texas, received $186,742 for polling and demographic research. Benchmark Research Group of Sacramento, Calif., collected $31,230 for polling and research. Huffington paid Moore Information of Portland, Ore., and Market Strategies of Southfield, Mich., $23,090 and $19,399, respectively, for still more polls and strategic advice. Competitive Edge Research of San Diego, Calif., billed the campaign $10,196 for providing opposition research.

Huffington paid McNally, Temple $321,012 for producing advocacy mailers and working to turn out the vote. The Michael D. Meyers Co. of Kirkland, Wash., received $10,550 for consultations on the persuasion mailers. Mason Lundberg & Associates of Orange, Calif., collected $235,404 for phonebanking, and Sandy Bodner Consulting of Marina Del Rey, Calif., received $22,282 for coordinating public relations efforts. For providing general strategic advice, consulting on the advocacy mailers, and buying air time, Huckaby Rodriguez of Sacramento received $126,241. With the exception of the $3,065,439 Gephardt spent on his reelection effort, Huffington's massive payments to his consultants amounted to more than any other House candidate spent on his or her entire campaign.

Gephardt placed a distant second to Huffington in spending on consultants, paying eleven advisers a total of $1,342,737. Doak, Shrum & Associates of Washington, D.C., received $97,632 for creating his television and radio commercials. The Media Company, also of Washington, collected $703,217 for placing the spots.

Unlike Huffington, who simply wrote personal checks whenever his campaign needed money, Gephardt had to raise the money he needed. In addition to a permanent fund-raising staff of eight who worked out of his Washington, D.C., campaign office, Gephardt paid three event planners a total of $27,792 for organizing events in Washington, Los Angeles, and New York. Malchow & Co. of Washington, D.C., and Gold Communications received $27,081 and $17,230, respectively, for their direct-mail fund-raising efforts.

Gephardt paid Gold Communications and The November Group $140,099 and $16,946, respectively, for creating advocacy mailers. Two was also the magic number for pollsters, with KRC Research of New York collecting $128,924 and Mellman & Lazarus receiving $78,821. Telephone Contact of St. Louis, Mo., collected $104,996 for phonebanking and mailing out follow-up materials to potential supporters.

Other House candidates who funneled at least $1 million through their consultants were Dick Chrysler (R-Mich.), $1,294,249; Dornan, $1,142,072; and Fazio, $1,090,711. Forty-six House candidates spent more than $500,000 through their consultants.

Spurred on by fears over redistricting or their constituents' anti-incumbent leanings, a sizable number of House incumbents dramatically increased their reliance on expert advice. Rep. William J. Hughes (D-N.J.) had not found it necessary to hire a media consultant in any of his previous nine campaigns, preferring instead to develop his ads in-house. For his 1990 reelection effort, Hughes had simply recycled spots from his 1988 campaign. "For eighteen years he ran a mom-and-pop operation," noted administrative assistant Mark H. Brown. However, faced with a well-funded Republican challenger and concerned with the widespread anger over tax increases pushed through by Democratic Gov. James J. Florio, Hughes paid the Campaign Group of Philadelphia, Pa., $210,030 for creating and placing four television commercials in 1992.

In addition to handing Rep. Richard J. Durbin (D-Ill.) a host of new constituents and a well-funded Republican challenger, redistricting placed him in a new media market. "Seventy percent of our district is now in the St. Louis market, and that means it's four times as expensive to advertise as before," lamented district staff director Michael E. Daly. While Durbin had not hired a media consultant in 1990 and had spent just $10,690 on broadcast ads, his new political reality forced him to invest $378,052 in such ads during 1992. Shorr Associates of Philadelphia, Pa., collected $340,265 for designing and placing ten television and radio commercials. Durbin spent nothing on persuasion mail in 1990, but in 1992 he invested $150,907 in brochures and advocacy mailers, $83,509 of which went to Campaign Performance. Durbin spent nothing on polls in 1990, but to help formulate his message and strategy in 1992 he invested $43,500 in surveys conducted by Garin-Hart. Fraioli/Jost received $29,521 for coordinating Durbin's Washington events—$10,621 more than he spent on fund-raising consultants in 1990. In all, Durbin increased his expenditures on consultants by $477,895—twenty-six times his 1990 outlay.

Redistricting drastically altered the campaign style of Rep. George "Buddy" Darden (D-Ga.) for his rematch with Republican Al Beverly. In the new District 7, Republicans pulled from Gingrich's old district had replaced those from Cobb County, who had become accustomed to voting for Darden. As a result, he drastically increased his communication budget for the 1992 race; along with that went a similar increase in his consultant budget. In 1990 Darden had paid the FMR Group of Washington, D.C., $9,425 to create his broadcast ads. For producing and placing his commercials in 1992, McKinnon Media of Austin, Texas, collected $143,850. Advocacy mailings had been produced in-house for the 1990 campaign, but in 1992 Darden paid Gold Communications $29,250. Kitchens, Powell & Kitchens of Orlando, Fla., received $18,100 for conducting the 1992 campaign's polls; no polls were done in 1990.

Pennsylvania's redistricting plan dealt Republican Rep. Robert S. Walker a constituency that was 50 percent new to him, and that translated into a $30,626 increase over 1990 in expenditures for advertising and persuasion mail. Faced with a 1990 opponent who spent less than $5,000, Walker had chosen not to hire a media consultant. Redistricting, not the $10,488 spent by his 1992 challenger, led Walker to hire Brabender Cox of Pittsburgh, Pa. The firm designed and placed Walker's broadcast and newspaper advertising and handled his advocacy mailings, for a fee of $58,226. Walker paid Maxwell & Associates $3,498, and, in turn, the event planners helped him collect about one-third more from political action committees than he had in 1990, when he hired no fund-raising consultants.

Not everyone spent more on consultants in 1992. For example, Rep. Tim Johnson (D-S.D.) faced a 1992 challenger who had

$60,992 less to spend than his 1990 opponent, so Johnson cut his spending by $89,123. Johnson slashed his spending on broadcast advertising from $204,852 in 1990 to $111,969 in 1992 by almost entirely cutting out consultants. While Struble-Totten Communications of Washington, D.C., had collected $20,000 for creating his 1990 broadcast ads, his 1992 spots were created in-house and produced at the DCCC's Harriman Communications Center. The Media Group of Columbus, Ohio, and Struble-Totten received $1,078 and $877, respectively, for miscellaneous production costs. Johnson's campaign placed its ads directly rather than turn that chore over to a consultant, thereby reducing expenditures on air time to $107,675 from $150,000. "It was a matter of cost effectiveness," explained John Y. Deveraux, Johnson's deputy chief of staff. "In a highly competitive race where you want to be sure each ad is correctly placed to get the most for your money, we would hire a consultant."

In 1990 Rep. H. James Saxton (R-N.J.) spent $454,178, or 62 percent of his budget, on consultants. The Media Team of Alexandria, Va., and Ailes Communications of New York designed and produced Saxton's broadcast media, receiving $42,179 and $5,000, respectively. Farrell Media of New York bought most of the air time for $295,274. Advanced Communications in Richmond, Va., handled phonebanking for $35,049. Pollster Tarrance & Associates of Houston, Texas, collected $21,250. Public Sector in Florence, N.J., collected $4,000 for providing general strategic advice. To help him raise money through the mail, Saxton paid Direct Mail Specialists of Ocean Springs, Miss., $48,626. Gurney Sloan of Washington, D.C., received $2,800 for planning fund-raising events.

Facing a 1992 opponent whose budget was roughly one-seventh of his 1990 challenger's, Saxton sliced his spending on consultants to just $66,128—a 587 percent reduction. The Media Team was called on once again, but this time they received just $23,735 for consulting and design work. National Media of Alexandria, Va., collected only $5,057 to place the ads. Tarrance conducted the campaign's polls, but their cost was reduced to $9,950. Direct Mail Specialists and Sloan helped with fund raising, receiving $21,034 and $3,150, respectively.

While some House candidates invested their resources with nationally known consultants, others turned to former staff members who had left government service to form their own consulting firms. Rep. Greg Laughlin (D-Texas) funneled more than one-third of the

$449,063 he spent on his 1992 campaign through Maverick Communications of Austin, Texas, a firm founded in 1989 by Laughlin's former congressional district director, Ken Bryan. Bryan collected $153,225 for creating and placing Laughlin's radio and television commercials, designing and placing newspaper advertising, managing a large phonebanking operation, conducting polls, and handling direct-mail fund-raising solicitations. Included in Bryan's remuneration was a postelection "winner's bonus" of $25,000.

The largest single expense listed by Rep. Thomas M. Foglietta (D-Pa.) under "actual campaigning" was a $20,000 lump-sum payment for "consulting" to Bob Barnett, his former chief-of-staff, on December 29, 1992. Barnett also received a $10,000 contribution from Foglietta in December 1991 for his unsuccessful bid for a seat on the Philadelphia City Council.

Mark Fierro, press secretary for Rep. James Bilbray (D-Nev.) until April 1992, collected $14,000 from his former boss's campaign for helping to create five television and three radio commercials. Fierro, like Barnett and Bryan, worked for no other congressional candidates during the 1992 election cycle.

However, all three are undoubtedly hoping to follow in the footsteps of Dolly Angle, former administrative assistant for Frost. Angle gave up her government job in 1991 to found Dolly Angle & Associates of Arlington, Texas, a fund-raising firm that earned $11,110 from Frost, $31,112 from Rep. Gene Green (D-Texas), and $50,242 from Rep. Chet Edwards (D-Texas) during the 1992 cycle.

Some members allowed their employees to launch consulting businesses while still on the government payroll. Freshman Rep. John T. Doolittle (R-Calif.) paid $48,774, or 67 percent of his fund-raising event costs, to Event Planners of Roseville, Calif. The firm is owned by Doolittle's congressional staff director, David G. Lopez, and Lopez's wife, although Lopez said he had no formal connection to the 1992 campaign.

Rep. James L. Oberstar (D-Minn.) paid Jim Berard Media Services of Washington, D.C., $77,058 to place broadcast ads, $11,030 to place newspaper ads, and $2,664 for coordinating press access to Oberstar during the 1992 Democratic National Convention. James A. Berard was also Oberstar's congressional communications director.

Some House members decided they could do very well without consultants. Rep. C. W. Bill Young (R-Fla.) increased his spending from $194,043 in 1990 to $458,366 in 1992. His spending on advertising and advocacy mailings rose by $307,397, but none of that increased spending went to consultants. Young personally wrote all his voter contact mail, television and radio commercials, and newspaper ad copy. The campaign bought the air time and placed the newspaper ads directly, leaving only the production to be done by others. As administrative assistant Douglas M. Gregory put it, Young believes that "after being in politics for thirty-two years, if he doesn't know what his constituents want, then how will some consultant know."

Rep. Earl Hutto (D-Fla.) felt the same way. While he looked to Frederick/Schneiders of Washington, D.C., for polling, Hutto, a former sportscaster and advertising agency executive, preferred to write and produce all his ads. "It saves money, and with the small amount I raise, I try to guard my funds," noted Hutto in explaining the paucity of outside advisers.

Outspent by nearly five to one in his primary contest with Rep. Terry L. Bruce (D-Ill.), Rep. Glenn Poshard maximized his $150,000 budget by creating his own commercials. "He's his own campaign manager, strategist, and creative designer," noted press secretary David D. Stricklin. Poshard emerged with 62 percent of the primary vote.

In an effort to reach younger, newly registered voters, Walter R. Tucker III (D-Calif.) wrote and produced his own campaign song with a decidedly upbeat tempo. "He's very artsy," said administrative assistant Marcus S. Mason. In addition to giving away cassette tapes of the tune, Tucker edited it into a sixty-second commercial that aired on two rhythm and blues stations. Tucker also developed what Mason described as "a more traditional commercial" that ran on CNN and Black Entertainment Television.

In 1989 Rep. Craig Washington (D-Texas) had spent more than $600,000 to win a special election, and he swore he would never let his spending reach that level again. "This job isn't worth $600,000," he proclaimed. In that spirit, Washington continued his practice of using consultants sparingly in 1992. Campaign Strategies of Houston, his only paid consultant, received $13,424 for designing a small persuasion mail effort. "I decide my own methods, come up with my own slogans," he explained. "I want to get me across, not some image of me."

SENATE CAMPAIGNS:
CONSULTANTS BY THE DOZENS

Virtually every Senate campaign was a consultant's dream come true, but the battle between D'Amato and Abrams proved to be the most lucrative of all. D'Amato pumped $6,762,965 through his consultants, which accounted for 57 percent of his total spending. The NRSC added $1,512,543 (see Table 7-10). Russo, Marsh & Associates of Sacramento, Calif., billed D'Amato $754,230 for creating his broadcast ads. Multi Media Services collected $4,982,589 from D'Amato and $1,507,718 from the NRSC for placing the ads. D'Amato paid Finkelstein $621,489 for polling and general strategic advice; the NRSC paid Finkelstein $4,825. For their organizational efforts, James E. Murphy of Gaithersburg, Md., and Serphin Maltese of New York received $24,884 and $23,000, respectively. Bernstein & Associates of Arlington, Va., handled opposition research for $30,275.

To pay for his campaign, D'Amato relied heavily on Barbara Klein Associates of Washington, D.C., who collected $61,243 for helping him raise $1,361,231 from PACs. MWM of Washington, D.C., received $257,775 for direct-mail fund raising. He paid Anne Hyde Co. of Glendale, Calif., $2,500 for coordinating a fund-raising reception in Los Angeles and American Telecom of Horsham, Pa., $4,980 for telemarketing.

Abrams paid fifteen consultants a total of $4,760,287, which represented 75 percent of his total outlays. The DSCC augmented those payments with checks totaling $1,500,316.

To win his caustic Democratic primary battle with 1984 vice presidential nominee Geraldine A. Ferraro, New York City Comptroller Elizabeth Holtzman, and black activist Al Sharpton, and wage an equally acrid general election campaign against D'Amato, Abrams invested 54 percent of his $6,374,304 budget in television and radio advertising.

Struble-Totten Communications of Washington, D.C., collected $411,384 from Abrams and $55,000 from the DSCC for creating and producing broadcast ads. Jan Crawford Communications of Paris, Va., received $748,786 from Abrams and $1,370,000 from the DSCC for buying air time. Abrams paid Geto & De Milly $2,717,531, including $2,262,199 for creative input to the ad campaign and additional purchases of air time. Media Strategy Associates of New York billed Abrams $6,000.

Abrams sank $667,674 into his direct-mail fund-raising efforts, including payments of $359,814 to A. B. Data, $54,032 to Penn & Schoen Associates of New York, and $13,704 to Craver, Matthews, Smith & Co. of Falls Church, Va. For coordinating fund-raising receptions, Fundraising Management and Pamela Lippe of New York received $95,536 and $99,543, respectively. Telemarketers Great Lakes Communications of Milwaukee and Meyer Associates were paid $28,431 and $3,457, respectively.

In addition to orchestrating Abrams's first direct-mail fund-raising solicitations, Penn & Schoen collected $171,000 from Abrams and $45,000 from the DSCC for polling. Jeff Gillienkirk of New York provided opposition research for $20,261, and the DSCC paid the Research Group of Chicago, Ill., $30,316 for additional opposition research. Speech writer Michael Sheehan of Washington, D.C., and general campaign consultant Anita Burson of New York collected $13,252 and $17,557, respectively.

Together, the Abrams and D'Amato campaigns generated consultant billings of $14,536,111. As astounding as that total was, it was not all that much greater than the $13,897,288 spent by Boxer and Herschensohn.

For their work on her successful Senate bid, forty consultants billed Boxer's campaign, the DSCC and the DNC a total of $7,469,121. Boxer employed thirty fund-raising advisers to help solicit donations to defray the massive bills rung up by media consultants Greer, Margolis; pollsters Greenberg-Lake; and general strategist Campaign Design Group. Craver, Matthews collected $744,060 from Boxer and $18,435 from the DSCC for orchestrating her direct-mail solicitations. Twenty-three of her fund-raising consultants planned events, including CT Associates of Seattle, Wash., which received $102,528 from Boxer and $23,250 from the DSCC. Boxer hired numerous event planners from California, including Janet Steinberg of Tiberon, who received $45,935; Francis Kidd of Culver City, $45,433; Gina Pennestri of San Francisco, $39,800; Donna Andrews of Los Angeles, $34,758; and Deborah Taylor of Panorama City, $24,094. Among her four telemarketers, National Telecommunications Services of Washington, D.C., made the most, billing

Boxer $66,000. Services for Organizational Renewal of San Rafael, Calif., provided telemarketing for $19,020.

Boxer's opponent relied heavily on consultants as well. Seventeen consultants billed the Herschensohn campaign $3,973,523, while the NRSC kicked in $2,454,644 for additional media buys.

In all, forty-three Senate candidates spent at least $1 million through consultants, including twenty-two who paid their advisers more than $2 million. When coordinated expenditures by the national party committees are included, forty-seven candidates generated billings in excess of $1 million, including twenty-seven whose consultants billed at least $2 million.

Table 7-1 The Top Fifty Media Consultants in the 1992 Congressional Races

			Payments from		
Rank	Company	Location	Candidate	National Party	Total
1	Squier/Eskew/Knapp/Ochs Communications	Washington, D.C.	$11,273,185	$1,195,674	$12,468,859
2	Greer, Margolis, Mitchell & Associates	Washington, D.C.	9,237,278	1,859,500	11,096,778
3	National Media	Alexandria, Va.	8,532,931	1,418,228	9,951,160
4	Multi Media Services Corp.	Alexandria, Va.	6,687,370	2,583,093	9,270,463
5	Target Enterprises	Hollywood, Fla.	4,195,056	4,904,599	9,099,655
6	Campaign Group	Philadelphia, Pa.	7,466,215	731,775	8,197,990
7	The Media Company	Washington, D.C.	6,133,757	966,000	7,099,757
8	Fenn & King Communications	Washington, D.C.	5,776,706	22,637	5,799,343
9	The Garth Group	New York, N.Y.	4,643,143	980,540	5,623,683
10	Morris & Carrick	New York, N.Y.	3,840,981	1,235,000	5,075,981
11	Sipple Strategic Communications	Washington, D.C.	5,043,919	0	5,043,919
12	Doak, Shrum & Associates	Washington, D.C.	2,430,061	923,000	3,353,061
13	Smith & Harroff	Alexandria, Va.	3,042,748	106,393	3,149,141
14	Pro Media	Needham, Mass.	3,079,210	0	3,079,210
15	Shafto & Barton	Houston, Texas	2,600,951	114,990	2,715,941
16	The Media Team	Alexandria, Va.	1,629,252	931,099	2,560,351
17	Shorr Associates	Philadelphia, Pa.	2,459,103	0	2,459,103
18	Hanover Communications	Raleigh, N.C.	1,790,218	560,928	2,351,146
19	Media Strategies & Research	Washington, D.C.	2,304,695	44,000	2,348,695
20	Geto & De Milly	New York, N.Y.	2,262,199	0	2,262,199
21	Jan Crawford Communications	Paris, Va.	769,219	1,370,000	2,139,219
22	Trippi, McMahon & Squier	Alexandria, Va.	2,092,307	25,000	2,117,307
23	The Perkins Group	Indianapolis, Ind.	1,637,987	452,415	2,090,402
24	Austin-Sheinkopf	New York, N.Y.	1,733,875	243,000	1,976,875
25	Media Solutions	Atlanta, Ga.	1,121,400	796,083	1,917,483

(Table continues)

Table 7-1 (Continued)

Rank	Company	Location	Payments from Candidate	Payments from National Party	Total
26	Twede-Evans Political	Salt Lake City, Utah	1,753,198	141,523	1,894,721
27	Profit Marketing & Communications	New Berlin, Wis.	1,498,586	290,919	1,789,506
28	Sandler-Innocenzi	Washington, D.C.	1,586,806	106,324	1,693,130
29	Axelrod & Associates	Chicago, Ill.	1,564,693	40,000	1,604,693
30	Struble-Totten Communications	Washington, D.C.	1,427,447	65,596	1,493,044
31	Eichenbaum, Henke & Associates	Milwaukee, Wis.	1,112,500	303,500	1,416,000
32	Mike Murphy Media	Washington, D.C.	1,186,083	107,000	1,293,083
33	Nordlinger Associates	Washington, D.C.	1,260,625	20,000	1,280,625
34	Joe Slade White & Co.	New York, N.Y.	1,134,869	142,795	1,277,664
35	Barnhart Advertising	Denver, Colo.	965,175	275,082	1,240,257
36	The Robert Goodman Agency	Baltimore, Md.	1,185,141	15,750	1,200,891
37	Media Plus	Seattle, Wash.	751,074	407,838	1,158,911
38	Mentzer Media Service	Baltimore, Md.	1,051,095	97,145	1,148,240
39	Schreurs & Associates	Waterloo, Iowa	836,838	304,072	1,140,910
40	Starr, Seigle & McCombs	Honolulu, Hawaii	1,115,551	0	1,115,551
41	Russo, Marsh & Associates	Sacramento, Calif.	1,110,591	0	1,110,591
42	Specialized Media Services	Charlotte, N.C.	1,089,540	0	1,089,540
43	Marketing Resource Group	Lansing, Mich.	942,819	50,972	993,791
44	Western International Media	Los Angeles, Calif.	980,970	10,000	990,970
45	Paul Kinney Productions	Sacramento, Calif.	654,112	333,000	987,112
46	Kranzler Kingsley Communications Corp.	Bismark, N.D.	881,797	25,000	906,797
47	Edmonds Powell Media	Washington, D.C.	777,635	89,669	867,304
48	Cottington & Marti	Edina, Minn.	735,261	108,322	843,582
49	John Franzen Multimedia	Washington, D.C.	826,447	0	826,447
50	Edward Mitchell Communications	Wilkes-Barre, Pa.	817,685	5,500	823,185

Table 7-2 The Top Twenty-Five Direct-Mail Consultants in the 1992 Congressional Races

Rank	Company	Location	Payments from Candidate	Payments from National Party	Total
1	Response Dynamics	Vienna, Va.	$1,763,935	$ 0	$1,763,935
2	Karl Rove & Co.	Austin, Texas	1,201,658	0	1,201,658
3	Gold Communications Co.	Austin, Texas	1,146,223	0	1,146,223
4	A.B. Data	Milwaukee, Wis.	844,558	0	844,558
5	Craver Matthews Smith & Co.	Falls Church, Va.	761,284	18,435	779,719
6	MWM	Washington, D.C.	600,913	0	600,913
7	Tim Macy & Associates	Sacramento, Calif.	523,914	0	523,914
8	Malchow & Co.	Washington, D.C.	479,047	0	479,047
9	Coyle, McConnell & O'Brien	Washington, D.C.	422,686	0	422,686
10	The Lukens Co.	Arlington, Va.	418,837	0	418,837
11	Polly A. Agee	Arlington, Va.	244,646	0	244,646
12	Mal Warwick & Associates	Berkeley, Calif.	230,730	0	230,730
13	Jim Wise Associates	Alexandria, Va.	218,575	0	218,575
14	Direct Mail Systems	St. Petersburg, Fla.	199,056	0	199,056
15	The Madison Group	Bellevue, Wash.	173,819	0	173,819
16	Lungren & Co.	Sacramento, Calif.	171,410	0	171,410
17	Odell, Roper & Associates	Golden, Colo.	150,146	0	150,146
18	Bennett & Associates	Raleigh, N.C.	131,623	0	131,623
19	Betsy Crone	Washington, D.C.	126,796	0	126,796
20	Losser & Associates	Washington, D.C.	119,472	0	119,472
21	Campaign Services Group	Austin, Texas	113,181	0	113,181
22	Winning Direction	San Francisco, Calif.	103,318	0	103,318
23	Fundamentals	Rock River, Ohio	76,474	0	76,474
24	James R. Foster & Associates	Carrollton, Texas	71,921	0	71,921
25	Marketing Associates	Charlotte, N.C.	70,797	0	70,797

Table 7-3 The Top Twenty-Five Event Consultants in the 1992 Congressional Races

Rank	Company	Location	Payments from		Total
			Candidate	National Party	
1	Pamela D. Needham	Washington, D.C.	$495,337	$ 0	$495,337
2	Fundraising Management Group	Washington, D.C.	432,577	0	432,577
3	Robert H. Bassin Associates	Washington, D.C.	429,676	0	429,676
4	Fraioli/Jost	Washington, D.C.	402,316	0	402,316
5	John L. Plaxco & Associates	Los Angeles, Calif.	395,138	0	395,138
6	Steven H. Gordon & Associates	St. Paul, Minn.	371,753	0	371,753
7	Springer Associates	Falls Church, Va.	371,616	0	371,616
8	Dan Morgan & Associates	Arlington, Va.	357,487	0	357,487
9	Erickson & Co.	Washington, D.C.	357,434	0	357,434
10	Paula Levine	Washington, D.C.	318,156	0	318,156
11	Creative Campaign Consultant	Washington, D.C.	310,366	2,700	313,066
12	Ziebart Associates	Washington, D.C.	241,115	0	241,115
13	Shelby/Blaskeg	Washington, D.C.	222,394	0	222,394
14	Maxwell & Associates	Alexandria, Va.	211,104	0	211,104
15	Joyce Valdez & Associates	Los Angeles, Calif.	208,897	0	208,897
16	PAC-COM	New York, N.Y.	201,772	0	201,772
17	Mary Pat Bonner	Springfield, Va.	198,763	0	198,763
18	Jim Wise Associates	Alexandria, Va.	183,578	0	183,578
19	Carey Hagglund	Sausalito, Calif.	180,854	0	180,854
20	Conroy & Co.	Washington, D.C.	158,906	0	158,906
21	Barbara Klein Associates	Washington, D.C.	157,409	0	157,409
22	Barbara Silby & Associates	Potomac, Md.	151,741	0	151,741
23	Kimberly A. Scott	Washington, D.C.	145,584	0	145,584
24	Hammelman Associates	Arlington, Va.	145,400	0	145,400
25	CT Associates	Seattle, Wash.	117,810	23,250	141,060

Table 7-4 The Top Twenty-Five Persuasion Mail Consultants in the 1992 Congressional Races

Rank	Company	Location	Payments from Candidate	Payments from National Party	Total
1	Campaign Performance Group	San Francisco, Calif.	$2,693,376	$ 40,847	$2,734,224
2	Karl Rove & Co.	Austin, Texas	370,111	479,833	849,944
3	McNally, Temple & Associates	Sacramento, Calif.	720,990	25,888	746,878
4	The November Group	Washington, D.C.	553,000	53,561	606,561
5	Direct Mail Systems	St. Petersburg, Fla.	563,922	33,480	597,402
6	Welch Communications	Arlington, Va.	492,753	101,959	594,712
7	Gold Communications Co.	Austin, Texas	593,872	0	593,872
8	Bates & Associates	Washington, D.C.	576,392	0	576,392
9	Russo, Marsh & Associates	Sacramento, Calif.	499,127	60,692	559,819
10	Roger Lee & Carol Beddo Associates	San Jose, Calif.	509,858	0	509,858
11	James R. Foster & Associates	Carrollton, Texas	456,771	47,500	504,271
12	Ambrosino & Muir	San Francisco, Calif.	436,106	0	436,106
13	Precision Marketing	Easton, Pa.	393,826	0	393,826
14	David J. Murray & Associates	Princeton, N.J.	302,340	53,540	355,880
15	Brabender Cox	Pittsburgh, Pa.	270,548	55,472	326,020
16	Brown Inc.	Santa Fe, N.M.	308,567	14,805	323,372
17	Campaign Strategies	San Antonio, Texas	288,547	0	288,547
18	Kevin B. Tynan & Associates	Chicago, Ill.	159,517	112,235	271,752
19	Marketing Resource Group	Lansing, Mich.	255,756	6,501	262,257
20	Clinton Reilly Campaigns	San Francisco, Calif.	241,524	0	241,524
21	Bay Communications	Edgewater, Md.	215,553	0	215,553
22	Blaemire Communications	Reston, Va.	194,015	9,110	203,124
23	The Madison Group	Bellevue, Wash.	148,395	31,726	180,121
24	John Grotta Company	Arlington, Va.	123,402	37,734	161,135
25	Pavlik & Associates	Fort Worth, Texas	158,061	0	158,061

Table 7-5 The Top Twenty-Five Pollsters in the 1992 Congressional Races

Rank	Company	Location	Payments from		Total
			Candidate	National Party	
1	Greenberg-Lake	Washington, D.C.	$1,255,391	$515,222	$1,770,613
2	Cooper & Secrest Associates	Alexandria, Va.	1,421,428	91,650	1,513,078
3	Garin-Hart	Washington, D.C.	1,061,152	340,368	1,401,520
4	Mellman & Lazarus	Washington, D.C.	1,038,464	286,438	1,324,902
5	Arthur J. Finkelstein & Associates	New York, N.Y.	1,099,269	10,439	1,109,708
6	Tarrance & Associates	Alexandria, Va.	861,495	28,900	890,395
7	Public Opinion Strategies	Alexandria, Va.	775,096	43,382	818,478
8	Hickman-Brown Research	Washington, D.C.	644,928	69,000	713,928
9	Penn & Schoen Associates	New York, N.Y.	475,268	84,800	560,068
10	American Viewpoint	Alexandria, Va.	533,185	7,000	540,185
11	Moore Information	Portland, Ore.	504,882	3,500	508,382
12	Hill Research Consultants	Woodlands, Texas	385,629	0	385,629
13	Fairbank, Bregman & Maullin	San Francisco, Calif.	351,872	32,500	384,372
14	Bennett & Petts	Washington, D.C.	210,610	164,834	375,444
15	Lauer, Lalley & Associates	Washington, D.C.	237,150	134,860	372,010
16	Frederick/Schneiders	Washington, D.C.	325,878	36,800	362,678
17	Market Strategies	Southfield, Mich.	274,771	29,500	304,271
18	Kitchens, Powell & Kitchens	Orlando, Fla.	292,250	10,000	302,250
19	Bill Johnson Survey Research	Mt. Vernon, N.Y.	247,200	0	247,200
20	Fabrizio, McLaughlin & Associates	Alexandria, Va.	229,576	13,500	243,076
21	Western Wats Center	Provo, Utah	43,718	196,415	240,133
22	Feldman Group	Washington, D.C.	78,586	146,619	225,205
23	Arnold Steinberg & Associates	Calabasas, Calif.	205,425	0	205,425
24	KRC Research	New York, N.Y.	190,106	0	190,106
25	Thomas Kielhorn & Associates	Oklahoma City, Okla.	186,250	0	186,250

Table 7-6 The Top Fifteen Campaign Management Consultants in the 1992 Congressional Races

Rank	Company	Location	Payments from Candidate	Payments from National Party	Total
1	Geto & De Milly	New York, N.Y.	$444,082	$ 0	$444,082
2	Kuwata Communications	Santa Monica, Calif.	261,419	0	261,419
3	RHM	Round Rock, Texas	200,538	0	200,538
4	Campaigns & Elections	Peoria, Ill.	188,433	0	188,433
5	Carville & Begala	Alexandria, Va.	156,657	0	156,657
6	Political Advertising Consultants	San Antonio, Texas	114,628	0	114,628
7	Hopcraft Communications	Sacramento, Calif.	96,205	0	96,205
8	Political Consulting & Management	St. George Island, Fla.	95,763	0	95,763
9	MBM Consulting	Richmond, Va.	91,631	0	91,631
10	Curt Stainer & Associates	Columbus, Ohio	87,977	0	87,977
11	Western Pacific Research	Bakersfield, Calif.	83,933	0	83,933
12	Attention!	Naperville, Ill.	79,842	0	79,842
13	Washington Political Group	Montgomery, Ala.	74,439	0	74,439
14	Hunt, Marmillion & Associates	Los Angeles, Calif.	69,866	0	69,866
15	Cutting Edge Communications	San Antonio, Texas	65,058	0	65,058

Table 7-7 The Top Fifteen General Strategy Consultants in the 1992 Congressional Races

			Payments from		
Rank	Company	Location	Candidate	National Party	Total
1	Arthur J. Finkelstein & Associates	New York, N.Y.	$340,281	$ 0	$340,281
2	Campaign Design Group	Washington, D.C.	182,715	39,686	222,401
3	Spencer-Roberts & Associates	Irvine, Calif.	212,498	0	212,498
4	Eddie Mahe, Jr. & Associates	Washington, D.C.	192,136	0	192,136
5	Maxwell & Associates	Alexandria, Va.	165,079	5,000	170,079
6	Joseph Gaylord & Co.	Washington, D.C.	146,999	0	146,999
7	Tony Payton & Associates	Arlington, Va.	139,331	0	139,331
8	Carlyle Gregory Co.	Falls Church, Va.	120,841	0	120,841
9	Richard Morris	West Redding, Conn.	110,333	0	110,333
10	Ridder/Braden	Denver, Colo.	101,333	6,841	108,174
11	Randy Hinaman	Alexandria, Va.	100,154	0	100,154
12	The Brier Group	Harrisburg, Pa.	93,043	0	93,043
13	Fabrizio, McLaughlin & Associates	Alexandria, Va.	88,441	0	88,441
14	Huckaby, Rodriguez	Sacramento, Calif.	85,746	0	85,746
15	Doyce Boesch	Washington, D.C.	85,380	0	85,380

Table 7-8 The Top Fifteen Campaign Get-Out-the-Vote Consultants in the 1992 Congressional Races

| Rank | Company | Location | Payments from | | Total |
			Candidate	National Party	
1	The Tyson Organization	Fort Worth, Texas	$567,098	$ 0	$567,098
2	Campaign Telecommunications	New York, N.Y.	441,077	94,807	535,884
3	Telemark	Wilsonville, Ore.	492,459	0	492,459
4	Payco American Corp.	Brookfield, Wis.	330,736	9,953	340,689
5	Timbes & Yeager	Mobile, Ala.	293,693	0	293,693
6	Optima Direct	Washington, D.C.	105,741	187,483	293,224
7	Campaign Tele-Resources	Omaha, Neb.	262,966	0	262,966
8	Mason Lundberg & Associates	Orange, Calif.	248,760	0	248,760
9	Cherry Communications	Gainesville, Fla.	158,047	5,000	163,047
10	Gordon & Schwenkmeyer	El Segundo, Calif.	111,157	2,500	113,657
11	Campaign Strategies	San Antonio, Texas	106,268	0	106,268
12	Parker Group	Birmingham, Ala.	101,071	0	101,071
13	Telemark America	London, Ky.	63,333	34,077	97,410
14	Matrixx Marketing	Ogden, Utah	88,494	0	88,494
15	Precision Marketing	Easton, Pa.	86,954	0	86,954

Table 7-9 The Top Fifty House Candidates' Spending on Consultants

Rank	Candidate	Candidate	National Party	Total
1	Michael Huffington,[a] R-Calif.	$3,054,032	$ 0	$3,054,032
2	Richard A. Gephardt, D-Mo.	1,342,737	137	1,342,875
3	Dick Chrysler,[a] R-Mich.	1,294,249	6,501	1,300,750
4	Robert K. Dornan, R-Calif.	1,142,072	0	1,142,072
5	Vic Fazio, D-Calif.	1,090,711	275	1,090,986
6	Gerry E. Studds, D-Mass.	892,042	15,137	907,180
7	John W. Olver,[a] D-Mass.	867,821	5,137	872,958
8	Jane Harman,[a] D-Calif.	865,330	0	865,330
9	E. Clay Shaw, Jr., R-Fla.	804,750	0	804,750
10	Linda Bean,[a] R-Maine	789,905	0	789,905
11	Michael A. Andrews, D-Texas	787,570	137	787,708
12	Bob Carr, D-Mich.	764,377	3,912	768,289
13	Lynn Schenk,[a] D-Calif.	767,675	0	767,675
14	Steny H. Hoyer, D-Md.	762,836	137	762,973
15	Terry Everett,[a] R-Ala.	749,890	0	749,890
16	Martin T. Meehan,[a] D-Mass.	727,531	10,000	737,531
17	Newt Gingrich, R-Ga.	683,437	44,880	728,317
18	Steve A. Orlins,[a] D-N.Y.	724,571	0	724,571
19	Thomas J. Downey, D-N.Y.	722,893	137	723,031
20	Peter H. Kostmayer, D-Pa.	698,460	20,137	718,598
21	Ben Erdreich, D-Ala.	697,212	10,137	707,350
22	Mike Synar, D-Okla.	700,758	137	700,896
23	Gerry Sikorski, D-Minn.	688,224	10,137	698,362
24	David E. Bonior, D-Mich.	694,254	137	694,391

25	Herbert C. Klein,[a] D-N.J.	682,903	0	682,903
26	Tom McMillen, D-Md.	656,478	17,637	674,115
27	Martin Frost, D-Texas	663,530	137	663,668
28	Charles Wilson, D-Texas	635,617	17,137	652,754
29	Ron Marlenee, R-Mont.	626,384	25,024	651,408
30	Les Aspin, D-Wis.	644,099	5,137	649,237
31	Richard Ray, D-Ga.	614,697	15,274	629,971
32	Pat Williams, D-Mont.	607,065	22,448	629,513
33	Dan Glickman, D-Kan.	610,101	5,137	615,239
34	Don Ritter, R-Pa.	613,053	0	613,053
35	Sander M. Levin, D-Mich.	590,148	16,176	606,324
36	Robert E. Andrews, D-N.J.	579,277	9,216	588,494
37	Jim Bacchus, D-Fla.	565,273	137	565,411
38	Jim Bunning, R-Ky.	545,633	17,804	563,437
39	Rosa DeLauro, D-Conn.	556,969	5,137	562,107
40	Dan Rostenkowski, D-Ill.	546,451	11,873	558,324
41	Richard H. Lehman, D-Calif.	525,411	25,137	550,548
42	Bob Filner,[a] D-Calif.	546,316	0	546,316
43	Jerry Huckaby, D-La.	518,919	20,537	539,456
44	Mark Neumann,[a] R-Wis.	537,903	0	537,903
45	Harold Rogers, R-Ky.	503,583	34,077	537,660
46	Jim Nussle, R-Iowa	470,133	54,975	525,108
47	Leslie L. Byrne,[a] D-Va.	506,975	15,000	521,975
48	Richard J. Durbin, D-Ill.	496,795	11,873	508,669
49	James C. Greenwood,[a] R-Pa.	465,904	35,771	501,675
50	Mary Rose Oakar, D-Ohio	498,882	137	499,020

[a] Nonincumbent or special election candidate.

Table 7-10 The Top Fifty Senate Candidates' Spending on Consultants

Rank	Candidate	Candidate	National Party	Total
1	Alfonse M. D'Amato, R-N.Y.	$6,762,965	$1,512,543	$8,275,508
2	Barbara Boxer,[a] D-Calif.	5,962,551	1,506,570	7,469,121
3	Dianne Feinstein,[a] D-Calif.	5,638,512	1,250,920	6,889,432
4	Arlen Specter, R-Pa.	5,700,962	980,540	6,681,502
5	Bruce Herschensohn,[a] R-Calif.	3,973,523	2,454,644	6,428,167
6	John Seymour, R-Calif.	3,896,617	2,449,955	6,346,572
7	Robert Abrams,[a] D-N.Y.	4,760,288	1,500,316	6,260,603
8	Lynn Yeakel,[a] D-Pa.	3,455,023	811,371	4,266,394
9	Wyche Fowler, Jr., D-Ga.	3,591,642	513,431	4,105,073
10	Dick Thornburgh,[a] R-Pa.	3,112,805	950,999	4,063,804
11	Bob Packwood, R-Ore.	3,739,763	29,000	3,768,763
12	John Glenn, D-Ohio	2,974,030	622,240	3,596,270
13	Bob Kasten, R-Wis.	3,101,893	402,589	3,504,483
14	Christopher S. Bond, R-Mo.	3,140,117	337,695	3,477,812
15	Harris Wofford,[a] D-Pa.	2,392,471	948,000	3,340,471
16	Mike DeWine,[a] R-Ohio	2,358,127	892,000	3,250,127
17	Daniel R. Coats, R-Ind.	2,482,915	452,415	2,935,330
18	Lauch Faircloth,[a] R-N.C.	2,234,583	560,928	2,795,510
19	Paul Coverdell,[a] R-Ga.	1,529,979	984,487	2,514,466
20	Carol Moseley-Braun,[a] D-Ill.	2,007,207	404,323	2,411,529
21	Christopher J. Dodd, D-Conn.	2,213,242	163,340	2,376,582
22	Terry Sanford, D-N.C.	1,787,468	532,000	2,319,468
23	Ernest F. Hollings, D-S.C.	2,150,614	111,396	2,262,011
24	Robert F. Bennett,[a] R-Utah	2,065,242	124,621	2,189,863

25	Don Nickles, R-Okla.	1,960,370	179,010	2,139,380
26	Richard Williamson,[a] R-Ill.	1,130,894	944,052	2,074,945
27	Rod Chandler,[a] R-Wash.	1,629,146	407,838	2,036,983
28	Richard C. Shelby, D-Ala.	1,879,184	85,282	1,964,466
29	Bob Graham, D-Fla.	1,931,007	0	1,931,007
30	Barbara A. Mikulski, D-Md.	1,912,394	10,714	1,923,108
31	John McCain, R-Ariz.	1,731,636	173,104	1,904,740
32	Brook Johnson,[a] R-Conn.	1,541,924	279,182	1,821,106
33	Les AuCoin,[a] D-Ore.	1,484,550	235,208	1,719,757
34	Terry Considine,[a] R-Colo.	1,359,597	275,082	1,634,678
35	Harry Reid, D-Nev.	1,513,837	108,805	1,622,642
36	Russell Feingold,[a] D-Wis.	1,188,623	336,910	1,525,533
37	Joseph H. Hogsett,[a] D-Ind.	1,294,454	194,800	1,489,254
38	Tom Daschle, D-S.D.	1,327,189	0	1,327,189
39	Ben Nighthorse Campbell,[a] D-Colo.	1,062,318	243,545	1,305,862
40	Daniel K. Inouye, D-Hawaii	1,243,202	0	1,243,202
41	Wendell H. Ford, D-Ky.	1,201,067	0	1,201,067
42	Geri Rothman-Serot,[a] D-Mo.	880,369	293,908	1,174,277
43	Kent Conrad, D-N.D.	1,112,509	55,812	1,168,321
44	Charles E. Grassley, R-Iowa	916,280	227,093	1,143,373
45	Patty Murray,[a] D-Wash.	751,596	373,730	1,125,326
46	Dale Bumpers, D-Ark.	1,111,170	0	1,111,170
47	Dirk Kempthorn,[a] R-Idaho	896,385	109,535	1,005,919
48	Frank H. Murkowski, R-Alaska	873,792	110,480	984,272
49	John B. Breaux, D-La.	925,749	8,872	934,621
50	Wayne Owens,[a] D-Utah	782,344	110,000	892,344

[a]Nonincumbent or special election candidate.

CHAPTER 8

Reform

The Broken Promise

Mr. Chairman, our charter was to provide real campaign
reform, not a sham, not campaign deform, not a mockery, not
an incumbent protection plan, not an embarrassment.
Rep. Robert L. Livingston (R-La.), Nov. 22, 1993, during
House floor debate on the campaign finance reform bill

I n May 1992 President George Bush vetoed legislation that would
have established, among other things, voluntary spending limits
of $600,000 in House races and limits in Senate campaigns rang-
ing from $950,000 to $8.9 million, depending on state population.
Adherence to these limits would have entitled House candidates to a
number of benefits, including the ability to tap public funds for as
much as $200,000 in matching funds for contributions of less than
$200. Among the rewards accorded to Senate candidates for agreeing
to the limits were taxpayer-funded vouchers for up to 20 percent of
their spending limit to purchase television air time.

Democratic presidential hopeful Bill Clinton's reaction to that veto
was sure and swift. "Well, I think his actions speak louder than his
words. . . . I hope they will take his veto, write another bill, make it
even tougher, and send it right back to him." Candidate Clinton
promised throughout the fall campaign to place campaign finance
reform high on his agenda. Following his election, Clinton included
such reform language in his legislative agenda for his first one hundred days in office, a document he dubbed "Putting People First."

Democratic congressional leaders seemed to agree. Appearing on
the November 29 edition of *This Week with David Brinkley,* Senate
Majority Leader George J. Mitchell (D-Maine) said, "I hope we're
going to pass a [campaign finance reform] bill—we passed a good,
strong, fair bill last year. It was unfortunately vetoed by President
Bush. We're going to come back early this year, because I think we

have to change the process, and . . . restore public confidence." Despite Republican objections over public financing provisions, Democratic control of the House, Senate, and White House seemed to assure that reforms would be quickly forthcoming.

Eighteen months later, the House and Senate had succeeded in passing significantly different campaign finance reform bills but had not managed to name conferees to work out the differences. One major stumbling block to compromise was political action committee (PAC) contributions, which the Senate sought to ban and the House agreed grudgingly to restrict to $200,000.

Realizing that the proposed ban would probably not survive a constitutional test, the Senate stipulated that if the ban was struck down, PACs would be limited to contributing $1,000 per election cycle; individual campaigns would be barred from collecting PAC money in excess of 20 percent of the spending limit. Many in the House sought to leave the current $10,000 maximum PAC contribution in place.

The reason for this fundamental disagreement was simple. While the typical victorious Senate candidate in 1992 depended on PACs for only 27 percent of his or her receipts, 180 victors in House races collected 50 percent or more of their money from PACs. Nearly half—216 of the 435 elected on November 3—collected more than $200,000 from PACs, or one-third of the proposed House spending limit. Cutting their PAC receipts to $200,000 would be painful enough, but slicing them to $120,000 to conform with the Senate's 20 percent cap was more than most House members seemed willing to do.

On paper, if this impass over PAC contributions could be resolved, the two bills seem to provide the possibility for real reform, although in reality they provide little more than cosmetic changes. Take for example the notion—implied by some, explicitly stated by others—that one goal of reform is to "level the playing field" for incumbents and challengers. For obvious reasons, few incumbents are likely to look with favor upon that concept, just as most view term limits as an unnecessary check on the wisdom of the electorate.

The current House bill provides both incumbents and challengers with up to $200,000 in matching funds, delivered in the form of taxpayer-funded communication vouchers that could be used to pay for television or radio air time or for printing and postage. However, the bill declares that access to the vouchers does not kick in until a candidate has raised at least $60,000 in small contributions, including the first $200 of each larger contribution. The threshhold was explicitly intended to discourage challengers. As Rep. Sam Gejdenson (D-Conn.)—Democratic point-man on campaign finance reform in the House—explained to his House colleagues during the November 22, 1993, floor debate on the reform package, "The threshhold, estimated to around $66,000 in 1996, is high enough so that we are not arbitrarily creating viable challengers where there would be none." In 1992 at least 311 challengers did not raise enough to gain access to the full $200,000 in matching funds. There was no incumbent who would have had difficulty raising enough to collect the maximum had they chosen to do so, particularly if they had been weaned off PAC funds.

GETTING AROUND THE LIMITS

While most members of Congress say they want "reform," the definitions of that term differ so vastly that any meaningful reform is unlikely. One thing is clear, if the conference committee produced anything closely resembling the House version of the reform package, it would be spending reform in name only.

For instance, while the $600,000 spending limit has been widely touted, it is, in reality, more of a floor than a cap. If a candidate wins the primary by 20 points or less—a still very comfortable 60-to-40 percent spread in a two-way race and a virtual certainty in a multicandidate primary—that candidate's spending limit is automatically raised by $200,000. Then, if a runoff is required, the cap is raised by another $200,000. If the current House bill had been in effect during the 1992 campaign, and if all 859 House candidates had agreed to abide by the limit, only 159 would have had to change *anything* about their campaign spending.

The current House bill further excludes from the spending limit the costs of legal services and taxes, as well as an exemption of up to 10 percent of the cycle limit for overhead, fund-raising, and accounting costs. Once the exemption for legal fees and taxes is taken into account, the number of candidates who would have had to alter their campaigns in 1992 drops to 150. Applying the 10 percent exemption for accounting and fund-raising costs brings down to 121 the number of House candidates affected by the legislation. Of that number, 93 were incumbents, 11 were challengers, and 17 were open seat candidates. Ninety-five of the 121 emerged victorious, which means that at most only 22 percent of those elected would have had to change their spending patterns in any way.

The equation is further complicated by the implicit but erroneous assumption that all candidates would agree to the limits. Under the House bill, the spending limit would be lifted and federal matching funds retained if candidates who had chosen to comply with the limits found themselves faced with opponents who rejected the limits. In the Senate version, candidates not complying with the limits would be subject to a stiff tax on campaign receipts.

Would Republican Linda Bean (Maine) have agreed not to spend $1,228,962 of her own money—85 percent of her total expenditures—in her attempt to oust Democratic Rep. Thomas H. Andrews? Most assuredly not. The current House bill calls for federal matching funds in the form of communication vouchers to kick in only after a candidate raises at least $60,000 in contributions of $200 or less, including the first $200 of each larger contribution. Since Bean raised only $60,066 from small contributors, and $123,304 from donors who gave her $200 or more, the total value of her communication vouchers would have been well under $200,000. Given that she invested $921,195 on broadcast ads and persuasion mailers alone, spending less in order to get $200,000 worth of vouchers would not have made much sense.

If Bean had opted not to abide by the voluntary limits, the $782,034 Andrews spent to defend his seat would have been, and should have been, permissible under the House bill. However, because Andrews raised more than $200,000 from small contributors, he would have been eligible for the full $200,000 cash infusion from federal taxpayers, who in effect would have helped protect an incumbent from possible upset by a well-funded challenger.

Would Dick Chrysler (R-Mich.) have opted not to dip into his personal bank account for $1,585,108 of the $1,762,128 he spent on his bid to unseat Democratic Rep. Bob Carr? Without the ability to self-finance an $849,340 broadcast advertising campaign and a $384,838 advocacy mail effort, Chrysler probably would not have come within 2 points of retiring Carr. Had Chrysler decided not to abide by the limits, taxpayers would have subsidized Carr's $1,353,305 campaign with another $200,000 in communication vouchers, which would have substantially reduced the $499,886 spending advantage on broadcast advertising and persuasion mail enjoyed by Chrysler.

It is highly unlikely that Michael Huffington (R-Calif.) would have agreed not to spend the $3.5 million he invested in upsetting Rep. Robert J. Lagomarsino in the primary or the $1.9 million he spent to dispatch Democrat Gloria Ochoa in the general election. If not, then the $706,338 Ochoa spent trying to win the seat would have been perfectly legal, and she would have received the $200,000 federal matching funds to further help her balance the spending mismatch. Again, had the current House bill been law in 1992, the taxpayers—people who lived throughout the country and did not have a stake in the outcome or who opposed Ochoa's candidacy—would have found themselves paying part of the bill.

Rep. Mike Synar (D-Okla.) would have been granted the additional $200,000 spending quota by virtue of his 43-to-38 percent primary victory over Drew Edmondson. Since Oklahoma election law requires primary winners who do not receive a majority of the votes to face a runoff with the second-place finisher, Synar's limit would have then been boosted by another $200,000 for the runoff. When the National Rifle Association weighed in with its $226,088 independent campaign, Synar would have been allowed under the current House bill to spend a comparable amount in excess of his normal spending limit, effectively raising his spending limit to $1,226,088. Synar would not have had to make any adjustments to his $1,185,676 campaign in order to come in under the limits.

At most, in a year marked by the greatest House turnover in fifty years, less than one-quarter of all House members would have been affected by the proposed spending limits. Instead of trimming spending substantially, the taxpayer-funded communications vouchers— which the Congressional Budget Office estimated would cost $90 million the first year—would free up campaign funds to pay for a host of other items only tangentially related to campaigning.

Rep. George Miller (D-Calif.) spent $657,215 on his 1992 reelection effort, $206,713 of which was spent on advertising and persuasion mail. After the various exemptions are taken into account, Miller's spending was just below the $600,000 threshhold. Miller would have had to trim his PAC contributions by nearly $62,000, which presumably would have necessitated additional fund-raising expenditures in order to meet the matching funds requirement. Dave Scholl, his Republican opponent, managed to raise just $61,888 in individual contributions and lacked the requisite amount of small contributions to qualify for matching funds. Had Miller opted to take the matching grant he could easily have qualified for, the taxpayer in essence would have picked up the tab for his $109,229 in contributions to other candidates, party organizations, and various causes. The $200,000 public grant would also have covered his $17,037 constituent entertainment costs and much of the $115,184 he spent on overhead.

Similarly, Jerry F. Costello (D-Ill.) spent $603,886 during the 1992 cycle, leaving him well under the limit after the fund-raising and tax exemptions are factored in. He collected only $145,175 from PACs, requiring no change in behavior. His individual contributions qualified him for the federal matching funds, which he did not need. Whether or not it was considered part of the exempt expenses, Costello's $84,000 payment to his lawyer to ensure that his interests were well served during the redistricting fight effectively would have been covered by taxpayers, as would the $42,961 he simply gave away.

By subsidizing Rep. Pete Stark (D-Calif.) in his reelection effort, the taxpayer essentially would have been picking up the tab for the Cadillac Seville he drove at campaign expense. Taxpayers would have been given the chance to pay the $30,390 constituent entertainment tab Rep. Leon E. Panetta (D-Calif.) racked up, and pay for his stay at the Maui Prince Hotel in Maui, Hawaii, where he attended a conference that he did not feel the taxpayers should pay for out of his congressional office account. As the examples in Chapter 2 illustrate, the list of excesses potentially billed, at least in part, to the taxpayer through this system is virtually endless.

The Senate bill includes a new federal tax on campaign receipts equal to the highest corporate tax rate, 36 percent. Those agreeing to abide by the limit established for their state would be exempted from the tax; those opting not to abide by the limit would pay it, in effect paying at least a portion of the cost of providing communication vouchers. Exemptions from the limits include legal and accounting fees, taxes, and travel between the candidate's home state and Washington, D.C. Exempted travel would include trips taken by spouses and children.

Had the Senate version of the bill been in effect in 1992, twenty-seven candidates would have either had to trim their spending or opt not to abide by the spending limits. Sen. Alfonse M. D'Amato would have had to slash his spending in the nonexempt categories by $4,392,335 to bring his spending below New York's $6,720,498 limit. Had he decided to live within the limits, D'Amato might have had a much more difficult time justifying the $156,729 he spent on campaign cars and the $163,098 he spent on meals, including $35,252 at Gandel's Gourmet in Washington, D.C. Living within the limit would have put his campaign spending on par with that of New York Attorney General Robert Abrams, D'Amato's Democratic opponent.

The Senate limits would have effected both candidates in only five states. In Pennsylvania, Republican Sen. Arlen Specter would have had to decrease his outlays by $4,587,902 to meet Pennsylvania's $4,828,388 limit, while Democrat Lynn Yeakel would have been able to get by with a modest $109,227 reduction. Had Specter decided to adhere to those limits, in all likelihood the seat would have gone to Yeakel. Rep. Les AuCoin (D-Ore.) would have needed to cut his spending against Sen. Bob Packwood by less than $400,000 after all the exemptions were taken into account, including the independent campaign adjustment. In order to meet Oregon's $2,004,000 spending cap, Packwood would have needed to slash his outlays by more than $5 million. Paul Coverdell (R-Ga.) would have needed to drop his spending by less than $60,000; Democratic Sen. Wyche Fowler, Jr., would have needed to reduce his spending by $2.1 million to come in under Georgia's $3,069,043 limit. Both Sen. Terry Sanford (D-N.C.) and Republican Lauch Faircloth could have made adjustments of less than $200,000 and met the North Carolina's $3,164,650 cap. Sen. Christopher J. Dodd (D-Conn.) would have had to cut his budget by roughly half in order to comply with the state's $2,004,000 limit. Dodd's Republican opponent, Brook Johnson, would have had to slice about $380,000 from his outlays.

Had the limits been in effect for 1992, Rep. Barbara Boxer (D-Calif.) would have had to figure out a way to slice nearly $1.7 million from the $9,947,007 in nonexempt spending she put into her open Senate seat contest. While she might have still prevailed against Republican Bruce Herschensohn, it would have been a decidedly different campaign.

Nevertheless, while twenty-seven Senate candidates would have been affected, forty-seven would not have been. Among those who would not have needed to change anything about their campaign style were Sen. Bob Dole (R-Kan.), who could have asked taxpayers indirectly to help pay his $265,827 tab for chartered airplanes or his $49,765 bill for constituent entertainment.

While both the Senate and the House bills intend to restrict the flow of PAC money, both bills would also have at least one unintended consequence. Campaigns would be forced by the economics of fund raising to significantly reduce or abandon direct mail and telemarketing, which would reduce the number of small contributions flowing into campaigns.

By eliminating direct mail and telemarketing from his fund-raising mix, Packwood could have saved $2,871,538 over his six-year election cycle. While some of that cost would have been shifted to standard fund-raising receptions, which generally yield a far greater return on investment, that one decision would have gotten him more than half way to the $5 million reduction he would have needed to bring him under Oregon's spending limit. However, that move would have also radically changed his donor profile. Packwood would not have collected anything close to the $3,728,299 he received from contributors who gave less than $200.

Locked in a tight open Senate seat contest, Boxer could not have afforded to slash her $4.3 million broadcast advertising budget. However, she could have brought herself under California's 1992 cap by eliminating her $2,003,533 direct-mail effort and shifting a portion of the savings into additional high-donor receptions. If that had been required, Boxer never would have been able to collect the millions of dollars she raised in small contributions from women all across the country who were excited to help elect another female senator. Without that outreach to other women, Boxer might very well have lost her primary contest with Rep. Mel Levine, who raised millions from large donors. Of the $10,431,140 Boxer raised for her campaign, $4,453,685 came from supporters who gave less than $200.

Rep. Robert K. Dornan raised $1,188,786 from small donors, only $143,158 from contributors who gave $200 or more, and just $75,978 from PACs. He could afford to do what most reformers say they want—restrict the flow of special interest money into his campaign—because he operated a $1,121,604 direct-mail fund-raising program that reached out to small contributors who share his philosophy. Had the spending limits been in effect and had he chosen to abide by them, Dornan would have been allowed to spend $800,000 by virtue of his 20-point victory in the primary, but his $1,552,281 budget would have left him $752,281 over the limit. Dornan gave away only $1,000; he spent $3,432 on constituent entertainment, $39,920 on overhead, $310,566 on direct appeal for votes, and had $46,024 in unitemized expenses. Reducing all those outlays to zero would have still left him $351,339 over the limit. He could not possibly have brought himself under the spending cap without gutting the direct-mail program he built to raise his small donations.

Ironically, the reform packages as currently written would have the effect of pushing congressional candidates into the arms of the very people who were considered the root of political evil in the 1970s—"fat cat" individual contributors.

OUR PROPOSALS

If the bills currently winding their way through the legislative process are seriously flawed, and we strongly believe they are, what are the alternatives? We believe that the path to finding those alternatives begins with the realization that the proposals currently under discussion evolve from the false premise that television advertising rates are responsible for the rising cost of campaigning. In fact, even in a year when incumbents were supposedly running scared, when there was a record number of open seat contests, and when challengers had considerably more money to spend, television and radio advertising accounted for 27 percent of all spending in House races and 42 percent of spending in Senate contests. House incumbents allocated only 25 percent of their spending to broadcast advertising; Senate incumbents invested 40 percent of their money in such ads.

The reform attempts also evolve from the misconception promulgated by many reformers that public financing will *automatically* lead to less costly campaigns. However, our research found that incumbents spent $3,828,682 on constituent entertainment; $1,689,952 on campaign automobiles, many of them Cadillacs and Lincolns driven in Washington, D.C., not the incumbent's state or district; and $1,901,812 on meals that apparently had nothing to do with fund raising or constituent entertainment, many consumed at fancy restaurants in Washington, D.C., or in other countries. While incumbents spent a total of $95,626,044 on broadcast advertising, they also invested $78,467,605 in overhead, $54,660,343 in fund raising, and gave away $10,653,432. Most candidates would have been able to meet the loose spending limits without altering their behavior in any way and, in fact, would have been able to effectively tap the taxpayer for as much as one-third of their spending.

No reform that allows candidates to spend campaign money on luxury automobiles and other items that do little more than enhance their personal lifestyles can be called reform. Campaign spending should be limited to campaigns. If members of Congress are serious about campaign finance reform, then Rep. William L. Clay (D-Mo.) should not be able to tap his campaign to pay the $799 monthly lease and repair bills on a car he drives in Washington, D.C. He should be forbidden from using campaign money to buy season tickets to Washington Redskins games or pay for travel to New Jersey for meetings with the Board of Benedict College and with the United Negro College Fund. He most certainly should not be allowed to use campaign funds to pay for his $310 dues at the Robin Hood Swim Club in Silver Spring, Md. If he wants to attend the Congressional Black Caucus Weekend retreats, his campaign should not pick up the tab, nor should it pay for expenses incurred on trips to Jamaica, N.Y., for meetings of the Clay Scholarship Board and for a reception for former Rep. William H. Gray III.

If Congress is serious about reducing the cost of campaigns, as opposed to the cost of politics, then Rep. Barbara-Rose Collins (D-Mich.) should not be able to spend nearly $9,000 over two election cycles on clothes and image consultations. D'Amato should not be able to tap his campaign treasury for $156,729 to lease and maintain two luxury automobiles, one of which is used by the senator in Washington, D.C., not in New York. Nor should D'Amato be able to spend campaign funds to cover a $4,439 harvest day celebration of New York agricultural products to which senators and their staffs are invited. Rep. Henry A. Waxman (D-Calif.) should never again be permitted to spend $4,500 of his campaign treasury to help defray the cost of a trip that he and his wife take to Israel or any other foreign destination.

Under anything that would pass for real reform, Rep. Louis Stokes (D-Ohio) would not be allowed to spend $4,111 on a reception at the

House restaurant for attendees of the National Baptist Convention, nor would he be allowed to tap his campaign treasury to cover the cost of his family's accommodations at Walt Disney World Resorts, as he did in April 1992, or to cover the $3,199 bill at the Washington Hilton and Towers, where he and his family stayed during a Congressional Black Caucus annual weekend bash. Sen. Bob Graham (D-Fla.) would not be able to spend $3,905 of his campaign funds on Super Bowl tickets given to his friends, nor would he be allowed to spend $4,156 on gifts, including boxes of pecans and "Florida ties" handed out to fellow senators and employees of the congressional barbershop and shoe-shine stand. Challenger Allan L. Keyes (R-Md.) would not be permitted to pay himself an $8,500 monthly salary from campaign funds should he decide to run again, a practice that brought him a $49,614 income during his challenge to Democratic Sen. Barbara A. Mikulski. Real reform would forbid the lavish, lifestyle enhancing expenditures of Senate hopeful Carol Moseley-Braun, who dropped $22,445 of her campaign funds during the four-day Democratic National Convention in New York. True reform would provide for a careful review of D'Amato's $35,252 tab at Gandel's Gourmet and the 220 meals of $200 or less consumed by Sen. Daniel K. Inouye (D-Hawaii) in the Washington, D.C., metropolitan area.

Real reform would ban contributions such as the $85,198 Rep. Paul E. Gillmor (R-Ohio) funneled from his own campaign treasury into that of his wife Karen, who waged a successful campaign for the state senate. It would prohibit Inouye from tapping his campaign treasury for a $150,000 donation to the Hawaii Education Foundation, an organization he founded to provide scholarships to Hawaiian high school students. While it may be a worthy cause, Inouye's foundation has nothing to do with campaigning. The $94,319 television campaign spearheaded by Rep. David E. Bonior (D-Mich.) on behalf of a proposed ballot initiative to give middle income homeowners a $500 property tax cut also had nothing to do with the 1992 campaign. The initiative was sponsored by the Michigan Homeowners Tax Break Committee, which Bonior cochaired.

When members find themselves in need of a lawyer to defend them against ethical and criminal charges, they should not be able to tap their funds to pay for legal counsel. Such expenses certainly should not be included in the list of exemptions from any spending limits that are imposed. Eliminating these expenditures would do far more to reduce the cost of campaigns than any of the spending limits currently under discussion.

No reform will be useful unless the Federal Election Commission (FEC) is given the power to act. Its current six-member structure, which mandates that the commission have three Republican and three Democratic members, was from the beginning an invitation to failure. While Congress seems unlikely to create an agency that truly has watchdog authority over campaign practices, that is ultimately the only path to true reform.

Rather than cutting the FEC's budget, as both President Clinton and members of Congress have proposed, the agency's budget should be increased. As our examination of the FEC's record of enforcing the $25,000 contribution limit demonstrates, no election law is worth anything if it is not enforced. At present, the FEC's budget does not allow them to pursue all the cases that we have routinely brought to their attention over the past four years.

Along with that increased budget, Congress should also give the FEC authority to conduct random audits of campaigns. The FEC should invest some of that larger budget in additional staff auditors. Following the 1992 campaign, FEC staff analysts identified forty-six campaigns that deserved an audit according to the agency's formula developed to score accounting problems. Citing insufficient staff, the FEC launched audits of only eight campaigns with the most egregious problems, including Moseley-Braun's.

Random audits might have discouraged some campaigns from spending money in questionable ways. A random audit of the 1989 and 1990 campaign books of Sen. Charles S. Robb (D-Va.) most certainly would have raised questions about purposefully misleading entries made by David K. McCloud, Robb's then-chief of staff.

In May 1992 McCloud plead guilty to authorizing the use of campaign funds to purchase an illegal audiotape of a conversation between Virginia Gov. Douglas Wilder and a supporter. The $2,375 bill from the law firm of Hofheimer, Nusbaum, McPhaul, and Samuels was originally rejected by the campaign because McCloud "could not pay the bill as submitted." The law firm then folded the charge into a $4,790 bill for "research services." McCloud also admitted to recording as fund-raising costs a $500 payment that was actually used to pay the travel expenses of an aide who went to Boston to meet with a woman who claimed she had had an affair with Robb while he was governor.

Random audits would also have uncovered that Rep. Carroll Hubbard, Jr. (D-Ky.) diverted $50,000 in campaign funds to personal use. This began in 1990 when he ordered his staffers not to report to the FEC campaign payments to him totaling $5,500. Such diversions were carried on throughout much of the 1992 cycle. He used the money to pay his home heating bills, school tuition for his daughter, credit card bills, and his ex-wife's cable television bills, among other things. He used his campaign assets as collateral to obtain a $15,000 personal loan, another violation of federal law. Hubbard routinely demanded that congressional staffers campaign for him and his current wife—who also sought a House seat in Kentucky—while on the government payroll. Hubbard's foibles accidentally came to light as a result of the investigation into the House banking scandal. In April 1994 Hubbard plead guilty to federal charges of conspiring to defraud the FEC, stealing government property, and obstructing justice.

The FEC should more carefully scrutinize those who routinely fail to itemize thousands of dollars in expenses (see Table 8-1). While it is possible that the campaign of Rep. Mary Rose Oakar (D-Ohio) spent $121,630 in two years on items that cost less than $200, the fact that this represented 10 percent of her total spending should raise questions. Rep. John P. Murtha (D-Pa.) should not have been permitted to list only the vendors on an $8,139 Visa bill without stating what he bought from each vendor or how much each item cost.

Roughly 10 percent of the spending reported by Rep. John D. Dingell (D-Mich.) was either completely unitemized or so vaguely described that it was impossible to tell how the money was spent. Dingell chose not to itemize $67,801 in expenditures of less than $200. Reimbursements to individuals for "campaign expenses" amounted to $27,991, including $17,593 paid to Dingell. Payments for "petty cash" totaled $12,000. Entries such as "campaign materials" or "campaign expenses" or "reimbursement" fail to provide any information that conforms with the spirit of the existing law and should be banned from the candidates' reporting lexicon.

Reform is possible, and in a system increasing characterized by voter cynicism, it is absolutely crucial that *meaningful* reforms be instituted. If, as Synar put it, "the American public made a bold statement about gridlock and change in Washington" in 1992, then artful dodges in the name of reform will only serve to deepen the public's distrust of politicians and the government they represent.

Table 8-1 The Top Fifteen Spenders in the 1992 Congressional Races: Unitemized Expenses

Rank	House		Senate	
	Candidate	Expenditures	Candidate	Expenditures
1	Mary Rose Oakar, D-Ohio	$121,630	Don Nickles, R-Okla.	$174,341
2	John D. Dingell, D-Mich.	107,792	Arlen Specter, R-Pa.	174,114
3	Ronald V. Dellums, D-Calif.	95,740	Charles E. Grassley, R-Iowa	119,203
4	Austin J. Murphy, D-Pa.	94,801	Tom Daschle, D-S.D.	102,447
5	Bud Shuster, R-Pa.	92,127	Bob Kasten, R-Wis.	99,948
6	William D. Ford, D-Mich.	91,875	Harry Reid, D-Nev.	92,586
7	Alan B. Mollohan, D-W.Va.	72,566	Barbara Boxer,[a] D-Calif.	79,570
8	Charles B. Rangel, D-N.Y.	70,686	Bob Packwood, R-Ore.	70,970
9	Harold Rogers, R-Ky.	68,397	Wyche Fowler, Jr., D-Ga.	68,846
10	Lynn Woolsey,[a] D-Calif.	64,455	Alfonse D'Amato, R-N.Y.	64,203
11	Bart Gordon, D-Tenn.	64,252	Carol Moseley-Braun,[a] D-Ill.	56,160
12	Jerry Huckaby, D-La.	63,170	Christopher S. Bond, R-Mo.	55,110
13	Mike Synar, D-Okla.	61,256	Steve Lewis,[a] D-Okla.	49,623
14	Joseph M. McDade, R-Pa.	59,468	Russell Feingold,[a] D-Wis.	47,728
15	Newt Gingrich, R-Ga.	58,682	John McCain, R-Ariz.	47,576

Note: Totals are for entire two-year House and six-year Senate cycles; both include special election expenditures.

[a]Nonincumbent or special election candidate.

Index

The page numbers in **bold** indicate tables and boxes. Congressional district numbers are shown in parentheses.